Sparks of Genius

The Inventive Photography of Bill Angove

Richard Goodwin

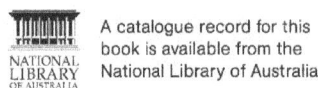 A catalogue record for this book is available from the National Library of Australia

Copyright © 2024 Richard Goodwin
All rights reserved.
ISBN-13: 978-1-923174-08-5

Linellen Press
265 Boomerang Road
Oldbury, Western Australia
www.linellenpress.com.au

Angove's photography ... "described as the work of a genius in photographic magazines both in Britain and in America"

Cyril Casellas
Weekend Magazine, Perth
4 June 1966

He hasn't set the Thames on fire but he's started a few sparks

Marjorie Angove
Undated newspaper clipping

There is no easy explanation of genius or talent: they exist and we accept them as facets of creative force. Some measure of artistic power or sensibility is inherent in all humanity; 'genius' is as good a word as any other to denote those exceptional beings in whom, unaccountably, it rises to full force.

A J A Symons
The Quest for Corvo

Chapters

Chronology 1

Introduction 3

A Sense of Adventure 9

Boy from the Bush 15

Lens, pens, brushes and war 22

Foundations in photography 31

Camera club years 39

The Lure of London 48

Framing life off Piccadilly 54

Sailing into early success 60

Frustrated painter goes 'crazy' 69

A London Canvas 80

Skeletons and ballet steps 88

The curtain rises 95

Crossways 102

Thoughts of home 112

Ambitions in Australia 119

The Sydney Years 138

Vogue and variations 148

Back to Britain 155

Australians and the Swinging Sixties 164

Independent studio 171

Working World 179

Home to new directions 188

Staying global 195

Showtime 205

A premature end 215

Acknowledgements 225

References 226

Chronology

WILLIAM HENRY NORTON **ANGOVE**

2 May 1924	Born in Albany, Western Australia (WA)
1930s	Childhood in Roelands (WA), holidays in Albany
1942	Finishes high school in Bunbury (WA)
1943-44	Enlists in army, trains in Northam (WA)
1945	Based at Kapooka camp, Wagga Wagga, New South Wales (NSW)
September 1946	Discharged from army
1947	Returns to Perth (WA), working as social photographer while studying
1947	Joins Western Australian Camera Club
February 1955	Moves to London, UK, working with various studios
November 1958	Returns to Perth
February 1959	Moves to Sydney (NSW)
1962	Returns to London
September 1970	Returns to Perth
1971	Joins Institute of Australian Photographers, included in exhibitions
1972	Starts teaching at Perth Technical College
1979	Exhibits at Art Gallery of WA, starts film and TV studies
5 February 1980	Dies in Perth, aged 55

A young Bill Angove (undated)

In memory of Ken Knox (1925-2020) whose friendship of eight years continues to enrich my life in ways unimagined at the beginning.

Introduction

On the evening of 26 March 1953 members of the Western Australian Camera Club assembled in the social club rooms of the state bank in central Perth for their monthly meeting. One of their rank, Bill Angove, who'd been in the camera club a few years, gave a talk on the subject, *The Meaning of Art*.[i] Twenty-eight-year-old Angove was already a young man of many tastes, acquired from a rural upbringing and fledgling career paths as an architectural draughtsman and regular photographer of social events around the city. His primary hobby was painting.

Angove pointed out to his audience that photography was the most junior of all the arts having been around not much more than a century. He felt this limited history created too shallow a legacy for a fulsome appreciation of creativity as demonstrated in the arts.

"The only thing we can fall back on is the history of painting, music, ballet, sculpture and other forms," he insisted before going on to discuss the various arts.[ii]

Angove set out to persuade the gathering of professionals and amateurs that to be a good pictorial photographer it was really necessary to show an interest in these other art genres. It was a conviction that drove the man for the rest of his highly productive but shortened life. He made his living with a camera but, for almost the next three decades, he immersed himself thoroughly in cultural settings around theatre, music, art, dance, film, travel, commerce and publishing. And in circulating well beyond Western Australia (WA) he made many powerful and casual connections with leading lights in these fields, principally in the United Kingdom and in Sydney.

I never met Bill Angove. Our paths did not cross. But I came to know his story years later through a mutual friend, Ken Knox, who grew up in the Hunter Valley of New South Wales. After World War II, Knox moved to Perth to work in the General Post Office (GPO).

I met Knox when I randomly photographed him at the Royal Perth Show in 2012. He was taking a break from demonstrating morse code in the heritage pavilion with a bunch of retired fellow GPO telegraphists. My picture of Knox ended up in the National Portrait Gallery in Canberra and, although 25 years apart in age, we became firm friends.

On my first visit to his home in Manning, an inner southern suburb of Perth, we explored a mutual involvement in the Western Australian Camera Club which was founded in 1917.

Knox told me[iii] that upon his arrival in Perth in 1948, he quickly found himself mixing in circles in which photography was popular, including among his GPO workmates and in what was then the state's only camera club.

Knox had first started to dabble in photography during his teenage war service as a signals operator in the jungle at Lae, Papua New Guinea. He owned a *Kodak Bull's-Eye* box-type camera and recorded aspects of camp life as well as the local natives using scarce 620 film sent to him, hidden in welfare parcels, by his parents. These pictures still exist and are located in his family's collection.

Knox initially moved into a boarding house in West Perth. Upon his arrival at the property, he says he encountered a man named Bill Angove sitting on the mantelpiece. Angove noticed that the newcomer had a "cheapy" camera in his possession and encouraged Knox to take his picture. It was the start of a great friendship and a serious journey in photography. Angove was best man when Knox married artist Thelma Mills in Perth in 1952.

Angove's early interest was in street photography which he pursued as a sideline while working as an architectural draughtsman. He would develop his prints on a table in the boarding house. One night, he suggested Knox accompany him to a competition meeting of the Western Australian Camera Club to which Angove belonged. Knox joined up and stayed for more than a decade by which time his mate Bill had progressed to far greater heights abroad and interstate.

During the next few years of our friendship, I engaged Ken Knox on the subject of the camera club's approaching centenary. I was secretary and undertook the task of compiling stories from its history and planning events to commemorate the milestone. He shared memories with me of illustrious figures from the club in the 1950s, Angove prominent among them. He handed me an article from a 1955 national magazine featuring a story and pictures of Angove's avant-garde approach to photography, which heralded his debut on the commercial photographic scene in London.

Among the illustrations accompanying the article was a small headshot of Angove with his camera on a plinth. I liked it because it epitomised the joy of capturing the world with camera in hand. I subsequently suggested to my club committee that we seek the publisher's permission to reproduce the shot and adopt it as a motif for our centenary given that it depicted a person who arguably became the most famous alumnus of our organisation.

Angove had long ago passed away so the approval to use the picture had to come from the magazine. It was forthcoming and so Bill with his Rolleicord was depicted as the 'hero' image for our club's anniversary posters, handbills and stationery. Never for a moment did I imagine that within a few years I would get to handle that very same camera.

Forty years after his friend Bill Angove had died prematurely at the age of 55, Ken Knox succumbed to old age in his 95th year. We had done so much together in the eight years of our friendship. Besides the portrait of Knox, which had earned both of us a bit of fame, and our respective involvement in the camera club, we had also managed to save Thelma's personal collection of her own rare art, which unfortunately had been neglected in the family home after her death in 2009. In addition, we had arranged donations of significant works from Ken's photographic archives to several leading institutions.

Angove and camera in 1955 'hero' pic

In fact, our work together forged such a close relationship that, after Ken died on 22 April 2020, his family asked me to deliver a eulogy at his funeral in Perth on 1 May. In the 10 days that followed, with the encouragement of archivist friend Joanna Sassoon, who had helped with his photography legacy, I wrote an obituary for the daily newspaper. Referencing Ken's early association with Bill Angove, it was published on 13 May[iv]. Among the interested readers that morning was Pinjarra businessman, Rob McLarty, who enthusiastically alerted his wife Meredyth, one of Bill's nieces. The family was keen to get in touch with me.

Meredyth McLarty explained that she, sister Beverley Angove and their other siblings, had inherited the custody of an extensive store of their uncle's documents, prints and photographic equipment, lovingly retained after his death by their late mother, Gwenda, Bill's only sister.

Meredyth wondered if I would be interested in seeing any of it. She recalled meeting the Knox family several times many years earlier. I was certainly keen and suggested they could also make themselves known again to Ken's daughter, Robyn, who lives in Perth.

Two weeks later, the four of us met at my home for a delightful afternoon of story-telling and exchanging memories. Bev and Meredyth brought along several boxes, a mere sampling as it turned out, of their uncle's materials. The caches included albums, catalogues, transcripts, letters, certificates, photographs and a few of his cameras. Among the gear was the Rolleicord, a medium-format twin lens reflex camera produced by Franke

& Heidecke (Rollei) between 1933 and 1976,[v] and that Bill had been pictured with in 1955. The nieces allowed me to borrow the vintage camera and I was able to take it back to our camera club to show the assembled members. This little bit of history, a record of our organisation's longevity as we chose to portray it, had momentarily returned home.

Beverley especially, supported by Meredyth, sister Jennifer and brother Peter, had long treasured their uncle's archive in the hope that one day it might provide a springboard for publicly preserving, and indeed celebrating, his legacy. I made the decision that first afternoon we met that I would help them in this quest. This story advances that mission.

Angove and Knox: Best Mates (circa 1950)

A Sense of Adventure

Bill Angove's most notable professional achievements occurred during his times working in London and Sydney in various stints between 1955 and the early 1970s. While his success was less prominent in his native Western Australia, it is clear that many of his personal traits, his passions and the standards he attained were strongly derived from his home base.

He grew up in the country, a descendant of a line of land surveyors for whom exploration was a fundamental pursuit. It's hard not to ascribe at least some of Angove's sense of adventure, demonstrated both in his travels and in his innovative approach to photography, to the qualities that his numerous ancestors displayed.

Angove inherited the desires and talents of a typical trailblazer. As his life journey progressed, he was surrounded by other influencers, especially from the arts, who in their own ways helped shape his pursuits and achievements.

He was born on 2 May 1924 to parents John Angove and Marjorie Butcher. On both sides of his family, there were adventurers.

Like so many others, his paternal great grandfather, Thomas Angove, came to Australia during the height of the Victorian gold rushes in the 1850s. He hailed from the English regions of Cornwall and West Devon, renowned for its historic mining industries. Aged in his early 30s, Thomas embarked from Liverpool in October 1855 on board the clipper *Schomberg* which was undertaking its maiden voyage. Clipper ships, the glamour vessels of the age, boasted huge areas of sail and were built for speed. The *Schomberg* was skippered by a famous Scottish seafarer, Captain James 'Bully' Forbes, who was determined to set a new speed record for the voyage between England and Australia. Both Forbes, known for his fierce and fiery temperament, and his boat were products of Aberdeen. The target was to complete the trip in 60 days.

Angove, accompanied by his brother John, recorded the journey in a diary, most of which survives to this day. The miner noted at the height of the voyage: "We have no less than thirty-three sails spread on different masts. There is not a ship afloat that carries so much canvas."[vi]

One morning the vessel found itself battling in a pre-dawn squall on the high seas. Angove was on deck to witness Captain Forbes issuing orders at a blistering rate. The passenger, thoroughly enjoying the exhilaration of the moment, wrote in his diary: "To hear the Scotch accent and to see him like a lamp lighter or I might say like a bounding kangaroo, hopping here and bounding there, it made a squall a delight to me, and to see our bark ploughing through the water was a satisfaction that led me to think we should not be long at that rate before we got to the golden lining."[vii]

Schomberg departs Aberdeen (Colour Lithograph by T. G. Dutton)

But alas nothing golden awaited. The *Schomberg* had already clocked up more than 80 days when, on Boxing Day, the ship ran aground on a reef east of Peterborough on Victoria's south-west coast, still a day short of Melbourne. Captain Forbes was reportedly below deck entertaining female passengers when the vessel was blown ashore at Curdies Inlet. Fortunately, Angove, alongside the other 430 passengers, and the ship's crew and cargo were all saved although the same couldn't be said for Forbes' career. The *Schomberg* was one of more than fifty ships that came to grief on what is called Victoria's Shipwreck Coast[viii] where, incidentally, I lived and worked for some years. It and another clipper, the *Loch Ard,* are probably the best known.

Angove's diary is richly descriptive, the product of a highly literate man. In one entry about a third of the way into the voyage, he reflects on the significance of the venture to the lives of all those travelling to the other side of the world: "I trust that now we have crossed the Equator that it will prove but the beginning of a new era in our lives and circumstances."

Exactly a hundred years later, his great grandson Bill made the same trip in reverse and it's fair to say he was filled with similar hopes and expectations.

Settling in Victoria, Thomas Angove moved to the goldfields of the Ballarat region and took up a role as a mining manager at nearby Clunes, the location of the colony's first gold strike in nearby volcanic hills[ix]. It was to prove a very profitable mining centre for the rest of the 1850s and the 1860s.

Within a few years, his family joined him in the colony. Son William Henry Angove, born in the village of Petertavy in Devonshire[x] in 1850 and migrating at age 11, was a student at one of Clunes eight schools and later studied at the Ballarat School of Mines, earning a job ticket in mining and land surveying. William had moved north to the Bendigo district by the mid-1870s where he married Emily Ripper. William then pioneered the family's migration to Western Australia where the Angove family fortunes were to reach greater heights.

William took up a two-year appointment as a surveyor with the Western Australian Government Lands Department in Perth in 1879. [xi] He surveyed the inner suburb of North Perth. One of the area's main arterial roads, Angove Street, is named in his honour.

William came to the attention of another surveyor, Alexander Forrest, who had for a time been in charge of the Albany district. Forrest offered Angove a business partnership which they ran for three years. After that they went their separate ways to work independently for the Western Australian Land Company, this time with Forrest, one of a steeped band of brothers engaged in exploration, commerce and politics, in Perth and Angove taking up residence in Albany. They worked on the development of a rail line from Albany to Beverley in the state's Wheatbelt[xii], built in the late 1880s and known as the Great Southern Line. He also surveyed the Dundas shire and the mining settlement of Norseman before later joining the Albany Town Council, of which he remained a councillor until almost the time of his death in Melbourne in 1912.[xiii] A lake and short stream in the vicinity of Two People's Bay at Albany carry the Angove name, an honour bestowed a year after his passing by fellow surveyor B W Ridley.

His son, John Henry Angove, born in 1888 and later father to Bill, followed in the same vein as a surveyor. Known as Harry, he was employed by the Lands Department and spent many periods of up to six months working in the bush. In Perth in 1920 he married Marjorie Butcher, who was born in 1892 in Sandy Bay, Tasmania.

Marjorie's father, Edward William Norton Butcher, had a similar professional history, engaged originally as chief clerk of Tasmania's Department of Lands and Survey.[xiv] Butcher later became a pioneer sheep breeder in the remote Murchison region of Western Australia establishing a 300,000 hectare station named Moorarrie north-west of

Meekatharra. Visiting this outback region today, you can still only describe it as extremely harsh and challenging for its occupants. It was a courageous choice of location to pursue a pastoral enterprise in the late 19th century.

The Butcher family also boasted a dazzling ancestor known internationally for his exploration, natural history scholarship, art, writing and cartography. Here was a person of whom Marjorie's son Bill would have been extremely proud. William John Burchell, Marjorie's great uncle, is credited with remarkable accomplishments[xv]. During a four-year scientific exploration of South Africa, he collected more than 63,000 botanical and zoological specimens. Starting in 1811, his expedition amassed 7,000 kms, travelling in a modified Cape ox-wagon which he used as a home, laboratory, art studio and library, demonstrating a competence "in aspects of practical mechanical engineering"[xvi]. He created 500 drawings and many landscape and portrait paintings during his travels. His mapping was hailed as a milestone in the cartography of the country. Later, he undertook a similar natural history mission in Brazil.

W J Burchell by Thomas Ernest Maguire 1854

Burchell has been described as a perfectionist[xvii] and those who have documented his story in journals and books cite numerous examples of his ingenuity, aesthetic artistry and brilliant mind. He named many species of plants, insects and fauna including Burchell's zebra, which boasted a distinguishable stripe pattern. A contemporary and friend of Charles Darwin, he "was on a course towards and tantalisingly close to evolution, but the destination eluded him"[xviii]. The authors of a tribute to Burchell in 2012 summarised his success thus: "He certainly knew a lot about a lot and could do a lot".[xix]

How much young Bill Angove knew of his illustrious forebear from 140 years earlier is unquantifiable but niece Jennifer Brodie-Hall says his mother treasured Burchell's history. Another niece, Meredyth McLarty, believes that in character and disposition, Bill had more affinity with his Butcher ancestral line than the Angoves. His parents included examples of favourite Butcher nomenclature, William and Norton, in his names at birth.

Third sister Beverley reflects on a line from a recent television series on Captain James Cook anchored by actor Sam Neil who observes: "Explorers push harder than most. That's what makes them unique." Bev adds: "It reminds me of William Burchell and I think Bill also had this quality."

An obvious talent Bill shared with his great-great-uncle was painting and sketching. They both trained in drawing and draughtsmanship in their youth. Here is part of a painting by Burchell dating from 1810 (below left) and one by Angove in 1947 (below).

Ancestral links with the painting of sailing ships

In another respect, the men were to have quite different experiences in London. Burchell, entering his 80s sullen and withdrawn, took his own life in Fulham in 1863 after being, in the words of his naturalist friend William Swainson, "so signally neglected in his own country".[xx] On the other hand, a century later, London was the honeypot for many of Angove's greatest successes. Although the concept of under-appreciation in one's homeland did arise again.

Boy from the Bush

Harry Angove served as a gunner in World War I. Aged 27, he enlisted in Albany in April 1916 and joined the 11th Field Artillery Brigade which sailed from Melbourne late the following year on the troop carrier *Port Sydney A15*[xxi] landing at Suez. The brigade was initially based in Egypt. Just six weeks before the end of the war, the troops found themselves in the Picardie region of France where fighting had prevailed throughout its duration. The 1916 Battle of the Somme is the most well-known engagement in this region, notorious for its heavy casualties, but further battles took place in 1918 including the one that Harry and his brigade fought in.[xxii] He sustained a severe gunshot wound in his right thigh. He was hospitalised and invalided out within a few weeks, and then sent back to Australia at New Year 1919 on the *Karmala*.[xxiii]

Just a year later he and Marjorie Constance Butcher were married in the autumn of 1920 in West Perth. Butcher's mother Elizabeth lived in the same suburb after the death of her husband at the end of their working lives in Tasmania and rural Western Australia, including Katanning, a farming town 170km north of Albany. That's likely where Marjorie and Harry met.

Recovered from his war injury, Harry had resumed work as a surveyor for the WA Lands Department. In the early years of their marriage, the couple spent long stints travelling in the bush in the State's south-west, moving between survey camps as Harry completed jobs. They also spent time further east, developing affection for the town and district of Esperance. According to a memoir of their daughter, Gwenda, published by her eldest daughter Jennifer and son-in-law Charles Brodie-Hall about 80 years later[xxiv], Marjorie had enjoyed the lifestyle. She saw being in the bush as an adventure. They had a camp cook and Marjorie loved horse riding.

By late 1923, Marjorie was pregnant with the couple's first child. Her granddaughter Meredyth explains why the family ruled out that her uncle, William Henry Norton Angove, would be born at one of the camps.

"Gran was tiny – only 4 foot 10 inches and, from what Mum described, quite frail," Meredyth says.[xxv] "I suspect Harry would have insisted she be in Albany near his mother."

It was also deep into autumn and typically cool in the southern regions, down to 10 or 11 degrees overnight, so by the time of Bill's birth on 2 May 1924 the family had retreated to Emily's eight-room stone home, *Terongie*, in Grey Street, overlooking the town's magnificent harbour. The birth actually occurred in what was called Albany's Cottage Hospital, conveniently located a few blocks away still in the vicinity of Grey Street. Bill was a big baby, according to Gwenda's account, and Marjorie being "very tiny" had a "bad time" with the birth.

__Marjorie and Harry on their wedding day.__

However, the difficult childbirth and baby Bill's arrival did not deter the couple from their simple way of life under the stars. They continued to go bush, apparently with gusto. In Gwenda's account, Marjorie is said to have had very fond memories of travelling with the infant in those days of horse and sulky along rugged tracks.[xxvi] Meredyth McLarty puts it this way: "Gran loved being on the camps and was a very strong personality."

Marjorie "risked her life" in giving birth to Gwenda four years later.[xxvii] At this time, the family was living in a flat in West Perth, on Thomas Street, facing King's Park. The accommodation in the big city was a recognition that the family was growing and was anticipating the need for Bill to soon start school. However, living in Perth meant long periods of separation because Harry was still undertaking surveying assignments for the government that typically kept him away for six months on end.

Marjorie and Harry with Bill and Gwenda (1929)

By the early 1930s, the children were missing their father. Six monthly visits no longer sufficed. So he switched jobs. Harry was appointed to the role of engineer in charge of the new Collie River Irrigation Scheme which was still being completed in the south-west. The family's initial move was to the major town of Bunbury, 170 kms from Perth and 60 kms from the coal mining town of Collie.

In Bunbury, the family was fortunate to live in an old house that had been occupied over some decades by the presiding magistrates of the district. The family knew it as *Timperley*, named after William Henry Timperley, the resident magistrate who had it built in 1896 at the corner of Stirling and Moore Streets.[xxviii] The WA Government's Public Works Department bought the property in 1904 and it was officially called *The Residency* thereafter. Coincidentally, the family already enjoyed a connection with the substantial brick and iron building because Marjorie's grandfather had been one of the magistrates who resided there.

Three years into Harry's employment on the irrigation scheme, the family moved to a new dwelling at a settlement called Roelands, on the banks of the Collie River, where his site office was located. The office was described as very basic for a reason to be revealed here shortly, and the house was only marginally better. Gwenda likened the residence to a mill cottage, some of which still exist in the region.[xxix]

Roelands at the time was a tiny village with one store, post office, school and hall, all located in a square around the corner from the Angove's family home. Europeans are thought to have started farming in the area in the 1840s, impinging on a local Aboriginal community that had occupied the fertile river plain for thousands of years.[xxx] One of the pioneering farming families, the Roses, called their property *Roelands Park*, a gesture to honour the colony's first surveyor-general John Septimus Roe. This later gave rise to a name for the village, Roelands. The name would no doubt have resonated favourably with the Angoves, given their family's long involvement in land surveying in fledgling Western Australia, immortalised in streets bearing the family name in Albany, Esperance, Norseman and Perth.

The Roelands area had a mixed agricultural history, with potatoes proving the best crop in the last quarter of the 19th century.[xxxi] The village itself really came to life after the Perth to Bunbury railway went through in the mid-1890s, according to recollections of old time resident James Kane in a letter he wrote for the local school's 75th anniversary in 1978.[xxxii] In the same way that major infrastructure can reshape economic fortunes today, capital works projects played a significant part in settlement and livelihoods in the 19th and 20th centuries as the economy industrialised. Roelands is a perfect example of such developments because, just a few years after the train line opened, the nearby breakwater for Bunbury's harbour was built with stone quarried in Roelands.

Although the Angoves arrived in town almost a third of a century later, they too had a connection with the railway and the harbour construction. To shift the huge granite boulders out of the quarry, a small locomotive called *Nunnagine* was used to haul rail wagons up a steep gradient. The loco had its own home, known as the Engine Shed.[xxxiii] By the time Harry Angove arrived to oversee the irrigation scheme, the Public Works Department had converted the engine shed into his site office.

In Kane's words, "it is an odd quirk of fate that the severe depression of the 1930s brought prosperity to Roelands".[xxxiv] The irrigation scheme, involving construction of the Wellington Dam on the Collie River, with main channels running north and south along the foothills of the Darling Ranges, carried water to farming land on the coastal plain. The engineering program provided jobs for many men on sustenance during the Depression.[xxxv]

His early years living close to Harry's construction project made a lasting impression on young Bill. One example of this is his painting of the Wellington Dam undertaken in his mid-20s while training as an architectural draughtsman. He would surely have remembered some of the adversity too.

Wellington Dam (1949) painted by Bill Angove

Because of those impoverished times, as Gwenda recalls,[xxxvi] none of the accommodation in Roelands had frills. The family dwelling had no electricity; just kerosene lamps for lighting. There was no refrigerator; just an ice chest and a Coolgardie safe on the back verandah. To have a hot bath, the family had to light the copper and then cart water in buckets from one end of the verandah to the other where the bathroom was situated.

Harry eventually convinced the Public Works Department to install a shower but it only offered cold water and so was confined to use in summer. Marjorie lacked a clothes wringer so the wet laundry went onto the line dripping.

The house had a Metters wood stove and an open fireplace in the lounge. Marjorie used an iron branded "Mrs Potts" which had to be heated on the stove top.

A dunny way down the backyard was serviced by what was known as a 'nightman'. Every Monday morning Mr Chergwidden would come to empty the toilet pan, kept clean in the meantime by Harry applying an early disinfectant called phenyl. Bill and Gwenda used to ride their bikes down to the toilet during the day time while chamber pots did the trick at night.

Bill's first cultural interests may well have been nurtured by a fascination with the start of the golden age of cinema. This was an era when much of the population turned to the big screen as their main recreational escape from the pall of the Depression. It also marked advances in colour film including Kodachrome[xxxvii], a world young Bill was to immerse himself in a decade or so later.

With sister Gwenda, he would regularly lean on Harry to take them six miles to the movies at the Brunswick Junction town hall on Tuesday nights. This was one of numerous venues in the state's south-west popularised by a travelling picture showman named Eric Kanzler. The bush circuit was Eric's responsibility while his brother Bert ran their silver screen business from a base in Albany.[xxxviii] Gwenda recalls the Aboriginal kids having to take the less attractive seats down the front.

Bill and Gwenda would travel by bus 14 miles each day in the opposite direction to attend high school at Bunbury. However, with the advent of war, the students had to board in Bunbury as a security precaution. Another student from the time, Marie of the pioneering Rose family[xxxix] recalls the conduct of air raid practice in the sandhills behind the school. According to Jenny Brodie-Hall, Gwenda remembered *HMAS Sydney* coming into Bunbury port in 1941 shortly before it was sunk with all lives lost, lamenting the fate of all the young men on board heading off to war.[xl]

Working in the irrigation industry had its foibles. Its busiest season was summer so Harry Angove could never take holidays at that time of the year. Instead, the family enjoyed a mid-winter break, tripping back down to Albany each year to stay with Harry's mother Emily in the same house that accommodated them at the time of Bill's birth.

Bill as a toddler

Harry loved going back to Albany. Getting there was a great overnight adventure. According to Gwenda's account, the family would take the train from Brunswick 100 miles across to Wagin from where they'd change onto the Perth-Albany steam train to reach their destination sometime next morning.[xli] This was part of the Great Southern Railway established in partnership by Harry's grandfather William almost half a century earlier.

"We always had a good time in Albany," she recalled.

Their days were spent in locations such as Middleton Beach and Strawberry Hill Farm, the oldest agricultural property in Western Australia. According to the National Trust, which owns the farm today, long before European settlement it was called Barmup, a meeting place for Menang Aboriginal people. In 1826, a government farm was established near the water course which fed a fledgling settlement. It was later purchased from Albany's soldier founder, Major Edmund Lockyer, by the pioneering magistrate, Sir Richard Spencer, in 1833[xlii] and, after a period of neglect, it changed hands in 1889, sold to Francis and Augusta Maude Bird. After restoring the house and farming the land for another 50 years, the Bird family was still living there in the era when the Angoves holidayed, and the children of each family became solid friends. Mrs Bird lived there until her death at age 94 in 1946. Her husband, who died almost 10 years earlier, at one time served as Chief Architect to the Western Australian Government.[xliii] Is that yet another clue to small factors that may have influenced the later direction of the young Bill Angove?

Bill and Gwenda with their grandmother Emily

Sapper William Henry Norton Angove WX41022

Lens, pens, brushes and war

In his later years at high school, 15-year-old Angove was given a camera by a cousin, Norman Chester, the son of Harry's older sister Emilie. It was a *Brownie Box*, typically the introductory camera of the era. He later described his initial foray into picture taking.
"[I had] early disasters in photography," he wrote, identifying attempts at Still Life and C/n [colour negatives].

It would appear young Bill was among the first to try *Kodacolour* negative film which happened to hit the market in his final year at school. It was film that the Box Brownies used in 120 format. As it transpired, he was destined to become a major colour practitioner and proponent in photographic circles 10 years later.

Despite the reference to disasters, he also noted that his "experiments" with the camera at high school [were] a PR "success", perhaps implying that his early exploits with the camera were popular with the people around him. Maybe this appreciation was a first good omen for what lay ahead.

The camera helped him become an enterprising chronicler of life in Roelands, described by Rose family member Nancy, as "a close-knit community where everyone helped everyone else".[xliv] In 2021 it was a delight to discover that Angove had photographed many of the town's inhabitants and landmarks – and these pictures survive to this day. Cousin Terry Butcher remembers Bill using the family bathroom for processing his film and printing his pictures.[xlv]

Student Bill's schooling tended to peter out after he gained his Junior Certificate in 1941 during which he studied drawing, woodwork and metalwork. You would be entitled to think these subjects provided a seeding of an appreciation for design principles that would later guide his professional pursuits.

The reason that the scholastic drive started to dissipate for Angove and the other boys in his class was the Second World War.

"By his final year of school, all the boys knew they were headed into the forces when they left school so studies became a bit irrelevant," Gwenda observed.[xlvi]

"Only one boy passed his Leaving [Certificate] that year and all went into the forces when they turned 18, including Bill."

Life in Roelands, captured by young Angove:

Rail station, local kids, general store and post office and his family's home.

After his summer holidays straight after finishing school in 1942, Angove enlisted in the Citizens Military Forces (CMF) based at Karrakatta in Perth in February 1943 and spent almost a year in that service. He was officially described as a 19-year-old science course student. He trained in Northam most of 1943. A month before Christmas he joined the Australian Imperial Force (AIF), signing on in Bunbury. The family was still living in Roelands.

"He was very much missed at home," his sister recalled.

During 1944 he trained as a radio operator. By early 1945 he was sent to Kapooka army camp in New South Wales, one of the chief training schools for the Royal Australian Engineers. He was assigned to duties as a sapper in the depot on the outskirts of Wagga Wagga.

"We were grateful he was never sent overseas," said Gwenda, "even though he volunteered."

"It was a very traumatic time and we regularly heard of friends killed or missing."

However, working at Kapooka was also not without its own risks. On 21 May that year 26 trainee sappers learning to make small, hand-held explosives, along with two of their instructors, were killed at the camp when their bunker blew up.[xlvii] To this day it's not known precisely what went wrong for the cohort of 17- to 34-year-olds who perished. It was the worst defence training accident in Australian history. The procession and burials in Wagga Wagga remain Australia's largest military funeral yet an occasion rarely remembered, according to the ABC, because of the lack of publicity it has drawn in the years since.[xlviii] How close Angove was to this catastrophic incident is unclear and it seems he never later referred to the calamity.

During his time at Kapooka, Angove involved himself in two emerging creative outlets: drawing and photography. Having acquired another camera at Wagga, he mentioned in personal notes years later that he became the official camp newspaper photographer at Kapoooka. He also had a library job at the base, fortuitously his first close contact with the publishing business.

On arrival in Wagga, Angove had bought a 1930s compact plate camera, a German-built *Kodak Recomar*, known as a folding bed camera. According to an antique photography collector[xlix], the Recomars were designed to be used with plates or sheet film, either in individual film holders or in film packs. Bill's used film packs. It came from the Stuttgart factory of Dr August Nagel, later purchased by Kodak but shut down in 1939 when war broke out.

Sketch from wartime Kapooka Camp

Reaching out to the researchers at the Australian War Memorial (AWM), I discovered that Kapooka, like other military camps, had its own army official photographer, in this case a man named William Martin. But the base newspaper relied on less formal input and its records were more ephemeral.

"In a more general sense, the work of a camp newspaper photographer is much harder for us to track down than that of an official photographer proper," AWM's assistant photographic curator Emma White explained.

Alas the memorial doesn't hold any of Angove's photographic work but he is represented in the art collection with a single humorous cartoon (on page 27).[l] Emma White says the cartoon is part of the collection of illustrations that mostly come from various army publications such as the pocket-sized magazine, *Salt,* which the AWM labelled "the Australian Army Education Journal". The publication's purpose was described as entertaining and informing Australian servicemen and women. It sought contributions from Australian and allied serviceman [sic] "in the form of letters, stories, articles, verse and drawings".[li]

"Sometimes the name of the maker is only known because the drawing was signed by them. I think our Angove is one of those."

"I think he wants to join the BMA, Doc"

Rural scene drawn by Angove

You can see it's in a style that became Angove's trademark, as demonstrated in this illustration (on previous page) six years later. It also reflects a style of drawing typical of Australia's pen and ink exponents in the first half of the 20th century, exemplified by famous names such as Stan Cross, Norman Lindsay, Phil May and David Low whose work appeared regularly in journals such as *The Bulletin* and *Smith's Weekly*.[lii] He may well have become familiar with these publications through his work in the camp library. Anyone who can create cartoons is demonstrating some flair and it's reasonable to deduce that Angove had begun to feel confident about parading his wares to the world.

Other sources of enrichment were on offer to young men like Angove at Kapooka. It actually functioned like a complete village, boasting a huge recreational hall which was used for theatrical purposes as well, hospital, sports grounds, post office and the previously mentioned library.

While the residents 'day job' included instruction in all types of demolition and bomb disposal work, camp life offered a wide variety of other activities. Some of these likely helped to shape the tastes of Angove, the 20-year-old from the back blocks of Western Australia.

For instance, Wagga's school of arts and dramatic society performed plays at Kapooka[liii] and the camp's sappers and non-commissioned officers (NCOs) staged a major art exhibition that featured pencil drawings, black-and-white work, water colours, oils, architectural plans, leatherwork and jewellery[liv]. The art show occurred just prior to Angove's time there but it illustrates the diverse cultural interests that the camp population shared and suggests an atmosphere in which those with any artistic talents might have felt encouraged.

In total, his military service covered 1300 days when he was discharged in September 1946. He was one of more than half a million men and women demobilised from the military in the year after the war ended. Angove was aided by a scheme called civil rehabilitation which offered advice on finding employment, training, housing and loans. Years later he told magazine journalist Cyril Casellas that joining the army was a turning point in his life. He said his participation in the rehabilitation program gave him the opportunity to weigh up the pros and cons of what he would do when he was discharged.[lv]

"Eventually [he] decided it would be better to 'go alone' and take on photography as a bread-earner," wrote Casellas,[lvi] although this decision may not have come with utmost conviction and determination because, 20 years later, he told another writer, Allanah McDonald, that he rather turned to photography for "something to do".[lvii]

Angove availed himself of the soldier Civil Rehabilitation Centre 1946[lviii][lix]

To embark on his new mission, upon demobilisation Angove bought his third camera, an old American press camera, to be precise a Graflex 3¼ x 4¼ Speed Graphic, from professional photographer Howard Sainsbury who ran a studio and camera shop in Perth's London Court.

Graflex Speed Graphic camera of the type Angove acquired after leaving the army[lx]

According to Casellas[lxi], Angove then went frantically searching for a good second-hand exposure meter.

"In this way, he luckily gained his first break," he wrote.

"He found what he was looking for from a commercial photographer in Cottesloe."

That man was almost certainly Kevin Radford, one of a band in Perth who made a living from what might be called social photography. They would shoot pictures of people in the streets - for which a licence was required under a 1947 State law - as well as at functions ranging through weddings, parties and similar events.

It appears Radford introduced Angove to a fellow street photographer named Len Cutts[lxii] who ran a photographic business called *Modern Photos* in Wellington Street, West Perth, and also employed other photographers. The business was one of about a dozen that formed the Outdoors Photographers Association at the time.

Cutts reportedly told Angove: "I'm a bit up to the neck for wedding engagements. How about filling in for a couple of weeks?"

The keen ex-soldier didn't hesitate in accepting the offer.

"He promptly jumped at the chance," wrote Casellas.[lxiii]

It proved to be the first step on the ladder to making photography his livelihood. And in the way these things happen, it opened other doors for the 23-year-old ready to embrace opportunities.

Bill's mother Marjorie and her sister Clarice photographed by him on a Perth Street in November 1952

Foundations in photography

Back in Perth, Bill Angove was earnest and eclectic in his attempts to make a mark in the world. He set himself on multiple paths to realise his ambitions.

His energy seemed boundless as he took on the wedding photography assignments, studies in architectural draftsmanship - combined with relevant work in a private practice and at the State Housing Commission - and classes in drawing and painting at Perth Technical College.

In his own words, he also devoted himself to further educating himself about photography.

"During this time," he later wrote,[lxiv] "I followed a period of intense self-study on photography."

To underscore and reinforce his immersion in photography, Angove also joined the Western Australian Camera Club which was to prove a springboard for his later advancement.

Eventually his passion for working with the camera led him to "withdraw from further study towards architecture in favour of the practice of photography".[lxv]

In a pattern typically useful for progression in a career or other field of endeavour, this period in Perth immediately after the war enabled Angove to develop a network of contacts that nourished his future direction.

The population of Perth was only around 250,000 and those who lived, worked, studied or gathered for recreational purposes in and around the central city probably only amounted to half that number. It wasn't a big place. Angove's circle of friends and acquaintances represented a cultural slice of the inner city, dominated by artists, designers, photographers, performers and entertainers although many of them would have had day jobs in other fields.

For instance, when he was tackling street and wedding photography for Cutts, he found himself in the company of six telegraphists from the post office whose interests in picture-taking propelled them into this line of weekend work.

It wasn't all fun. Angove's friend Ken Knox recalls that the band of social photographers was issued with Leica cameras that sported very small viewfinders.

"Their hands would bleed after a day of working with the Leicas."[lxvi]

For Angove, the social photography generated at least two valuable rewards: personal development and scope for innovation.

"The weddings involved talking to a lot of people," he later confided,[lxvii] "and this broke me out of my shyness."

A close friendship that was to help professionally a few years later also arose from mixing around at weddings and parties. Like Angove, Rolf Harris had a beard and, even at 20 years of age, possessed a heap of talent. Harris, an art student and champion swimmer, was frequently hired as an entertainer at these events.

"Rolf was wise-cracking and playing the piano," Angove recalled.[lxviii] The pair became life-long friends. Harris was influential in encouraging his mate to try to make a name for himself in London, something Harris achieved on a major scale as a TV performer and artist.

The street and event photography gave Angove insights into people, business and confronting new boundaries.

"In eight years after the war, I went to about a thousand weddings, plus christenings and other functions," Angove recalled.[lxix] "

"Calculating on two and a half ounces of cake at each function, I must have eaten more than a ton of cake at that time."

On one occasion, he was assigned to a funeral and wake and, judging by some notes he later scribbled, appeared somewhat surprised by the experience of photographing a corpse for the first time.

His partners in this line of work, who included Radford, exposed him to a knock-about world that undoubtedly prepared him for adventures ahead as a stranger in unfamiliar settings.

"Why don't you do something useful like use a shovel," Radford teased him.[lxx]

At one stage, after morse code operator Ken Knox, newly arrived from his home state of New South Wales, joined him in his West Perth boarding house, Angove showed his capacity as a self-starter.

"One day Bill took a picture of me looking out the window of a train," Knox said.

"That started a [a line of] business for him … shooting [passengers] on interstate trains."

Over an initial period of about seven years Knox and Angove supported each other in numerous directions as fruitful friendships can often do.

The connections started to feed off each other. Knox met his future wife, Thelma Mills, through Angove. He and Thelma were contemporaries at the Perth Technical College, both studying drawing and painting. Knox's daughter Robyn tells the story that one evening her father went to the college to meet Bill at the end of his class.[lxxi]

"Bill and Thelma were walking to the gate together and then they all walked together to Thelma's bus stop," she says. "I'm not sure of the arrangements after that except they lived happily ever after."

Indeed, Knox and Mills married in 1952, and Angove was best man at the wedding. When their son Leslie was born a few years later, Angove became his godfather.

Best man Bill Angove with groom Ken Knox (1952)

While Thelma was formally studying art in her own time at the college, she was working as a commercial artist at the long-established publishing company of J Gibbney & Son, a powerhouse of printing and plate making in Western Australia.

This firm, founded by James Gibbney as block-makers and engravers in the mid-1880s, worked with Winthrop Hackett at *The West Australian* newspaper and the *Western Mail* in St Georges Terrace.

Gibbney's stable of apprentice process engravers and graphic artists included many who later became notable painters such Robert Juniper, Brian Taylor and Leon Pericles and, a generation earlier, Hal Missingham, Iris Francis and Harald Vike. Illustrators who later took their talent to the news columns of the papers also found their feet working for Gibbneys.

Thelma worked alongside Juniper in the business. He was at the next desk. Although she mainly produced illustrations of shoes for advertising, Thelma was working in an environment that nurtured strong artistic talent. And through friendship and a shared love of art, Angove became part of that same environment.

"Gibbneys was one of the few places where artists could earn a proper living at the time," says Philippa O'Brien, an artist, author and educator.[lxxii]

"It was a crucible for the development of fine art practice in Western Australia."

Virtually all visual material produced in WA in the 1940s and 50s came from this studio. It was a place where artists had a paid livelihood and became imbued in an ethic of professionalism.

Thelma Mills came under two strong influences in this setting: enrolment in classes at the nearby technical college, where luminaries such as Howard Taylor taught, and support and guidance from Gibbney's long-serving artistic director, John Lunghi, who became a personal friend. He was also an exhibiting artist and keen collaborator.

While Mills and Angove studied together, the latter never formalised his coursework. He told his supervisor, John Fawcett, a ceramicist and the college's deputy director, that he wasn't going to sit for exams.

Meanwhile, he and Thelma began to share a circle of friends and associates. John Lunghi was prominent among them. Angove names Lunghi at the top of a list of professional and personal contacts at the time.[lxxiii]

"Lunghi was a very culturally sophisticated Englishman who worked at Gibbneys for more than 35 years from 1937," says Philippa O'Brien.[lxxiv]

"He introduced his artists, like Thelma, to many other people and influences."

Many of the Gibbney artists combined their employment with studying or teaching at the technical college so these connections nurtured much talent in the WA art industry, and Bill Angove certainly found himself in that company.

Together with friends and family, he was fond of describing himself as "a frustrated painter". Yet he produced a lot of work to earn that self-deprecating status. His so-called frustration never seemed to deter him. The college itself became a favourite and enduring institution because two decades later he was back there teaching and experimenting with a new artistic form that combined screen-printing with photography.

While Gibbneys and the Perth Technical College might be considered among the cornerstones of the local art sector in the mid-20th century, the other major aligned institutions, closely linked and influential, were the newspapers of the era. By any national and international standard, Perth was a fairly small publishing town at the time.

One modest but relevant example of mutual interests was the long-time support for fine art and photography demonstrated by the proprietors of WA Newspapers who regularly hosted exhibitions in a public gallery at Newspaper House on St Georges Terrace. To reinforce the connections that prevailed at this time, this was the venue that staged the inaugural commercial exhibition of artworks by Rolf Harris in September 1950.

Though this 'Perth-boy-made-good' (Bill Angove) is among Britain's topline photographers he says . . .

'I'm really a frustrated painter...'

BILL ANGOVE

from CYRIL CASELLAS in London

"I'M a frustrated painter really," the small, wiry chap with an equally wiry beard confessed as he refilled my glass with red wine.

My attention was diverted from the eye-catching paintings on the walls of Bill Angove's bachelor flat in Bayswater, London.

"Yes," Angove declared, "I'm where I am now because I never really hit it as an artist."

And where is the Albany-born, Bunbury High School-educated man now? He's at the top of the tree in his field of work as a creative colour photographer in Britain.

Angove studied art in Perth, qualified as a draftsman but never felt that this was what he wanted to raise himself to the pinnacle of success.

The turning point in his life, which has now carried him to a highly self-satisfying and remunerative career, came when he was in the Army. Angove weighed up the pros and cons of the rehabilitation scheme in regard to what he would do when he got out and eventually decided it would be better to "go it alone" and take on photography as a bread-earner.

Like most successful photographers, he had an early grounding in the usual way — dabbling in snap-shooting with a box camera.

ANGOVE bought an old American Press camera and then frantically went in search of a good second-hand exposure meter. In this way he luckily gained his first break.

He got what he was looking for from a commercial photographer at Cottesloe, who suggested: "I'm a bit up to the neck for wedding engagements — how about filling in for a couple of weeks?"

Angove jumped at the chance, a camera was pushed into his lap, and he has never looked back.

"The weddings involved talking to a lot of people and this broke me of my shyness," he confided.

Angove's assignments at weddings sparked off a close friendship with another West Australian who has struck it rich in the creative world in England.

Also bearded, Rolf Harris, is one of the big hits in London show biz. Angove frequently was at weddings "where Rolf was wise-cracking and playing the piano."

Bill Angove's work — described as the work of a genius in photographic magazines both in Britain and in the United States — invariably is not seen and appreciated by the general public.

His work is essentially colour advertising and though some of it appears in popular magazines and such, much of it is produced in technical and scientific journals.

The highly dedicated photographer earns his own personal rewards and, though sometimes it means working on eight different locations in three days in various parts of the country, he can rake in $375 in two days and has reached a peak of cashing in to the tune of $500 for one day's work.

Continued

Paintings by Angove from his Perth Technical College years in the early 1950s

At least two leading lights from the city's thriving newspaper scene ranked among Bill Angove's inner circle of friends and associates, Paul Rigby (1924-2006) and Norman Aisbett (1921-2000).

It's not hard to discern the basis of the relationship between these three. They had much in common; each multi-talented, versatile and ever-willing to traverse new ground in their professional lives.

Rigby, born in the same year as Angove, left school in Melbourne at age 15 to work in a commercial art studio and then as a freelance commercial artist and book and magazine illustrator. After the war, he worked as a commercial artist and teacher before moving to Perth as an illustrator for West Australian Newspapers (1948–52), notably on the *Western Mail*.[lxxv] For the next half-century, he worked across Australia, the United Kingdom (UK) and the United States (USA) before retiring back to Western Australia in 2003. He settled in Margaret River, about three hours south of Perth, to concentrate on oil painting and run his own art gallery. In the mid-1970s he published a guide to drawing, influential among aspiring artists and cartoonists.[lxxvi] Bonds between him and Angove would seem a natural fit.

Norman Aisbett was notably a member of the Gibbneys studio stable of commercial artists prior to Thelma's time there. He then crossed over from advertising to editorial, making his name as a newspaper artist. As well, he gained a reputation as a painter and sculptor.[lxxvii] In the 1950s he was creating work depicting subjects as diverse as oil drilling and ballet. The latter was an abiding passion of Angove's. Aisbett's work, which also included portraiture, still occasionally appears in salerooms.

Both Aisbett and Rigby featured in exhibitions of work by press practitioners at Newspaper House over successive years in the early to mid-1950s. The reviewer of the 1954 display opined: "The newspaper artist is the galley slave of art. The present show brings out the technical skill and knowledge of composition so necessary in newspaper work."[lxxviii]

It's not hard to imagine that among the viewing audience for such shows would have been their friends Bill Angove and Ken and Thelma Knox. They socialised a lot. Prior to his departure for London in 1952, Rolf Harris was also one of the gang, in part because he and Thelma had become friends through their membership of the Bassendean swimming club.

Robyn Knox says the photographic mates often caught up at Angove's flat in South Perth to "do some darkroom work".[lxxix]

"I think Dad said Bill didn't like printing much. Then they went out for curry. Sometimes Thelma would visit with Dad and they would sit in Bill's courtyard having a beer."

Angove's numerous artistic pursuits, a source of growing affiliations and no doubt mounting aspirations, probably reached their zenith when he entrenched himself in the only camera club operating in Perth at the time.

Bill Angove with sister Gwenda (top) and Thelma and Ken Knox on a bush picnic

Camera club years

The Western Australian Camera Club was celebrating its 30th anniversary the year Bill Angove joined, newly arrived in Perth from war service. The club had been a meeting place and forum for devotees of photography since its foundation on a cold winter's night in 1917. Here Angove was to share his passion and sharpen his skills. He also proved to be a major contributor to the knowledge of others.

In Western Australia 1917 was also significant for the completion of the transcontinental railway, the admission of women to the police force and the arrival in Perth of a young Victorian, John Curtin, to edit a union newspaper. World War I was still raging in Europe.

A group of 34 people met in an accountant's office at the top of St George's Terrace at the invitation of the Colonial Secretary and Education Minister, Hal Colebatch.

At its formation, the Western Australian Camera Club prescribed its purpose as "the encouragement of the science, art and practice of photography, and the interchange of knowledge of such amongst members".

The foundation committee had strong ties to the recently established University of Western Australia (UWA).

The university's first professor of biology, William Dakin, was elected the inaugural president of the camera club.

Its foundation committee included a Scottish physicist who became a UWA Vice-Chancellor, Alexander David Ross, a future Minister for Health, Richard Sampson, and a future WA Government Astronomer, Harold Curlewis.

By the time Angove joined in 1947 an honour roll of club members had achieved distinction in the world of photography. For a spirited, energetic young man, it offered a conducive learning environment shaped by a string of former and current distinguished practitioners.

Dakin, for instance, later ran the zoology department at Sydney University and authored a seminal text on aquatic biology, *Australian Seashores*. More pertinently he worked with the famous Sydney photographer, Max Dupain, in advising Prime Minister John Curtin on military camouflage in World War II.

Alexander Ross and William Dakin

Ross accompanied a famous Goldfields photographer, John J Dwyer, on an expedition to photograph the solar eclipse at outback Wallal in 1922. Ross, a music lover and popular and witty broadcaster, later lived in Albany and served as patron of the club until the 1940s.

The strength of the links between the university and the club may have been, at least in part, due to the fact that the pioneers of each institution included numerous newspaper proprietors and editors, including Colebatch, Sampson and John Winthrop Hackett. Their legacies continued to leave their mark on the arts, education and publishing spheres in which Angove participated from the late 1940s.

A few earlier camera clubs had begun in Western Australia but did not survive. In July 1899, a club was established under the leadership of the police commissioner Colonel Phillips but he died within a year and the club did not survive. In the early 1900s, according to the *Kalgoorlie Miner* newspaper, a club was set up in neighbouring Boulder in the booming WA Goldfields but apparently waned.

In its early years, the WA Camera Club's membership was dominated by scientists and professional photographers, probably a reflection of the expense and complexity of photographic technology and processes.

The club divided its members into categories or sections, such as the "intermediate workers class" and the "advanced workers class", depending on their level of proficiency.

This practice persisted for decades. It was designed, in part, to assist beginners in finding their feet in photography as well as ensuring members could compete fairly in a range of ranked competitions. By the time Angove joined, the sections had been reclassified as grades A and B.

"The As won all the prizes," recalled Ken Knox, one of the GPO telegraphers who joined the club[lxxx], "because they could afford bigger paper."

Illustrating the club's commitment to education, its workshop talks and demonstrations were always a strong feature. Topics in the early years included a discourse on panchromatic film and light filters, lantern slide making, the carbon process of printing and *Pictorialism*. Among guest speakers at the club was the famous Antarctic and war photographer, Frank Hurley. Speakers were also drawn from its own ranks, a practice that was to see Angove rise to prominence among his peers.

Another hallmark of the WA Camera Club is its long tradition of competition and exhibition. Starting with its first public display which opened on 22 August 1917, the club held annual exhibitions of members' work. The early displays were mounted in venues such as St Georges House, the art rooms of the university, Boans department store and the Kodak Salon at 672 Hay Street.

Exhibition and competition subjects covered various categories such as landscape, street scenes, portraiture and human interest, architecture and branches of natural history, namely animal life and plant life. These broad themes are still well represented in the output of club members today.

From 1920 onwards photographs by members were exhibited in the Art Gallery of Western Australia and frequently over the years at Newspaper House on St Georges Terrace. In 1924 works by members of the club were included in an exhibition by the WA Society of Arts in Industries Hall, Barrack Street. These traditions would have appealed to Angove years later, keen to have his work shown in public. Indeed, his fine art prints made it into the state's premier gallery almost 60 years later.

Over the century it is estimated that more than a thousand people have joined the ranks of the WA Camera Club. Many achieved great distinction. Among the high flyers still active in Angove's time were Hilda Margaret Wright (1903 – 1990), who was honoured with a medal in 1938 by the Royal Horticultural Society in London for her mono wildflower photographs, and Fritz Kos (1927 – 2006), one of Australia's pre-eminent architectural photographers and founder of Mt Lawley College Photo School.

Club president in the late 1950s, Ted Roche, ran a portrait studio in London Court and was considered an inspirational leader and educator in the WA photographic world. He convened the meeting at which a peak body of camera clubs, known as the WA

Photographic Federation, was founded. The Federation's first president was a club colleague of Knox and Angove, Eddie Edwards, a postal engineer and former World War II Sunderland flying boat operator.

The club played an important and often pioneering role in the growth of popular photography in Perth and other regions of Western Australia, thanks to the likes of Bill Angove and other trailblazers.

Angove first attracted notice in the club in July 1947 when he took second place in a competition for which the set subject was "High Key Still Life". [lxxxi] He followed up with more competition success in 1948 responding to the topics of "Harbour and Shipping" and "Genre".[lxxxii]

Still Life was a recurring theme for Angove because, during the early 1950s, he indulged himself in this genre in both painting and photography. It can be seen as a forerunner to his proficiency in abstract imagery and the use of industrial and theatrical props which was to become a hallmark of his later commercial work.

By 1950 Angove had emerged as a prominent and instructive figure in the camera club. In September that year, he delivered the first of a string of presentations to his fellow members and visitors. His subject, Psychological Art, drew upon his two compelling preoccupations, painting and photography.

"There are two types of artists," he reportedly observed,[lxxxiii] "the visual type who depicts his art through his eyes and paints what he sees, and the haptic type, whose art expresses his emotions and, therefore, is often quite out of proportion."

The understanding of how a work of art can be viewed as "a combination of aesthetic symbols aimed at arousing emotions in people," seems to have been largely articulated by a Soviet psychologist during the first third of 20th century, Lev Vygotsky, who completed a dissertation in 1925 on the psychology of art.[lxxxiv] Others have reinforced it since.

The word 'haptic' was new to me. So I asked art curator and writer, Paola Anselmi, for help.

"It's a rarely used term," she explained, "but it means an artist whose work is not a mere visual translation of what they see but encompasses other factors, senses as well as emotions.[lxxxv]

"It has been used to describe performative work too which engages motion as well as sight."

Anselmi thinks the idea of haptic art is that it brings together in a work or a series of works or as part of an artistic aesthetic a complex web of associations … emotive, temporal, memorial, historical, philosophical and [a] list [that] can be endless.

The journal and website, *Frontiers of Psychology*, teases it out further: "The concept of haptic aesthetics has its foundations in the phenomenological insight that engaging with works of art involves more than vision alone. The haptic, as an aesthetic term, emerged in late 19th and early 20th century German art-history [and] evolved in Walter Benjamin's writings during the 1930s."[lxxxvi]

Benjamin also wrote about the social importance of photography[lxxxvii].

A modern scholar, Laura Marks,[lxxxviii] describes haptic visuality as a 'kind of seeing that uses the eye like an organ of touch.'

Presumably, Angove learned something of this analysis. Was it part of his art studies at the technical college? Did it come from his private reading?

Whatever the answer, it is a clue to unlocking photography from what many people like Angove may have perceived as a straight-jacket. He seems to be saying a certain type of artist is driven to parade the emotions experienced in an act of creativity and thereafter challenges a viewer to search for an emotional response as well.

This is relevant on at least two levels. It may well be the key to Angove's embrace of the abstract in photography. It is also consistent with the way photographic judges to this day are encouraged to evaluate competition works. What emotional response does an image engender? What message or meaning is conveyed by the photographer?

In summing up his talk in 1950, Angove insisted that you cannot judge a work of art without knowing the background of the artist and the reason why they created the picture. The club commended him on the amount of preparation he had devoted to the presentation.

He delivered another talk in July 1952 on the subject of stereoscopic photography. According to a press report, [lxxxix] he discussed ways of obtaining stereographs, the best type of film to use and the correct way to mount the prints. He also told his audience black and white transparencies could be made on lantern plates and viewed by transmitted light. Ever willing to explore the cutting edge, Angove said he found stereo photography so interesting that he would spend a lot of his time in this branch of photography.

By 1953 Angove's role in the club was firing up. A few months earlier he had been elected to the committee of management and delivered the aforementioned exhorting lecture on the value of embracing all the arts because photography had only a 100-year history. He also earned a prize for another Still Life and was elected president of the club's colour section. The latter role found him running sessions on topics such as "People" from a colour perspective.

Angove was among a select group that was represented in a public exhibition conducted by the club that year in the Kodak Gallery. The work was described as being of "a very high standard"[xc] and a means of conveying a "good impression" of the club's activities. For him in particular such shows gave him an appreciation of the value of effective public relations, a consideration implicit in many of his commercial undertakings in the future.

His print, *Hole in the Wall*, portrays the beginning of a style and selection of elements that were to emerge as signatures of his work over time: the deployment of jagged shapes and textures, later taken to new heights in his abstract output, and the enlistment of female models.

Hole in the Wall

Around this time, Angove also played a part in the critiquing of the members' monthly competition entries. This is a job that demands conscientious application and a capacity to provide articulate feedback. Furthermore, Angove's exploration of photographic art, both in his own work and that of others, reflected an ability which he later demonstrated as an author of photography articles and an educator.

The following year his camera club involvement remained ascendant. He led a debate on big versus small cameras.[xci] He argued in favour of the latter, another foresight into his equipment choices during a successful, agile and far-flung career. At that same club meeting, members submitted their prints in the monthly competition which was on the set subject, *Pin-Up Girl*.[xcii] He didn't earn a placing in the category that night but was no doubt reinforced in his liking for a genre in which he later excelled.

Angove also hosted an evening of colour travelogue movie films and stills from a contributing member, enthralling the audience with scenes of England and Europe.[xciii] He could hardly have imagined as he enjoyed the session that, within the next decade, he would be shooting pictures in such exotic locations for use in tourist literature.

Angove's leadership of the colour push culminated in two other episodes.

According to Knox,[xciv] his mate Bill obtained the first roll of a revolutionary colour film called Dufaycolor at the club, a product cheaper than others such as Kodachrome and compatible with "typical snapshot cameras"[xcv]. It was a breakthrough for amateur darkroom enthusiasts because they could process Dufaycolor at home almost as easily as black-and-white film.

Angove also reached out to Kodachrome users in the eastern states to send across their slides in exchange for a batch from the WA club.

So many of the things Angove tackled demonstrate that he would constantly strive to be at the cutting edge.

He was a keen participant in all other facets of the club, including workshops and excursions. The club's official records show Angove in various photographs taken at such events. In hand-written notes summarising milestones in his life, he rated the camera club among the major early influences. His list of friends, beyond the Knoxes, included club luminaries such as Fritz Kos and David Jukes. These relationships appear to link well with his tastes and interests because Kos was renowned across Australia for excellence in architectural and engineering photography and Jukes was a prolific and revered theatrical photographer. Angove came to love the theatre and always had a strong propensity for utilising design elements in his work.

Angove and Knox prominent in club activities (1954):
Picnic at Yanchep (above) (Pic: Ted Roche)
and demonstration at clubrooms (below)

Another friendship, nurtured in these camera club years, was with Jack Lorimer, a one-time science student and drama society member at UWA. Lorimer had previously undertaken draughting studies at Perth Technical College where the pair likely met. Later an exploration geologist by profession, Lorimer was "a highly proficient amateur photographer … [and creator of] a wonderful historic record of Perth and regional Western Australia during his lifetime".[xcvi] He and Angove joined the committee of the camera club at the same time. They shared a fondness for theatre arts and a friendship with Rolf Harris, a connection which flourished when they both later found themselves in London.

Lorimer ventured there with a friend, Leslie Marchant, a future professor of history, six months after Angove. The three men enjoyed enduring bonds. Twenty years later, Lorimer studied photography under Angove back in Perth, their mutual regard well established.

Both his passion and his practical achievements from the eight post-war years delineate Bill Angove as a man who wouldn't always be satisfied with the limited stimulation and success available in the modest settings of Western Australian art and photography. By the start of 1955, he had bigger ambitions to realise.

With fellow West Australian David Jukes

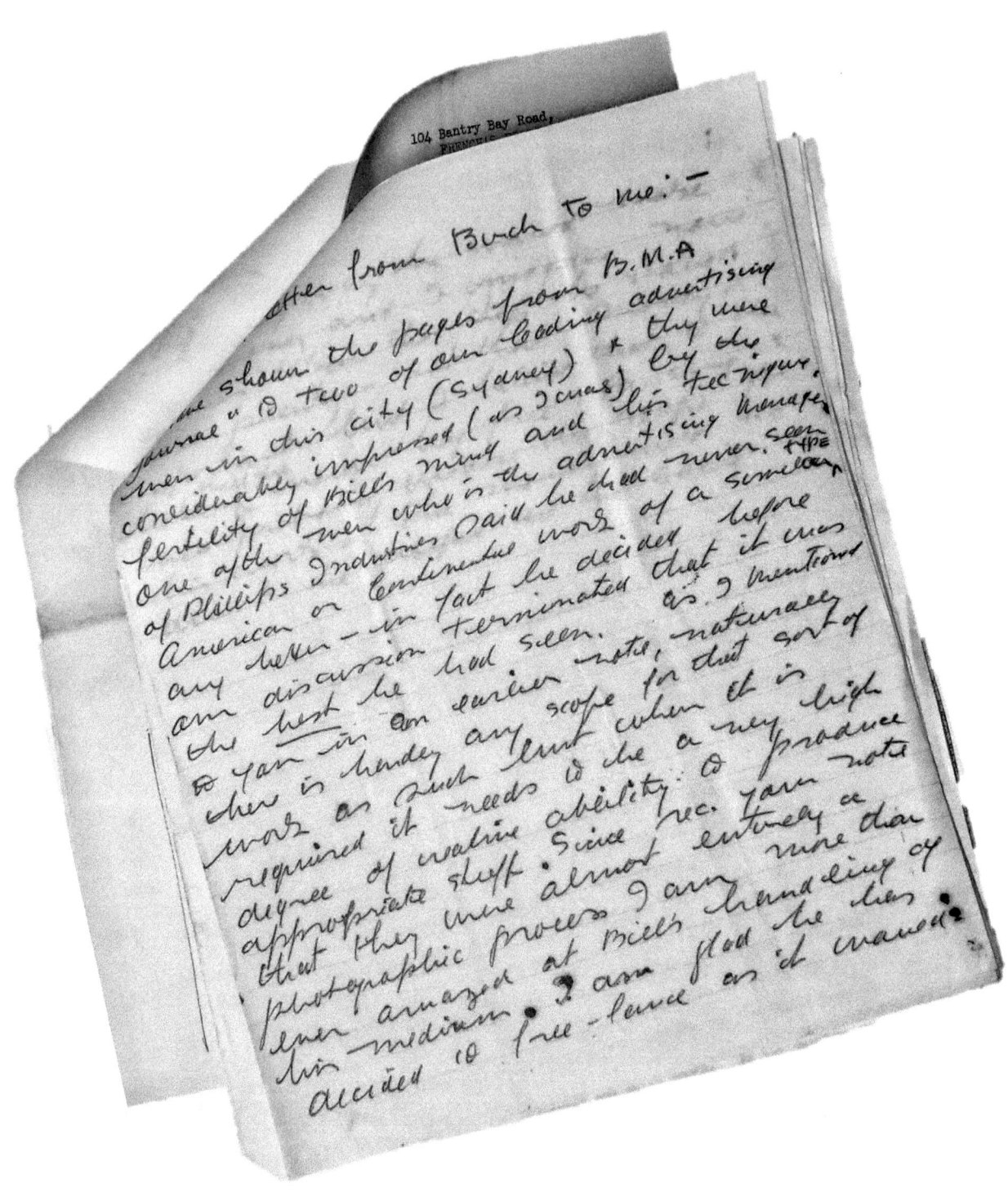

Letter from Burchell Butcher

The Lure of London

Angove spent the Christmas of 1954 with family down in Albany. He was at a crossroads.

With the hindsight afforded by history, and evidenced in a stream of archived materials I have had at my disposal researching his story, it is no exaggeration to declare Angove an emerging polymath by this time. The man demonstrated a keen appetite for learning, for stretching his boundaries and for performing in multiple spheres, seemingly in a hectic way at times.

For instance, by the end of 1954, he was a leading light in "a loosely-constituted group of people working together as the Art Club" in Perth.[xcvii] Angove was represented in an art exhibition at Boans' [department store] fashion gallery by "a bewildering variety of drawings and paintings". The *West Australian* newspaper's art critic labelled three of the works reasonably successful and, offering advice, suggested "perhaps concentration would develop an individual style".[xcviii]

In the same year, while working part-time for the State Housing agency, Angove was running a life drawing enterprise, the Perth Life Class, founded some years earlier by friend John Lunghi, the Gibbney's studio director, artist and educator. According to an old press clipping, the Monday evening classes in Cremorne Arcade off Hay Street had "an atmosphere of earnest effort" and "little direction except for mutual criticism".[xcix] No doubt Angove would have said this was precisely how you explore and learn. For him, it was the start of a long-time practice in the art of the nude.

All this immersion came on top of his social photography assignments, camera club participation, drafting work and art and photography studies.

So Christmas found him mulling over his future plans. Among the options on his mind was the example set by a member of his close friendship network, Michael Barrington-Martin.

Barrington-Martin was a Perth music graduate and piano teacher who had married Peggy Loneragan in 1949. Throughout his life, Angove often expressed a love for music.

"My taste is for classics," he wrote towards the end.[c]

It's likely he met the couple at one of their concerts or at a wedding he was photographing. They became part of his inner circle. Barrington-Martin's father was a portrait photographer in England, well known in the entertainment community, and by the end of 1952 Michael and Peggy decided to move to London to pursue similar directions.

Throughout the next two years, he and Angove continued to correspond and shortly before that Christmas break in his birthplace, an unfulfilled Bill Angove received another letter from his mate.

Barrington-Martin suggested the time was right if Angove himself was interested in heading to the UK.

"I realised I would never find my goals in the Perth of the time," Angove recalled much later.[ci]

But at the time he agonised.

"It took me a great deal of decision-making over whether to do the trip or not," he told niece Beverley towards the end of his life.[cii] That's despite admitting later that he was feeling in a rut in his native state and had a hankering to apply his talents to a more creative side of photography.

Magazine writer Allanah McDonald summarised this turning point more than a decade later: "Instinctively he felt that Western Australia was not the place in which the creative talent he felt sure he possessed would develop."[ciii]

He recalled in his conversation with his niece: "I had enough money. I could work the trip. The fare over by boat - in a six-berth cabin – was about ninety Australian pounds at the time."[civ]

The Barrington-Martins offered to put him up for some months and suggested he could take on some jobs with his friend, who by then was making a name for himself in the photographic world, specialising in theatrical portraiture based around the Great Windmill Lane entertainment district in London's West End.

Another enticement for Angove was the urgings of his friend Rolf Harris who had also ventured to London in 1952. A graduate of the University of Western Australia and Claremont Teachers' College, Harris enrolled to study visual art at the City and Guilds Art School in Kensington.

During this time, he came to the attention of a well-known fellow Australian artist named Hayward 'Bill' Veal, who had gone to London in 1951 to teach and paint.[cv] Veal, who had extensive experience including eight appearances in the Archibald Prize and managing art schools in Sydney and Melbourne, both inspired the young Harris and provided practical guidance to develop his artistic craft. Within a year, Harris also debuted on British television as a cartoonist-storyteller.[cvi] By 1953 his mentor Veal was elected President of the Australian Artists Association in London,[cvii] illustrating the momentum that had developed around expatriates spreading their wings abroad. Harris considered him "a father figure".[cviii]

The progress of Angove's mates - one a photographer and one an artist - must have helped Angove's eyes light up at the prospect of tackling the UK because he thought of himself as having a foot in both camps.

Angove consistently labelled himself an artist willing to give up paint for the camera "but who thinks and feels still as an artist".[cix]

The decision of Angove's friends to try their luck in London was part of a significant trend on the Australian cultural scene in this decade. Although there were early pilgrimages to England and the Continent by Australian visual artists, such as E Phillips Fox and Frederick McCubbin throughout the first half of the 20th century[cx], the period had been disrupted by two world wars. The 1950s suddenly opened the window much wider.

In a seminal essay in the literary magazine *Meanjin* in 1950, Melbourne-based critic, writer and teacher A A Phillips identified a trend he dubbed the 'Cultural Cringe', a phrase that henceforth entered the Australian lexicon.

In the words of one of Phillips' distinguished students, historian Geoffrey Blainey,[cxi] the term "referred to an old-time Australian tendency to bow down in the presence of English culture".

Phillips' entry in Wikipedia is more expansive in describing the cultural cringe:

> *It explored ingrained feelings of inferiority that local intellectuals struggled against, and which were most clearly pronounced in the Australian theatre, music, art and letters. Phillips pointed out that the public widely assumed that anything produced by local dramatists, actors, musicians, artists and writers was necessarily deficient when compared against the works of European counterparts. The only ways local arts professionals could build themselves up in public esteem was either to follow overseas fashions, or, more often, to spend a period of time working in Britain. In some professions this attitude even affected employment opportunities, with only those who had worked in London being treated as worthy of appointment or promotion. Thus the cultural cringe brought about over the early to mid-20th century a pattern of temporary residence in Britain for so many young talented Australians across a broad range of fields, from the arts to the sciences.*

Contemporary author and historian Don Watson identifies a prevailing attitude in post-war Australia in a 2001 essay: "Our publishing and literary taste was largely determined in Britain, our graduates studied in British universities, our intellectual and creative talents expatriated themselves to Britain."[cxii]

Any examination of the lives of Australians who came to enjoy success in the arts and letters during this epoch will reveal scores, if not hundreds, of examples. I merely looked into the timelines of a handful I came to admire or have an association with.

In no particular order, there's Fred Williams, "surely Australia's greatest and most innovative landscape artist of the 20th century"[cxiii], arriving in London in 1952. Sidney Nolan, who is credited with "changing the nature of Australian art"[cxiv] and who, like Angove, had served in the Australian Infantry Forces (AIF) in rural Australia during the war, first travelled to London in 1950 and again to stay in 1953[cxv] having by then become famous in Australia.[cxvi] Angove was to cross paths with Nolan in their adopted homes.

Another man Angove later came to know, the illustrious David Moore, "the first Australian photographer to work consistently for the international picture magazines during their grand era … of the 1950s",[cxvii] went to London in 1951 to advance his career.

A young newspaperman named Graham Perkin, "a transformational figure in the history of the media in this country"[cxviii] who was to be my first editor at *The Age* in 1972, headed to London for a year in 1955 to learn how journalism was undertaken on Fleet Street. Like Angove, he spent his childhood in the bush, a setting that tended to produce self-starters.

The pattern is confirmed.

In a study of Australian photography of the era, curator Gael Newton describes the 1950s as "a difficult time for creative photographers concerned with working in a meaningful way personally or professionally."[cxix] She says that, for this reason, many chose to go overseas.

But for Western Australians like Angove, there may have been even more of an attraction to London. In a history of Australian women photographers, the authors make the observation: "For serious artists and photographers in Western Australia the links with other countries, particularly England … always competed with any pull exerted by the culture of the distant eastern states. For travel, pleasure and learning, Europe was not much further or expensive."[cxx]

However, the aspirations of colossal emerging talents such as those mentioned cannot be entirely attributed to a cultural cringe or, in the case of West Australians, convenience. The place they chose to go to was offering something mightily alluring. English journalist and broadcaster, Katharine Whitehorn, in an article in 2007,[cxxi] looked back at the 1950s as times when "everything was getting better". She observed that these optimistic years ushered in new personal and political freedoms as well as bolder entertainment, literature and fashion. And more was to come in the next decade.

By the end of the 1954 Christmas holidays, Angove had made up his mind.

"I wrote to Michael and told him I would come."[cxxii]

"Every Australian photographer should go overseas,"[cxxiii] he later observed, "not just to observe but to stay and improve their techniques. And when you are young is the time. Otherwise, one becomes bogged down with a complex studio and other commitments.

"In a place like London, it is difficult to get into things so a short stay offers little more than sight-seeing opportunities in the photography world. One must spend a couple of years to make any worthwhile headway in the experience field in the eyes of British and European photographers."

In his own words, this was a clear re-statement of the mission that had guided him as he boarded the new P&O ocean liner, *SS Iberia,* at Fremantle on the second leg of her maiden voyage back to the UK.

the faces behind the names at *Mayflower Studio*

Teamwork is the secret of the unique service provided by Mayflower Studio. Although it is one of the largest and best equipped studios in the West End (4,000 square feet), Art Directors get the same personal kind of service they would expect from an individual. Who are these individuals?

HOWARD BYRNE
photographic director

'artists and photographers working together as part of the same team can inspire and stimulate one another'

First, there's Howard Byrne, Managing Director and Creative Head. We put him first, because he's the boss! He looks and talks like Jimmy Cagney—the same energy and drive—and you can't help but feel at ease in his company. Versatility is one of his outstanding characteristics. He obviously likes a lot of balloons in the air and much of the enjoyment he derives from photography is probably due to the fact that it gives him so many points of contact with life.

During the war, Howard Byrne was a front-line correspondent for the U.S. Army newspaper 'Stars and Stripes'. At the end of the war he swapped his typewriter for a camera and never looked back. He first made his home in England twelve years ago and formed MAYFLOWER STUDIO. Now he commutes at least twice a year between London and New York.

Byrne delegates most of the assignment work for clients to his capable studio staff, which enables him to concentrate on producing a steady stream of photographs for the ever-growing MAYFLOWER STUDIO LIBRARY.

His chief hobby is sailing—he keeps a cruising yacht and speed boat for water ski-ing at Birdham Pool, Chichester, and lives with his artist wife and 3 children on Coombe Hill, New Malden in Surrey.

BILL ANGOVE

Bill Angove is a bearded Australian expatriate who has fallen in love with London twice, and now its for keeps. He worked for Mayflower several years ago before homesickness took him back to Australia to work for Vogue Australia magazine but when his nostalgia for Europe regained ascendency he returned to London and re-joined Mayflower.

Angove is a photographic impressionist who produces colour photographs that look like modern paintings. He likes to work in the abstract or to take on assignments for clients who want something off beat. He experiments ceaselessly and has even boiled colour transparencies and printed three colour negatives on top of one another in his striving for a new image. He achieves some of his most original effects by painting on the back of his transparencies, which gives them a lift and sometimes completely transforms them. Kodak were so impressed by this exciting technique that they have made dye transfers prints of a number of Angove's transparencies for exhibition purposes.

No—this is not the Phantom of the Opera. Just Bill Angove—our Studio Manager dressed up for a fancy dress party.

Angove who had a couple of years at art school before turning to photography, is always striving to press back camera frontiers.

Carol Davy—who is probably the first person you will talk to when you phone MAYFLOWER STUDIO. She commands the switchboard and acts as receptionist-secretary—sees that the pictures get to the post on time, sign releases and that the models are pretty enough to be a model herself and did in fact do a modelling stint before joining MAYFLOWER.

Framing life off Piccadilly

The voyage was an entirely new experience for Angove who had never left Australia before. The ship's first stop was Colombo, the commercial capital of what was then called Ceylon, a former British island colony in the Indian Ocean. It excited the young photographer. Despite finding the place scruffy and the people quite different to those he'd previously encountered, Angove considered it picturesque.

He recalled later that it was the start of a liking for exotic Asian cities.

"I felt I had benefitted already," he said.[cxxiv]

Bombay (now Mumbai) was next on the itinerary, adding to Angove's fascination with a new culture.

After travelling through the Red Sea and Suez Canal, the ship finally arrived at Tilbury dock in London on a very dark March morning. It was snowing. And although he recorded that he had never previously felt so cold, he also admitted to being excited.

Unloading their own luggage, passengers endured what Angove described as the "terrible business" of going through customs that day.

It was here he encountered the first of his international challenges. He had bought a £10 studio camera in the port of Aden but the British Customs Service wanted to charge him another £60 of import duty.

"I didn't have the money," he explained, so the camera was warehoused until such time he could later declare it and pay the impost.[cxxv]

Michael and Peggy Barrington-Martin were waiting on the wharf for their friend and finally collected him. First order of proceedings was a whirlwind tour of the famous sights of the West End. Then it was off to Michael's parents place in Ladbroke Grove, a reasonably affluent former estate of Victorian dwellings between North Kensington and Notting Hill which included many artistic types among its residents. It was to become a counter culture mecca during the 1960s, a decade that was to mark Angove's second and longest stint in London.

In early 1955, Angove settled into the neighbourhood and lived out of a suitcase for about three months.

Barrington-Martin's recently acquired studio was in Great Windmill Street, just behind the Windmill Theatre, with the main transport connection through nearby Piccadilly Circus station.

"Michael ran quite a mixed photographic business," Angove recalled. Due to its location in the heart of an entertainment district, the studio's work ranged from portraiture to stills of theatrical performances to advertising shots as well as images for "cheap dolly bird" magazines.[cxxvi]

Beginning within days of his arrival in Britain, Angove's first job - as became the trend in the early starting points in his career - was in the darkroom. In fact, a decade later he wrote an essay called *Darkrooms I Have Known* in which he referred to the many he'd seen and worked in as black, slimy holes.[cxxvii]

In the darkroom of the Soho studio of Barrington-Martin, Angove set to work for the first time in his new country. One of the business's good earners was processing pictures for the neighbouring Windmill Theatre which had its own photographer. Angove did all the chap's developing and printing.

"I never had to go and see the shows across the road because I got to see all the negatives and the finished versions as well," he explained.[cxxviii]

The theatre, on the corner of Great Windmill and Archer streets, just off Shaftsbury Lane, had opened in June 1931 as a small play-house, but the unpopularity of its first play convinced owner Laura Henderson and her manager Vivian Van Damm to use the theatre as a variety house with non-stop performances and undressed showgirls.[cxxix]

A collection of photographs from the theatre's heyday in the 1950s, the time a freshly-arrived Angove encountered it from his darkroom duties, came onto the sale market in 2017. The auctioneer commented: "The fantastic archive of photos from the Windmill Theatre provides a peek into a wilder side of the 1950s than we are used to seeing.[cxxx]

"It is a world of glamour, youth and beauty, not words we normally associate with 1950s Britain."

The Barrington-Martin studio seemed to be among the hotspots of this parade of flesh and fashion. One of the firm's assistants, David Nye, recalls Peggy as "the brains of the business"[cxxxi] and Michael's fondness for the models, hence he "regularly had the studio door locked after a shoot".[cxxxii]

Another man who says he worked as a messenger for the studio a decade later posted online in 2015: "Can you imagine being a young teenager … working in a fashion and advertising studio in London's West End, around the corner from Carnaby Street; the Beatles recorded *Let it Be* on a roof not far away?"[cxxxiii]

It's not hard to imagine that this environment of showmanship and gloss was part of the edginess and spark that the young Western Australian photographer and artist was craving for when he left Perth. It proved to be the start of a long association with performance and glamour evidenced throughout both his international and later career.

This first overseas gig also introduced Angove to an emerging legion of famous names in entertainment and the arts, as Britain was striving to re-establish its *joie de vivre* after the devastation of the war. The Windmill, "infamous for its risqué dancing girls",[cxxxiv] was "a magnet to many of the new wave ex-servicemen comedians … but it was a tough crowd for comedians [because] not too many patrons were there for the jokes."

'It was post-war, the country was looking for distractions and these extravagant performances must have certainly provided some with those."

Angove was dazzled by the stars of stage and screen he discovered around him, initially in the environs of the Windmill.

"Many became great comedians," he reflected years later.[cxxxv] The list of names he encountered included Jimmy Edwards and the Goons - Sellers, Secombe, Milligan and Bentine - while the Windmill in that same era also helped advance the careers of Tony Hancock, Tommy Cooper, Benny Hill and Bruce Forsyth among many others.

Angove talked about a little club in Broadwick Street where the comics used to meet and where the original Goons had got together.

By the time Angove came to London, the Goons were radio regulars on the British Broadcasting Corporation (BBC) and obviously had an impact on him because he later admiringly summed up their modus operandi, "quite spontaneous, joking among themselves and [with] their style of humour."[cxxxvi]

A US magazine writer labelled the Goon Show as "avant-garde", "surrealist", and "abstract".[cxxxvii] He could have been talking about the talent of Bill Angove because it was from a similar mindset that his breakthrough photographic work was to emerge and capture attention before 1955 was out.

Working in the precinct of the Windmill Theatre was inevitably a stimulating experience for the ex-pat. He saw a slice of life that contrasted sharply with the relatively drab staidness of where he'd come from.

"One Thursday afternoon [in those early weeks] I came out of Michael's studio," he recalled.[cxxxviii]

"I think it was Archer Street, full of people, full of men hanging around talking in groups. I couldn't understand it [at first but then] it used to happen regularly.

"I found out later on that the musicians' union had its premises there. They all came in to get their gigs for the week and their payments. They'd then get together and go up to the pubs nearby.

"This was near the Rupert Street markets. There were all the wheelbarrows with fruit and veg. In Compton Street in Soho, there were all the beaut cheese and bread shops. For me, coming from a pretty plain city as Perth was at the time, it seemed very exciting."[cxxxix]

Settling into the great metropolis of London was a constant adventure of course. The underground rail system took some getting used to, he once complained.[cxl]

He said there was no way of knowing how far apart two stations were so he often found it preferable to walk. But even that had its challenges during that first winter.

"I got lost in the snow at Covent Garden," he said. "Just couldn't find my way back around the corner. It looked so different. I'd gone out in the morning and came back in the afternoon. I had no idea where I was."

Within a short time though he found his way around London.

The darkroom at the Barrington-Martin studios was suspended between the ground floor and the basement, according to Angove's description.[cxli]

He observed that it was an advantageous location because while he was printing pictures he could use a peephole into the studio, "able to enjoy a private view when clients hired [it] and provided their own models".[cxlii]

The darkroom, the Australian's first workspace in England, was confining.

"No daylight ever penetrated," he noted, "and wet reject prints littered the floor where they were trampled underfoot, giving off a peculiar odour which never dissipated."

Working in his host's darkroom was merely a holding operation and stepping-off point. By June, Barrington-Martin noted in a written job reference that Angove, whom he described as diligent and trustworthy, had familiarised himself with the London scene and "now feels he has sufficient local knowledge to obtain permanent employment which he desires in darkroom and/or actual photographic work."[cxliii]

"I had to find my own job," Angove explained.

"I started taking around what few examples I had of my own work with me, trying to find studios and places that might take me on."

Angove generated some interest from the operators of an enterprise called Mayflower Studio, situated off Piccadilly. He initially thought he might find a better offer but after a little contemplation, he decided to accept their modest deal to work there. It proved to be an ideal match-up.

Mayflower Studio was a large and well-equipped photographic agency located right in the heart of the West End. It ran darkrooms, a printing shop and numerous studios for portraiture and advertising shoots. It produced original work – especially in the field of fashion - which it regularly sold to the press, provided finishing services for other photographers' output and took on regular commissions from commercial UK and international clients.

1 Dover Street today

It occupied premises at 1 Dover Street, situated across the road from the Ritz Hotel in Mayfair. The building had been constructed in 1883 as a grand six-storey residence designed by Scottish architects Weatherley and Jones. Later, it became Hatchett's Hotel and White Horse Cellars.

Between the world wars, the place had been subdivided into offices. Mayflower, starting in the early 1950s, occupied a section that had previously housed photographic studios. They had an auspicious past that Angove was later to discover. In fact, Dover Street had a reputation for culture. Chopin had stayed there a century earlier while giving recitals in London and it had accommodated numerous photographic studios and fashion houses over the decades. Its predominantly Jewish entrepreneurs dressed and photographed actresses, dancers and musicians, a tradition that endured into the mid-1950s when Angove arrived on the scene.

Although he was destined for another darkroom initiation at Mayflower, Angove had equipped himself with a repertoire from his days in Perth that was to be instrumental in securing his breakthrough job in the heart of London and placing him on the first rung of recognition in world photography.

Advertisement for the services of Mayflower Studio

Sailing into early success

Bill Angove struck gold when he joined up with the partners who had established Mayflower Studio. He stepped into an international stable of entrepreneurship and talent. The business belonged to two energetic and visionary North Americans, a Canadian named Howard Byrne and a big tall Texan, Leon "Lee" Israel.

They were citizens of the world and quickly became sources of encouragement and opportunity for the young Australian.

At the job interview, Angove produced his secret weapon, a set of highly experimental and innovative prints that had travelled with him from Western Australia and marked him as a would-be avant-garde practitioner with film, chemicals and camera. This folio of work, which in a sense straddled photography and painting, particularly piqued the interest of Israel.

"Lee first recognised from my samples what I was trying to do," Angove recalled. [cxliv] "He was interested in the same kind of thing."

This was Angove's entrée to a studio with many business tentacles, reflecting the tastes and expansive thinking of the firm's owners. It's not hard to see a shared thread of adventurism in the pair and their new recruit.

Howard Byrne was a former photo-journalist who had worked from a base in New York City for the US military's newspaper, *Stars and Stripes*, during World War II. His career as an army press correspondent included covering stories such as the liberation of a grim prisoner-of-war camp holding Soviet, American, French, Italian and Serbian soldiers at Bad Orb in Germany in 1944.

After the war he fell in love with the West Sussex coast of England and settled around the historic and artistic city of Chichester, an area renowned for its idyllic harbour and sandy beaches. Spectacular coastlines would have been a ready-made subject for discussion with Angove whose Albany roots had endeared him to similar beauty.

Post-war professionally, Byrne "swapped his typewriter for a camera and never looked back".[cxlv] That was in large part due to the fact that he took charge of his own destiny, building a corporate empire based on supplying words and pictures for clients and media outlets.

Byrne, "a jolly little fellow",[cxlvi] was a sailor too. He owned a cruising yacht and commuted between Chichester's marina at Birdham Pool and New York at least twice a year.[cxlvii]

Appropriately given their origins, Byrne and Israel named their studio after the cargo ship *Mayflower* which had been hired by a band of purist pilgrims to sail from Plymouth in England to Cape Cod in Massachusetts in 1620, leading to the first permanent settlement by the English in the colony of what later became the USA. The studio's logo was a simple, stylised version of the ship (below).

Logo of Mayflower Studios

The pair's internationalism and fondness for the symbolism of the *Mayflower* was demonstrated by participation in the project to build a replica of the famous ship in Brixham, England, in the mid-1950s. The ship was a gift to the people of America from the people of England in honour of the friendships formed during World War II.[cxlviii] When it sailed from Plymouth in the UK in 1957 across the Atlantic to Plymouth, Massachusetts, Lee Israel was on board as one of 33 crew members. His official designation was as cameraman, suggesting he shot film footage as well as stills. The *Mayflower II* was captained by an Australian, author and photographer Alan Villiers.

The transcontinental characterisation of the business had other manifestations. Byrne founded his own press agency, the Transatlantic News Service, which gave him licence to travel around the globe, often under sail, writing feature stories and shooting pictures for sale and syndication to newspapers.

A profile of Howard Bryne in the company's catalogue ascribed to him "the same energy and drive" as the actor Jimmy Cagney.[cxlix] He revelled in promoting transatlantic connections, exemplified at one time by his strong backing in London publishing circles for a famous biography of Winston Churchill's New York-born mother, Jennie.

"Versatility is one of his outstanding characteristics," the piece continued. "He obviously likes a lot of balloons in the air and much of the enjoyment he derives from photography is probably due to the fact that it gives him so many points of contact with life."

It sounds like the adventurous Angove had met kindred spirits in Byrne and Israel.

"They made me an offer that was very small, about seven pounds a week, beginning in the darkroom," Angove recalled of his probationary start without any regrets.[cl]

It quickly became obvious that although he was initially low in the Mayflower pecking order, Angove appreciated the environment, respected the talented colleagues around him and continued on a valuable learning trajectory.

The working spaces at 1 Dover Street were numerous and connected in a rather haphazard fashion, according to Angove's records. The layout combined offices with studios via large connecting corridors. The retouchers had their own backroom. The negative rooms comprised a large converted passage which had been starved of daylight for many years.

The darkrooms were occupied mainly by young men who, he observed, "seemed quite satisfied with their conditions" even though their equipment was pretty old but obviously functional.[cli]

"We had a lot of film people working there and they were quite interesting to work with," the recruit recalled.

Mayflower employed seven or eight photographers at the time. Angove said they largely worked on their own assignments or brought clients' jobs back into the studios for a more experienced colleague to execute.

Much of the output, done on tight deadlines, entailed fashion shoots because Mayflower supplied pictures to a string of demanding daily papers. Among Angove's colleagues was John Antill, a man steeped in fashion photography whose work is still considered collectable today. Antill did work for big fashion houses like Pierre Cardin and also worked with record companies and entertainers like Duke Ellington. Even from these early days, you can recognise that Angove was in a mecca of big names, a potential platform to fame.

The Australian found that by working overtime a couple of evenings a week, he could bring his salary up to about £10.

"Slowly I was able to pay off the £60 I had borrowed to get my camera back [from customs] within the six-month time frame," he noted. In the meantime, he'd only had what he described as an "old beat-up" camera but had the advantage of borrowing better gear from the company's stocks.

That first year in London was a financial struggle for Angove and indeed he was still watching his pennies four years later as his first stint there wound up.

Cousin Terry Butcher, who worked in films and arrived in the UK a few months after Bill, was surprised at his relation's frugality.

"I thought he was doing very well financially," he recalled, citing an occasion when Angove suggested they do dinner in Soho.[clii]

"I was expecting a slap-up affair on the town but we ended up having just a hot dog."

The variety of work which went through the Mayflower darkroom was quite a contrast.

"In the darkroom, we worked hard at printing not only glamorous pictures but also very plain industrial stuff," Angove recalled.[cliii]

He cited as an example photographs of drawings of motor car tyres, which had to be accurately printed with extreme precision.

Within a short time, Angove's prospects in the firm were on the rise, matched by his ability to learn from those around him.

"I found that by starting at the bottom and working hard, they were pleased with me. They took me out of the darkroom and made me a general studio assistant and negative developing boy. This at the age of 30!

"I still got the same money, same overtime, but this negative developing area was straight next to the darkroom and we had to load the 5 X 4 films up and develop them very quickly and pass them straight through for printing. The finished prints were carefully retouched for the newspaper work.

"I saw what they did with the lighting and noticed different approaches and techniques by different photographers."

Angove took all these insights on board. In the meantime, he was still rising to challenges in the darkroom.

Around the middle of 1955, the noted British photographer Cecil Beaton was looking for new laboratories for printing his work. It was quite an achievement for Mayflower Studio to be in contention for the contract.

Beaton (1904-1980) had a huge reputation as a society portraitist, fashion leader, interior and set designer, illustrator, diarist, film and theatre costume designer and painter. He was "renowned for his images of elegance, glamour and style".[cliv] Britain's National Portrait Gallery considers his influence on portrait photography to be profound and enduring.

Studio head Howard Byrne was larger than life at the best of times, according to Vic Singh, a London photographer who worked at Mayflower as a junior assistant more than sixty years ago. Singh says Byrne's booming voice always reminded the staff who was boss.[clv]

Bill Angove was on the receiving end of the Canadian's spirited exhortations – and trust - when the first 'trial' assignment came in to the business from Beaton.

"Howard gave me the job of producing two of Cecil Beaton's famous images," he stated.^{clvi}

Handed the negatives, Angove was told to do the best possible prints he could.

"I don't care how long you take," Byrne said in his loud accent, "you gotta do the best job in the world, kiddo.

"You're in the hot seat, kid."

Angove recalled that he was given plenty of time.

Finally, he produced a satisfactory print of two of Beaton's pictures: the classic image of St Paul's Cathedral smouldering after a bombing in London (below), and a group of ladies in a Middle Eastern harem.

Beaton's St Paul's classic image

"They were very difficult negatives [to work with] because Beaton was a bit of a guesser," he said. "He wasn't an exposure meter man."

The outcome was a win for Mayflower and Angove.

"Anyway, we eventually got the account. It generated a lot of work."

Beaton, at one point, hired a lighting set-up from Mayflower, with the requirement that the lights had to be accompanied by a couple of staff. Studio manager Walter Michaels and Angove were chosen to undertake the assignment with Beaton. For Angove, the gig was a first close-up brush with a world of celebrity and glamour he was to get to know well over coming decades.

While he might have been inspired by Beaton's flair, Angove's professional progress was particularly aided by working with the other Mayflower staff and by tackling a wide variety of shooting jobs for the studio.

Michaels was one of them, considered quite a character. A pre-war refugee from Germany who smoked a pipe constantly, he was "very good as a photographer in an old-fashioned way, well-trained in the German schools", according to Angove.[clvii]

Another colleague was Derek Stubbs, a rear gunner who served in the Royal Air Force (RAF) and lost a leg. He'd turned to photography and was hired by Mayflower.

Vic Singh started at the studio as a teenager in the early 1960s when Angove was back in Australia for a few years. Singh's role and salary of three pounds a week was more lowly than Angove's had been in 1955.

"My job was to sweep the floor, make tea, get on a bus and deliver prints," he recalls.[clviii]

No doubt, like Angove, Singh found Mayflower Studio a hub of enterprise, innovation and enduring experiences.

"Sometimes I assisted Lee on shoots. He shot interiors and used a flash gun with large flash bulbs, firing them from different positions to light up a large space while leaving the shutter open on 5x4, a very inventive technique."

That capability was something Israel shared with Angove.

Mayflower was the first syndication agency in the UK, according to Singh.

"Models, male and female, were photographed to depict various characters in black and white," he says.

"When I used to sweep the studio floor and take cups of tea to the models changing room, I met some beautiful women in lingerie which left an unforgettable impression on a teenager's mind."

For Singh, access to the models soon helped him create his first portfolio and a ticket to a better job when he moved on from Mayflower.

Angove had a similar recollection in 1980: "I met some very charming ladies at the time, the 1950s, who were models. Much more demure young ladies than they are today."

After model shoots, ten- by eight-inch contact sheets were made and sent to various clients who could order prints. Singh was promoted to the mailroom, which despatched pictures worldwide.

Mayflower Studio boasted about its commercial offerings. Its slick and aggressive pitch to the market claimed it had a new approach to advertising photography.

"We get the ideas, we shoot the pictures, you look them over from our contact sheets and use what you like," Mayflower touted in a whole page in *Advertiser's Weekly*. [clix]

It outlined its business model: "You pay a reproduction fee only after [a] client has approved your scheme. Once you are a subscriber to Mayflower Studio Library, you get a steady stream of new photographic ideas on a wide range of themes pouring across your desk. Yet you are not involved in expensive creative fees … [and] model fees have been paid on all pictures."

Howard Byrne was also always ready to hire out his staff for customised jobs.

"The same team of crack photographers who produce these brilliant library shots are available to carry out your assignment work in our modern west end studio," he flagged.[clx]

"Photographers [are] sent anywhere day or night. Rush work [is] our specialty."

It was a savvy enterprise with North American flair and an ambition to win new business.

Having Bill Angove on board was a mutually rewarding arrangement. He admired the place, impressed by the talent around him and "a lot of fun going on".[clxi] Mayflower's leadership reciprocated the sentiment.

Angove's breakthrough moment with the firm came on the back of the folio of work he'd brought with him from Perth, a showcase of experimental images that the company's owners had found so beguiling and had helped secure his employment. It was to become known as his "crazy" output and marked him for soaring success.

Mayflower catalogue entries

Frustrated painter goes 'crazy'

In their constant drive to promote their studio's energetic and gifted stable of photographers, Byrne and Israel recognised they had someone out of a different mould when Bill Angove joined the ranks.

To help aid their recruit's emergence in the business and to boost his own career outlook, the pair decided that Angove's original set of Australian-produced slides he'd initially used to dazzle them deserved a wider audience.

The goal was to attract publicity for Mayflower and the photographer.

They arranged for Angove to be interviewed by the London correspondent for the *Australian Women's Weekly*, Win Bissett, who was based in Fleet Street.

"She got a story out of it," he recalled.[clxii] The resulting double-page spread, featuring six of his most inventive pictures accompanied by a head and shoulders portrait holding his Rolliecord camera, was published in November 1955.

The headline screamed *'Crazy' Pictures Won Him London Job*. Ms Bissett's article began: "Crazy pictures photographed in Australia by West Australian Bill Angove have been acclaimed in London as the work of a genius."[clxiii]

Acknowledging him as an important member of the Western Australian Camera Club before he went to England, her story quoted him saying each time he showed his slides there, members called them "old Angove's crazy pictures".

"But when Howard Byrne ... saw the pictures ... he gave Angove a job on the spot."[clxiv]

The article then repeated Angove's perennial self-description as a frustrated painter.

The leading picture in the magazine, *Perpetual Motion*, (on page 70), was referred to as a camera study created 'by keeping the shutter of the camera open while his model moved from [a] standing full face position to a profile study seated.'"[clxv]

The spread of reproduced images paraded the range of techniques Angove deployed to achieve his strikingly different results.

In *Spilt Milk*, (next page, bottom left) only one component was photographic, a milk jug on its side. The rest of the image comprised a drawing by Angove on newsprint depicting a smug-faced cat and the spilt milk.

In *Applause*, (next page, bottom right) Angove first created a set of varying sized and coloured cut-outs of hands and a laughing mouth which he then photographed on a neutral backdrop. The caption noted that it all added up to an intriguing surrealistic study of audience applause.

Perpetual Motion

Spilt Milk, and Applause

A picture called *Fantasy* (above) was an artistic and photographic tribute to a Perth musician named Judy Coleman. It featured painted musical notes and swirling lines around Coleman's superimposed face surrounded by ivy, a candlestick and a music box. *Fantasy* took its name from Coleman's composition. Incidentally, the candlestick was an artefact from the Butcher family's time in Lowlands, Tasmania, where they were once robbed by bushrangers. The candlestick, along with a teapot, eluded the thieves and both items remain in the possession of descendants today.

Using just a torch, Angove made *Man at Boulevarde Café* (next page) in total darkness. The shutter of his camera was left open and yellow and red filters were placed alternatively in front of the lens for the different colour sections.

Morning Archer, (next page, upper right) is a study of Perth ballet dancer Judy Schonell. The photographer initially applied a red filter to establish the background and then made a second exposure in darkness. The bow was drawn with a lighted torch.

The final picture in the magazine spread was "in sinister colours" and entitled *Horror*, showcasing Angove's versatile art skills. He made the grimacing mask from paper mâché and painted it as the focal point of his horror study. He used other objects from around the house: the paper snake, old-fashioned glasses and photo album.

Man at the Boulevarde Café,

Morning Archer

Horror

Crazy photos sell product ideas

ADVERTISING, MARCH, 1959

● "Crazy" photography involving negative distortion has become a popular vogue with English advertisers who want something startling says former Perth photographer Bill Angove who recently returned from London. Angove said that photographs for advertising illustration are more favored by London agencies than is the case in Australia.

PHOTOGRAPHIC abstractions in press advertising are regarded by some London advertisers as first-rate attention getters said Bill Angove, former Perth photographer who recently returned from London to join Sydney photographic firm Bruce Minnett Ltd.

Bill Angove

Angove said that during his four years in London he had found a steady demand for his photographic abstracts.

These were created by various distortion techniques.

"I found that they could prove the answer to the cry of some advertisers for 'something different, something not done before'," said Angove.

"The method is used to sell the idea or experience connected with a product rather than convey material volumes.

"People either like it or decry it but one way or the other it gets a lot of attention.

"It is commonly known as 'crazy' photography and some of it gets categorised as being in the 'horror' class.

"Pharmaceutical product manufacturers have made effective use of more startling examples in medical publications and direct mailers to the medical profession."

One for the anti-biotic terramycin captioned "Asian flu can kill", produced for advertising agents Napper, Stinton and Woolley after other methods had failed to satisfy the advertiser, achieved a satisfactory degree of horror with a reverse white on black head of a man 20 generations from the original negative.

The result was a ghostly effect with nose and mouth accentuated in white.

A series of three full page color advertisements which appeared in the British Medical Journal for Charles Pfizer and Co Inc for terramycin on such subjects as "When will the last patient die of TB?" and "Does man really have a limited expectation of life?" was described as "amazingly fanciful" by the London Advertiser's Weekly.

A part of the body was the nucleus of each, bleached out photographs of a girl's head, a male torso and a girl's hand.

"They were only vague resemblances but I had to introduce the human element in some way," said Angove.

"It was a matter of symbolising various aspects of medical science against an outer space background.

"An out-of-focus torch and little balls of plasticine took on the appearance of a great sun surrounded by satellites.

"It was all achieved by multiple exposures on color film."

Minimum copy

Crazy photography was a welcome relief from more mundane photography Angove said. While many of the London advertising agents were keen to use abstract photography most advertisers wanted something more down to earth.

"The current theme in London is more towards extremism in reality than to abstracts," he said.

"It is generally recognised that photography has more impact than artwork.

"People still adhere to the idea that 'the camera cannot lie' — whereas really the camera is the most subtle liar of all.

"In London advertisers are using the photograph a lot more than they do in Australia.

"Best advertisements feature a photograph blown up as big as possible with a minimum amount of copy.

"Some clients want heavy use of copy and this invariably precipitates a battle with the agent.

"Most of the photography used is straightforward, rather than creative."

An Angove subject that achieved wide sympathetic reaction was a life-size photograph of a worried, middle-aged businessman which Bengers published on an eight foot direct mail piece.

This was straightforward — there was no need for distortion.

Angove said that distortion did not necessarily mean that the result must be "crazy". Most artistic atmospheric advertisements such as the Bective shoe advertisements he had done for Vogue were possible by trick negative treatment.

It was possible to highlight the product and tone down the background with high artistic effect by negative distortion.

Striking realism

Agents in London had often called on him to solve such photographic problems as the illustration of the stickiness of Cellotape for the Monsanto Chemical Co.

Angove said he was called upon when several other types of illustration had failed to satisfy the customer.

He sent to a London butterfly farm for a large moth and imprisoned it in a cobweb of cellotape. The resultant photograph made the grade for an important chemical and plastics trade journal.

High key photography—shadowless subjects obtained by bouncing strong indirect lighting from all angles— was popular Angove said. This technique used with a white background gave the subject striking realism.

The "bleaching out" technique in half-tone giving a silhouette effect plus some detail was also very popular.

Angove's commissions for "crazy" photography he said were the result of a double page color spread of experiments he made before leaving Australia, published in the Women's Weekly.

The spread created much interest in London agencies and gave them the idea of introducing similar photography in advertisements.

Sydney magazine story on Angove's advertising work

Angove was delighted with the prominence his abstract folio gained in those early months in London. The creativity this work demonstrated for the times was a key to his subsequent success. The studio apparently acquired a supply of copies of the *Women's Weekly* edition, which coincidentally featured on its cover a 28th birthday portrait of Princess Margaret by Cecil Beaton. The magazine quickly became a calling card for attracting new work for the Aussie newcomer.

"I started to get a lot of important work as a result of that [coverage]," Angove said.[clxvi]

None was bigger than his breakthrough assignments for the international drug company Pfizer.

Pfizer was founded a century earlier by two German migrants to the USA, who began the business as a fine chemicals manufacturer based in New York. By the early 1950s the firm branched out internationally, establishing sites in nine countries, including a medicines factory at Sandwich in the UK.[clxvii] The same period produced a major milestone in the company's history. Its own scientists developed its first antibiotic, exploiting a micro-organism found in a soil sample near one of its laboratories in the American Mid-West. The antibiotic, Pfizer's follow-up to penicillin, was called *Terramycin*, derived from the Latin for "earth fungus".[clxviii] It was the company's first proprietary drug and it transformed its business model and its market reach.[clxix]

Pfizer had engaged a Soho advertising agency named Napper Stinton and Woolley (NS&W) as a prime marketing arm for drumming up business in Europe. The agency seems to have been a cutting-edge player in the industry with strong connections to influential entities. For instance, the England cricket captain, Ted Dexter, at one time served as an executive in the firm, while a public relations practitioner on its payroll, Jennifer Cross, had worked for the editor of the *British Medical Journal*.

Among those impressed by Angove's 'crazy' photographic output was a smart rising art director at NS&W named Burt Greene.

"They were at the time a fairly new firm in advertising," Angove recalled, "but growing very rapidly thanks to employing clever young men like Burt Greene."[clxx]

It was Greene who awarded Angove his "first direct assignment"[clxxi] since arriving in England.

"I was given a brief for a very abstract [image] to promote *Terramycin*. Greene gave me the space and the copy to produce something 'out-of-space-ish' but it had to be connected with the copy [text] for the drug.

"In fact, everything I put into it, I had to be able to explain."

The advertisement carried the heading: "When will the last patient die of TB?"[clxxii]

The first lines of the text read: "Will it be 2000AD, 2500AD, 3000? Or is this modern scourge due for defeat tomorrow? One thing is certain. The future will bring its own medical problems. How, for instance, will the doctor treat stress conditions caused by space travel?"

The rest of the copy dwells on gentle speculation about what the future of medicine holds, postulating that TB and even carcinoma will, by some future juncture, already have succumbed to newly discovered treatments.

"Possibly it will be a micro-organism, as yet unisolated, that rids mankind of these and other maladies. And what of progress in the field of anti-biotics. Will *Terramycin*, for instance, still be the 'wonder drug'?"

It is brilliant copywriting, pitched perfectly at the readership of the *British Medical Journal* where it appeared as a full page, which it's plausible to argue, appeared half disguised as editorial content (see below).

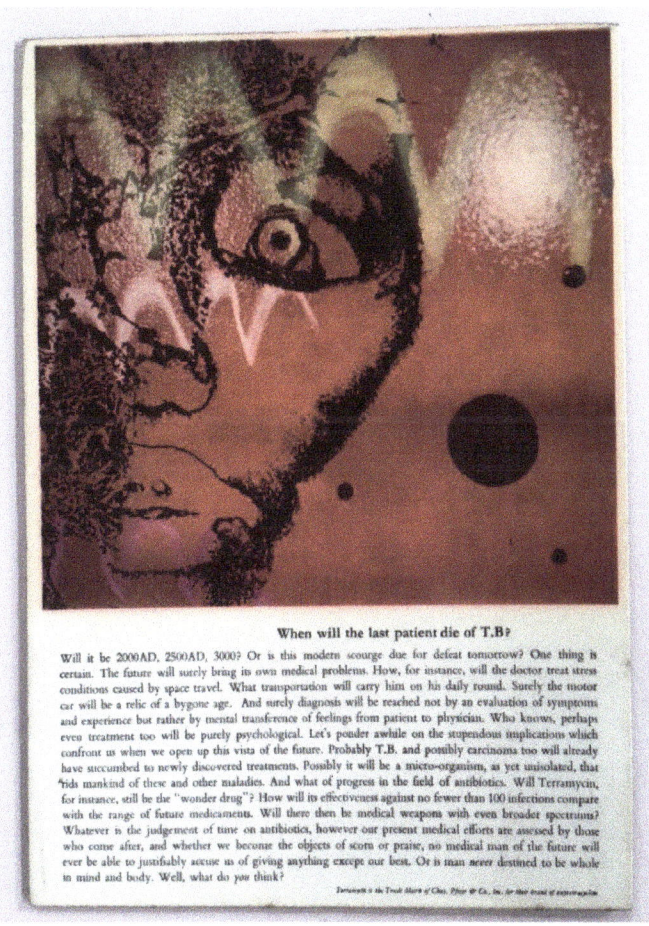

First of the Pfizer colour plates in the British Medical Journal

The *British Medical Journal* had been published weekly since 1840. Now known as The BMJ, it boasts that "over the decades, news of many important medical advances was broken in the pages of the journal."[clxxiii] For example, in its first decade, it ushered in news about the best use of undiluted chloroform in anaesthetics. Twenty years later, it published the seminal papers on antisepsis by Joseph Lister. In the years immediately before the work of Angove, Greene and NS&W pushed Pfizer's new offering on its pages, the journal carried Richard Doll's research papers on the causal effects of smoking on lung cancer and other causes of death. So it was undoubtedly a proven and powerful vehicle for reaching Britain's medical fraternity.

The first advertisement was followed by two more for the same product deploying similar themes. Greene and Angove continued their collaboration on both.

Angove wrote on the back of one of the published plates: "Everything in the photo had to be relevant to the copy. I had to research medical libraries and supply half-plate transparencies ready for the blockmaker."[clxxiv]

Angove working on his Pfizer photographs at Mayflower Studio

The advertisements relied heavily on the art photography. Consistent with the message, Angove created futuristic imagery, hinting at improvements in medical science, pharmaceuticals and life expectations. *Terramycin* was always labelled as a wonder drug and this status was backed up in the text by a claim that it was already effective against more than a hundred infections.

The three colour plates he produced for this project drew on a number of Angove's tastes and techniques. There's evidence of work from a paint brush, multiple exposures, light painting, tonal abstraction and the manipulation of props. The *Women's Weekly* pictures held clues to all these tools. You would expect that his studies in art and photography would also have implanted examples from which he could take inspiration. For instance, the influence of the American painter and photographer known as Man Ray is likely to have triggered some of Angove's penchant for the avant-garde. Ray and other photographers had embraced affinities with movements such as surrealism and dadaism, producing a notable abstract aesthetic in photography in the decades during which Angove was developing his art vision.

It's not hard to imagine the excitement the Pfizer assignments generated for Bill Angove. Here was a striking step up in his fledgling international career and it was achieved on his own terms, in that he had found a commercial client for whom his highly inventive approach was apt and rewarding.

The UK journal, *Advertiser's Weekly*, ran a regular feature called 'Photography in Advertising'. Columnist Ben Freeman enthusiastically reviewed Angove's "amazingly fanciful shot for Pfizer".[clxxv]

"There is no purpose to be gained by trying to analyse this from any general pictorial points of view," Freeman wrote. "Either you think it comes off or you do not. Personally, I do."

He then reproduced the copy and the image, unfortunately only in black and white, for his readers to judge.

Angove recognised he had something different to contribute to the world of press and magazine advertising.

"I had a flair for experimental work, which I was able to develop for pharmaceutical advertising," he said, referencing work with another drug company, Wyeth, which was prominent in this era of emerging polio vaccines and oral contraceptives.

The pharmaceutical folio also cemented an important relationship between the artist and the progressive advertising agency from which other work was to flow.

The Pfizer contract came with one drawback or regret for Angove although ultimately it was to prove to be of no consequence. The first two *Terramycin* advertisements were undertaken while he was still engaged on salary at Mayflower Studio. He looked to Howard Byrne for a pay rise in recognition of the valuable assignments for Pfizer but his request was turned down.

"I still had one more [in the series] to produce," he observed years later.[clxxvi] He received an offer directly from NS&W to complete the trio. While acknowledging "it was a bit naughty of me"[clxxvii] he undertook the third picture independently of Mayflower.

"I borrowed Michael's [Barrington-Martin] studio and did it there as a direct job. I think I upset Mayflower. I realised years later that I probably did the wrong thing by Howard."

Angove was soon to move on from Mayflower anyway and eventually returned to Australia for a few years but he retained a reciprocated loyalty to Mayflower because he was re-engaged there a second time.

The spirit of the place and the initial breaks he gained there remained in his heart. This had been his professional launching pad in his mighty adventure abroad. His affection and admiration for Mayflower Studio resided in particular in the nexus between joint founder Lee Israel and the Pfizer jobs.

By the time he returned, a cause for sad reflection descended on him.

"I learned on my second time back that my good friend Lee Israel dropped dead of a heart attack on the railway station waiting to go home one evening at five o'clock," he related as he himself lay dying in hospital in 1980.[clxxviii]

"Lee was aged 40. It was very sad. He was the man there who understood me best."[clxxix]

Those words speak loudly. It was the Texan who had first seen merit in Angove's antipodean folio and it was surely that endorsement, amplified by the *Women's Weekly* publicity, that gave him and his workplace colleagues the confidence to succeed with the Pfizer briefs. Here was vindication that Angove's abstract creativity had a potency in the world.

Pfizer was the first of a string of big corporate accounts that Angove was to work on. They were to include some of the biggest brand names in the UK and some of the most enterprising advertising accounts.

Another pharmaceutical contract came from a more familiar quarter, namely his homeland. Nicholas, the Australian company that first produced Aspro in 1915, had broken into the British market in the late 1920s to supply the UK and European populations. In 1956 the company was renamed Aspro-Nicholas and built a new factory in Slough.[clxxx] The firm stepped up its advertising and Angove was a direct beneficiary.

"We seem to have got our foot in on the Aspro account which is good as they do a lot of advertising here," Angove wrote at the time.[clxxxi]

"Aspro-Nicholas has been remarkably successful here, all through advertising."

His reflections on this subject arose from a travel episode he had done in the summer of 1958. He described it as a long trip. He'd had to go to Swindon, two and a half hours by train from London and then a half-hour drive added on, to photograph a woman for an Aspro testimonial advertisement.

"It was quite a wearing day," he complained, "with all the travelling then having to cope with a nutty family and get some decent shots of Mum (the nuttiest) rather took it out of me for the rest of the week."

A fortnight later, he was on a similar assignment.

"I went up to a town called Preston in Lancashire to do another of those Aspro testimonials. Eight hours travelling and half an hour's work! Meals on the train [were] rather expensive but [the bill] was on the firm."

Creativity can sometimes be a slog. While Pfizer was fun, Aspro was taxing.

Meanwhile, Bill Angove's photographic talents were demonstrated as many and varied because in parallel with his body of commercial work, he excelled in other branches of the arts and photography.

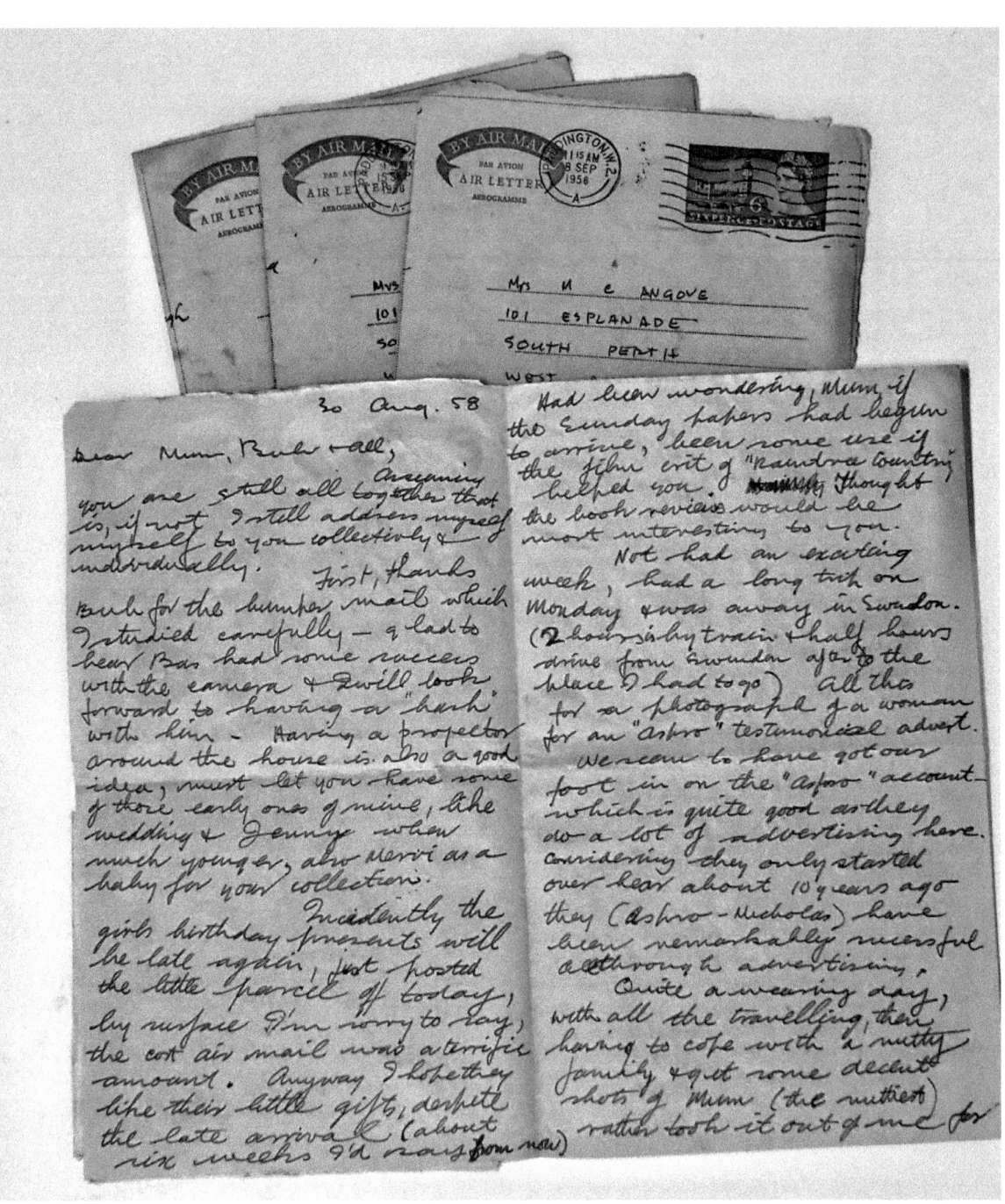

Letters home

A London Canvas

Never at risk of confining his career path to a straight-jacket, Bill Angove's first period of London years, 1955 to 1959, was characterised by energy and a have-a-go attitude. Buoyed by his first big commercial success with the Pfizer campaign, he committed to two immediate goals: to nurture Australian connections in his new environment and to pursue a passion around the human figure, both parading fashion and performing on stage. Underpinning both pursuits was a continuing practice in art and design.

On a personal level, he found numerous photographic subjects for documentation as he set about exploring his new city. His street photography portrayed slices of the post-war struggle and endeavour in London. His folio from this time also includes work that shows him applying his sense of humour.

A selection of Angove's work in his early London days (1955-58)

Angove set about strengthening his ties with ex-pat Australians, both on a personal and professional level. For instance, the painter in the image below is the South Australian-born actor Keith Michell who was an art teacher back in Adelaide before he moved to the UK in the early 1950s. Angove came to know many other Aussie artists over time.

As his career advanced at Mayflower during that first year, Angove felt he couldn't stay any longer with the Barrington-Martins. He discovered that one of his old friends from Perth, George Palmer, was in town. He tracked him down.

"He was very pleased to hear from me," Angove recalled, "and he invited me straight away to [stay at] his flat which he had been sharing with four or five other guys." clxxxii

"George was working as a draughtsman. He must have been earning more than me because he offered to pay half the rent of the flat at the time which was a very big place up at Kilburn. It was about seven pounds a week."

Kilburn, in north-west London, was popular with foreigners, with Angove noting a particularly large Irish population that loved to fill the local pubs.

It transpired that Palmer's flatmates, who had supposedly all gone away on a short holiday, had in fact deserted him.

"They didn't come back, leaving George with a massive bill to pay. George wouldn't let me pay any more than my one-fifth share."

Angove later told a long and amusing story about how he forgot to take his house key with him one day when he went shopping. Palmer had gone away for a few days. When Bill returned home, he climbed the stairs of the pre-war block of flats to the seventh floor and realised he didn't have his key. He peered in through the letter slot in the door and spotted his keys on the kitchen table. The police suggested he hire a locksmith and managed to find a chap who had lived in the same building decades earlier. Angove paid his bill and offered him a unique gratuity on top of the fee.

"A crate of apples had just arrived from Albany," he explained.[clxxxiii] The apples came from C E Bolt Pty Ltd in Albany where Bill's brother-in-law Basil worked with his father, Charlie Bolt.[clxxxiv] Their fruit trade to the UK ceased when a ship load of apples was held up in the Suez Canal during its blockade at the time of the Suez crisis. Apparently, the apples rotted in the Egyptian heat, turned into some pungent form of cider and oozed over the decks into the canal. This resulted in a significant financial hit to the company from which it never really recovered, according to Basil's son Peter.[clxxxv]

"I used to get a crate of Granny Smiths off every ship [arriving from Western Australia]. It went down very well at first. But eventually when the family business was dissolved that had to stop.

"I offered him [the locksmith] some apples but he didn't want any. However, he had a boy with him and he took half a dozen so everybody was happy."

A short time later, Palmer's errant flatmates all reappeared on the doorstep, wanting to move back in. They did so but Angove took some delight in recording the fact that George occupied the best room in the place and he had the second best so the miscreants had to settle for any of the other spare bedrooms.

By day, Angove was mixing in the slick and glamorous world of commercial photography, shoulder to shoulder with art directors, models and performers but on the personal front he had quite a humble existence.

"We lived on sausages, mashed potatoes, green peas and the scrag ends of meat, the cheapest things you could buy," he recalled.[clxxxvi] Occasionally they managed rabbit "as a treat".

"We found that we were all getting very ill. I developed abscesses. My doctor gave me something to put on them. That's all he did. [The medicine] stained your clothes.

"So I decided the best thing to do was to eat properly.

"You can't sacrifice your proper diet. So savings would have to be made in other directions. Gradually, I improved. I learned a lot from that [experience]."

The poor diet wasn't the only hazard Angove encountered at the Kilburn block of flats. He came to despise conditions in the high-rise building, concerned about the unreliable lift, the stink of garbage and the risk of fire. He felt so negative about it, on one occasion he wondered out loud how it survived the war-time bombing of inner London.

One reprise on the health and safety front was a series of weekly walks he and George did around nearby destinations in the countryside, typically accompanied by other Australians he'd kept in touch with from the boat. Using buses or trains to get out of town and a small guide book published by a local newspaper, they enjoyed picnics and pub visits which Angove described as "all very picturesque" and freeing participants from the "hurly burly of the big city".[clxxxvii]

Eventually, Palmer and Angove "were fed up with communal living and sought out somewhere better". They found a house in Lancaster Gate, configured as a bed-sitter. Its location was extremely central, in Westminster close to the entrance to Kensington Gardens.

"We were offered one big room to share, with two beds, a big old-fashioned maple fireplace and a wash basin in the corner," Angove recalled.[clxxxviii] It had a large window and a hot water pipe that ran through the room keeping it warm in winter.

"There was a gas cooker with a one-ring burner in the corner which served us very well for our meals. It's amazing what you can cook on a one-ring burner."

Palmer's English relatives, whom he only occasionally mixed with, had given him a device that went underneath the cooker and served as a kind of side extension on which you could keep another pot warm while preparing a meal. After a while, the pair also invested in a second-hand pressure cooker.

"Slowly that house built up with all our other friends coming over from Perth. There were ten to twelve of us from Perth living in that place in the end. We got two marriages out of there."

Two of the men's WA architecture mates, Bill Weedon and Ron Facius, married brides they had known previously back home.

Angove reflected that, during his time in this house, he began to build a circle of friends of his own. He also appreciated the location, close to Piccadilly Circus and his work location.

On the back of the recognition he'd earned from the *Women's Weekly* spread and the Pfizer contract, Angove came to the attention of one of Mayflower's rival businesses, Woburn Studios, located near Russell Square in Holborn, and he accepted their offer of a job.

His primary motivation was to work heavily in the fashion scene. Fashion photography was reaching new heights at the time. Besides the British press, the industry's key drivers were the large international magazines such as *Vogue, Harper's Bazaar* and *Vanity Fair,* to mention just a few. Its leading lights included legendary global practitioners such as the aforementioned Beaton, Edward Steichen, Irving Penn, Richard Avendon, David Bailey, Helmut Newton, Eve Arnold, Lillian Bassman and Norman Parkinson.

Interestingly, Angove became aware some time later that he'd had a close encounter with Parkinson's work back at Dover Street. Prior to Mayflower moving into the building, Parkinson had operated his studio there.

"I used to see 10X8 negatives that were his being kicked around in the offices," he admitted. [clxxxix]

"I regret the day now that I didn't salvage a few. They wouldn't have been of great interest in those days but Parky of course had gone onto greater things and became a well-known character."

Woburn Studio was a large commercial establishment when Angove joined, lured by the prospect of undertaking fashion shoots.

At least part of what stoked Angove's interest would have been the sorts of clients Woburn was working with. Unfolding before his eyes - and those of all the world's fashion followers – was a revolutionary young designer named Mary Quant.

The curator of a retrospective Quant exhibition in Bendigo, Australia, in 2021, Emma Busowsky Cox, told *Art Guide Australia* [cxc] that in 1955 Quant's first London boutique, Bazaar, was something of a phenomenon.

She said Quant's approach differed radically from the demure style of clothes retailing until that point. Bazaar launched with a party, stayed open late at night, and featured extravagant, arty window displays with mannequins in lively poses and "crazy things like having a lobster on a lead."

That lobster on a lead could have been straight out of the imaginative Bill Angove playbook to be explored here shortly.

And who shot Quant's work? Woburn Studios no less.

A young Swede, Carl Lindhe, who worked as an assistant there, later described it in an interview with an English webzine called *The Pictorial List*. He said the place accommodated a raft of staff photographers, "each in a separate studio with two assistants, shooting commercial pictures, anything from perfume bottles to specially built interiors."

The reference to specially built interiors is pertinent to Angove's role there. As well as photography, he also engaged in set design at various points throughout his working life.

His duties at Woburn Studios included the job of "background artist". He had serious ambitions to foster this line of work - alongside his photography - because during this period he enrolled in part-time art studies at Regent Street Polytechnic.

"[They] concentrated on theatrical design," he recorded years later.[cxci]

"My former architectural studies were a help here and I was able to use the theatrical design studies in making sets and painting backgrounds for our studio settings."

Incidentally, adding to the cultural trends of the era, this polytechnic also played memorable roles in the emergence of popular music legends. Three students there formed the band Pink Floyd and a visiting Jimi Hendrix had his first jam session in London on the campus with Eric Clapton.

British photographer Howard Grey worked at Woburn for several years during the late 1950s and early 60s. He told me[cxcii] there were about 10 studios in a big building. One was particularly large because the business had ambitions to shoot cars for advertising purposes.

As well as a senior photographer and assistant engaged in each studio during a shoot, Grey said there was a team of people called "pinners". It was their job to ensure the clothes hung properly on the models. The pinning of garments often required a ruthless method involving bulldog clips. The fitting and display of corsetry and suspenders entailed an inverse set of marionette puppetry strings, in this case deploying fishing line.

Among the models who worked at Woburn during this era was the famous Jean Shrimpton who was feted as an icon of Swinging London.

As Grey tells it, [cxciii]the work of the studios extended beyond fashion into the more racy field of glamour, where a pin-up star named Pamela Green headlined alongside a steady stream of young French women. The company's creative director, Jack Buss, chose the models for each shoot in "sordid little audition rooms", according to Grey. By the societal standards of today, these practices sound alarmingly predatory.

Woburn could be considered an advanced outlet for Angove's talents and interests. It immersed him further in a world of striking innovation and progressive movements. These were liberating times, leaving behind the hugely weighty burdens of the first half of the 20th century.

Grey has a theory about the exciting and culturally revolutionary 1950s onwards.

"The end of national service meant that young people's creativity was no longer being suppressed."[cxciv]

It's a sentiment not far removed from Bill Angove's view of his future work ambitions when he left the army.

The schedule of assignments at Woburn Studios had a chronic shortcoming. The output was structurally spasmodic.

"It was mail order catalogue work," Angove complained, "which meant it was very seasonal."

The two major fashion catalogues shot by Woburn staff were branded Grattan and Trafford.

Grattan was a Yorkshire-based clothing retail company founded in 1912.[cxcv] It typically produced four mail order catalogues every year for most of the 20th century. *Trafford World* was a catalogue produced by Great Universal Stores (GUS) offering home shoppers exclusive access to fashions from high-end designers such as the royal dressmaker Norman Hartnell.[cxcvi] GUS plc was founded in 1900 as a mail-order business in Manchester.

"I spent most of the time planning and shooting for a season's catalogue and then you'd have six weeks in between. [It meant] you had to go out and try to get more business but it really takes you longer [to succeed]. I'd lost touch."

Howard Grey, a third-generation photographer and cousin of singer Alma Coggan, endured the same hiatuses.

"There were two things we used to do during the long weeks between catalogue shoots," he said. One was painting the studios and the other was studying exams on "The Knowledge", the famous familiarisation with London's streets and lanes required by drivers to obtain and retain their taxi licences.

The "fits and starts", as Angove described them, eventually left him despondent at Woburn.

"I found I had to get out of there because I wasn't getting enough commercial work."

But an enduring professional partner, art director Burt Greene at Soho's NS&W agency, continued to be a significant force in sustaining Angove's creativity and London connections.

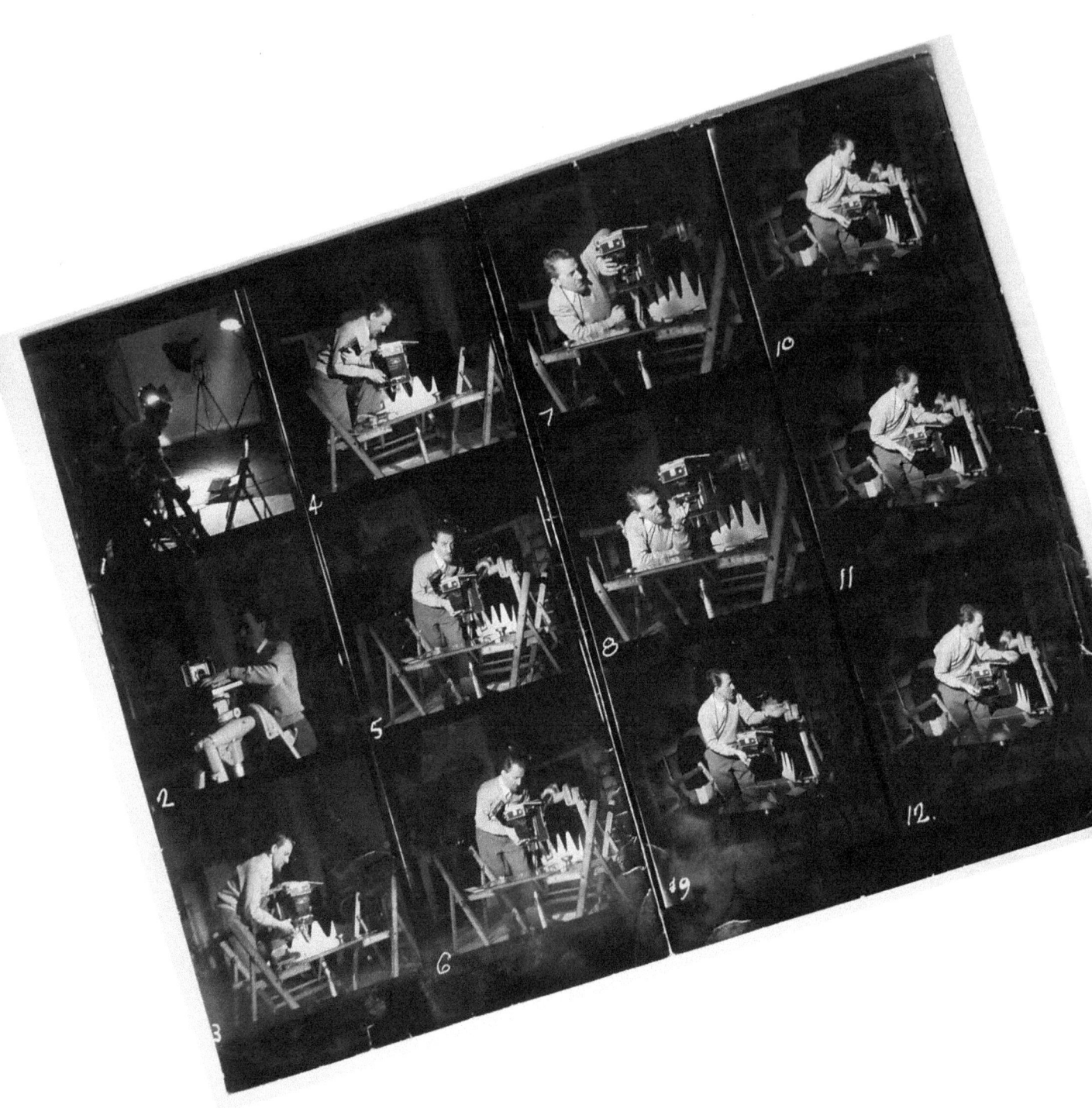

Angove working on a table top picture

Skeletons and ballet steps

Before he moved on from Woburn Studios, Burt Green sourced a memorable commercial assignment for Bill Angove, one that came to typify his emerging reputation for innovation and improvisation. He was heavily into sourcing props.

Green's assignment entailed another pharmaceutical advertisement and he wanted to deploy a skeleton to illustrate the human back.

"[It] was up to me to get the skeleton and he didn't care how I did it," Angove said in retelling the story years later.[cxcvii]

"I looked through the Yellow Pages which was my constant source … or practically my bible. I found that there was a firm of taxidermists and a firm [dealing in] medical educational supplies. Both had the same name but were not connected although there had been some family relationship.

"So I rang up … and asked if they had skeletons. 'Oh, yes, no trouble at all,' they said.

"They were all used for demonstrations in hospitals.

"So I said I'd come over."

The trip took Angove past St Pancras Station.

"It was one of those grey, dreary days. The road must have once [boasted] beautiful old houses and big gardens in the front but they now all just had high tin walls with double doors for vehicles to go through and a small door for single humans.

"I buzzed on the electric squawk box which opens the door to let you in. I said to the taxi driver 'hang on, I won't be long'.

"I made my way up a cinders path, passed a few tin sheds with cobwebbed windows – which felt like the right atmosphere – and then got to the main house.

"It was a bit of a gothic splendour inside, all clean and white, polished just like a hospital atmosphere and there's these skeletons hanging up from hooks in their heads.

"A young lady came down and said: 'There you are, which one do you want?' So I chose one.

"She asked me how was I taking it. I said I had a taxi outside.

"The only thing I could do was to slip off my raincoat and drape it over the shoulders of the skeleton and then carry it out like a body. I opened the front door. The taxi driver was reading his newspaper in the watery sunshine. It's very difficult to surprise a London taxi driver.

"The man really shot up. I said: 'Where're we going to put him, guv?'

"We supposed the only thing was to put him in the back seat with me. So we drove all the way back. Every time we got [near] a lot of people at traffic lights or a bus stop, he slowed down. I sat back and we moved the thing forward.

"We didn't get many looks. About the time of the old film with Dirk Bogart, *Doctor in the House*, he had a similar episode with a skull in a box on a London bus so people probably thought it was probably a stunt for a film."

Back at the studio, Angove hung the skeleton by fishing line using the hook in the head. He had to position the arms and legs with fishing line too to create the desired pose and then photograph it against a black background.

The job went well and so too the return trip with the skeleton. Angove prided himself in improvisation. From his Woburn days onwards, he successfully combined this gift with his art practice in theatrical design.

In an untitled and unattributed two-page typed manuscript retained in his archives,[cxcviii] the author of what appears to have been the draft of a magazine or press story observes: "This [Angove's art studies] has proven very useful in the studio, designing sets for advertising photography.

"Among the more ambitious efforts have been a golf club porch, the inside of a country club, and a beach, not to mention innumerable backgrounds for fashion shots."

Later in the article, the author notes that Angove's familiarity with London is to some degree due to his expeditioning to find props for different photographic assignments.

"He can find you practically anything to hire – a ton of clean beach sand, a genuine Regency table, a stuffed fox, a handful of artificial eyes, a suite of the most modern furniture or a human skeleton."[cxcix]

Although it's not mentioned in any surviving materials from Angove's archives, you wouldn't be surprised if he'd taken great delight in another quirky potential source of props at Woburn. As Howard Grey tells it,[cc] a miffed great-grandson of Madam Tussaud, Louis Tussaud, ran a rival chain of waxworks across Britain and the US in the early 1900s. Louis died in 1938 but his wax heads, reputed to bear poor resemblance to their supposed characters, were still stored in the bowels of Woburn Studios until the 1960s. We can only speculate as to whether Angove ever came upon them and used one or more in a photo shoot.

The mention of wax figures echoes another feature of the work at Woburn: the pinning and stringing of fashion garments worn by the models being photographed, previously outlined by Howard Grey. The models and their clothes could almost be said to have been treated much like waxworks, and it annoyed Angove.

He complained that the fussy prepping of the garments - such as pins and fishing line in every pleat of a skirt – would leave models virtually static. He compared them with cardboard cut-outs. The same result was required with men. Their trouser pleats had to be like a knife-edge.

"No creases were ever allowed to show," he said.[cci]

"I couldn't stand that type of work. I tried to introduce a bit of originality but it didn't go over too well. Even when high-speed electronic flash was introduced and firing off, they still pegged the girl down.

"I often photographed three models in a group. Each had to be made up and pegged down and backgrounds all arranged. That took so long that it only gave the photographer ten minutes to do his final photography which was rationed to three sheets of 8 by 10 film.

"It was not exactly creative work. But I learned a lot - again – learned a lot about people.

"The man who said to me 'I'm the best friend you've got in this firm, if you've got any troubles come and see me and I'll sort it out' … turned out to be the one who stabbed me in the back. But I was on the move anyway."

This is when Burt Greene came to the rescue. The young advertising executive introduced Angove to Ken Wells, a move that opened a third chapter in Angove's rapid progress in London. Greene suggested the pair join forces because the K. John Wells Studio in the heart of Soho was pumping out a lot of advertising and fashion work.

Angove recalled his first encounter at the Wells Studio just off Wardour Mews.

"It was in an area that was all cobblestones, terribly Dickensian, with barrow boys' stuff all around," he said.[ccii]

The studio was housed in a building that he described as "very picturesque" in its own way. The main studio was on the top floor with a big darkroom one floor below, all accessed by stairs. On the next floor down was what he labelled "Ken's small darkroom", while the floor below that accommodated "the headquarters" of a Maltese prostitute. Around the base of the building, the boys kept their barrows.

He remembered a winter of snow there, which he admired as it fell on the skylight, but when it melted it got inside the building's walls and dripped all over the equipment. He eventually concluded that, overall, it was a "bad old building" that deserved to be demolished.

The photographers worked closely together at the Wells site, both literally and collaboratively. Their advertising brief included another range of work for a major pharmaceutical company, most likely still Pfizer, contracted by Greene's agency, although Angove later directly sourced similar work from a rival firm, Wyeth.

Among his memories of the place was an urgent job that prompted him to volunteer to go in to work on a Sunday. It entailed another of his signature "special effects" treatment which required "a lot of repetition".[cciii] He also seemed to have surprised another inhabitant.

"[When] I finally finished, the lady prostitute downstairs said I could have seen her coming up and down the stairs with her customers and having a cup of tea with her maid discussing her previous customer. She said she didn't know I was up there, otherwise she would have invited me down for a cuppa too.

"She was one of those fat, happy souls but I didn't really want to get involved with that little lot. It was quite amusing."

Out of hours, Angove mixed socially with the crew from NS&W advertising agency mainly on a Friday night at a "jolly place" called the Bath House. One of their advertising colleagues was an Englishman named David Davies, who later migrated to Western Australia where he ran a successful Perth ad business.

The Wells Studio later moved a few blocks away to Frith Street to a basement below an employment agency. It proved to be a shot in the arm for the business. Wells took on another staff member, a young man named Mike Busselle, who initially did the printing for the company. Busselle went on to become a worldwide publishing success with more than 50 books on photography, travel and wine, selling millions of copies.[cciv] His educational titles include *Master Photography* and a series called *Better Picture Guides*. He was an earnest and prolific writer and lecturer on photography, in many ways, a likely model Angove would have followed had he lived longer.

Angove said the team at the Wells Studio worked hard to build the business despite having limited equipment.

"We worked out quite well in the end … and turned out quite interesting work," he reflected, "we always pleased the [advertising] agencies."[ccv]

Innovation was fundamental to achieving the studio's commercial imperatives.

"[The agencies] always used to say 'we want to see something we've never seen before. Do something different, do something we've never seen.'

"It was very difficult to keep up all the time [with that demand]. It's not the sort of thing you can learn at school either so we had a bit of an advantage there. Anyway, we got ourselves established."

Meanwhile, Angove was engaging with more Australians. Prominent among them were dancers from various companies. From his time at Kilburn, he had become familiar with a large nearby cinema where the Festival Ballet occasionally performed. Marilyn Burr and Mary Duchesne were two young Australians in the troupe. The pair had performed for the National Theatre Ballet (predecessor of the Australian Ballet Company) in the first full-scale Australian production of *Swan Lake* in Melbourne in 1951. Both then went abroad and enjoyed long and acclaimed international stage careers starting in London.

Figure 4: Linley Wilson, c. 1930, Perth Photograph by Axel Poignant.

Marilyn Burr (NLA) and Linley Wilson

"I just really talked my way in," he said. "I got myself permission to do some photography. I went on to become a sort of friend of the company. Everybody accepted me quite well."ccvi

At the same time, Angove connected with another friend from Perth, Robin Haig, studying ballet in London.

Robin took up the story in an interview with me in 2021: "I think I first met Bill when I was maybe a 17-year-old at Linley Wilson's ballet school in Perth. He was photographing some of us."[ccvii]

Wilson is credited with running the first classical performing ballet company in Perth from 1926 until the late 1960s.[ccviii]

"We met again in London when I went to study at the Royal Ballet," Haig continued.

"London was going through a transformation. I loved the A-line or tent dresses made fashionable by Mary Quant. The place had such a good feel.

"I remember Bill as being so active. He was in and out of so many of our lives. He seemed to be here, there and everywhere. Always part of the crowd."

They chummed up and initially ventured to a favourite entertainment venue for homesick Aussies.

"Rolf Harris was trying to get himself established and he used to sing on Thursday nights at the old *Down Under Club* off Earl's Court. It used to be packed out. I took Robin and introduced her to that place," [ccix] said Angove.

He also mentioned introducing Robin to a café called *Jimmy the Greek's* in Soho, noted for its generous meals and another venue where he had started to mix with ex-pats.

"It must have helped a lot of hungry young dancers as well." [ccx]

The hospitality with Robin Haig was reciprocated. He accepted an invitation to drop in for a meal at the digs shared by Haig and a girlfriend Ann on Portobello Road.

"The meal was very economical," he recalled. "The friend had done boiled eggs and cooked cabbage in the same water so what they got were green eggs. But it was life-sustaining!"[ccxi]

Angove was able to enlist Haig and other dancers from the Royal Ballet to do some photographic work. Wearing leotards and tights, Robin featured in an advertisement for milk that Bill shot in a studio. Other work featured classical dance. This output was used largely for supplying photographic libraries – what's known as stock images.

The curtain rises

A Perth architecture-trained mate and noted artist, Ron Facius, who became a successful industrial designer in London around this time, helped Angove forge other ties.

"Through Ron's wife we met Albert Tucker, an Australian painter who became quite famous," Angove recorded later, alongside a wry observation about Tucker's path to success.

"He used to nurture millionaires and such people. He priced his work very high. He got his work bought by the American Museum of Modern Art [in New York]. That's what set him up."

Tucker, 10 years older than Angove, had based himself in Paris since the late 1940s. Having been repulsed by the destruction and evidence of violence he had seen in post-war Japan and Germany, the man was known for his sense of wrath and his art took on dark, catastrophic subjects, according to author and gallery director, Patrick McCaughey.

Apparently, Jan Facius had first encountered Tucker and his American wife Mary Dixon in Italy where she had worked as a 'sort of nurse keeper' for film actress Jackie Collins' family, then friends of the Tuckers. The artist and his wife later moved to London and lived close by to the Facius family.

"Whenever Mary was away, Bert [Tucker] would turn up around tea time. 'Oh no, I haven't eaten' [he'd say], 'oh no it doesn't worry me, no, no … well, if you insist.' So we all cut off a bit of our meat and a bit of our vegies.

"He always only had one cigarette in his packet at the time … but this [story] could be considered slanderous so one would have to be very careful about using that material."

Tucker, in turn, introduced Angove to Sidney Nolan. The two painters had a long-term friendship, forged at the Contemporary Art Society in Melbourne from the late 1930s. By the time Angove met him, Nolan had emerged as a big name in Britain, his fame and acclaim outshining his standing back in Australia.

Nolan was instrumental in showing Angove and his friends the delights of the aforementioned *Jimmy the Greek's*, a popular Soho basement restaurant opened in 1948, famous for its cheap eats and poor wine.

"We'd get served enormous amount of food for very little money. It made life very good."

They all became regulars there. Sid Nolan, recognised as a great networker with connections to practitioners in a broad field of the arts such as opera, ballet, theatre and music,[ccxii] would have been seen as a kindred spirit and a likely influence on Angove in other ways, to be outlined shortly.

Having what Angove called "my dozen Australian friends" came in handy on a professional level, too, around this time. The studio had been commissioned to do an advertising campaign for a product called Loxene medicated shampoo.

The ad agency insisted the photographer enlist "ordinary people" in the shoot rather than models.

"So I had twelve ordinary people to use straight away," he retold the story. His flatmate George Palmer was one. Another friend who obliged was Barrie Carter, head of a metals trading firm in London, who later married a daughter of the founder of the Japanese Honda empire.

"Everybody got into the act. They were paid three pounds each, and that didn't go astray."

This episode opens a window on understanding the sort of personality Angove possessed. It's a picture reinforced by Robin Haig's descriptions of her friend.

"Bill was never pushy, never obnoxious," she said.[ccxiii]

"He was very openly engaging. Such an interesting person with interesting looks.

"He always dressed comfortably. I saw him as a Toulouse-Lautrec type of figure in my mind, short, bearded, craggy face in folds, he always looked the same.

"He had a great laugh and he was always curious about things. And he was an excellent photographer."

Bill Angove's first four years in London proved to be highly productive. It's a clear sign of his application, determination and prowess that he advanced professionally in his core direction, his commercial photography. He also made progress with his art and design and engaged in an expanding social scene in which he felt at ease, indeed, revelled.

The whole buzz generated by an awakening Britain, especially in the arts and popular culture, appears to have been a constant source of stimulation and enjoyment for Angove.

Author Mike Hutton, decades later, summarised the nation and the city in *Life in London in the 1950s:*[ccxiv]

> *After the trauma of the Blitz and wartime restrictions, London embraced the arrival of a new decade. Austerity was slow to loosen its grip, but the Festival of Britain pointed a tentative way forward. Two years later saw the birth of a new Elizabethan era that was greeted with an almost naïve enthusiasm. This was a time when class still dominated*

and divided. Despite the introduction of the welfare state, grinding poverty still existed. The rich were also suffering under a barrage of punitive taxation. The artistic community set out to challenge the bounds of perceived decency. As always, London spearheaded change. Twin sets and pearls gave way to a new elegance in women's fashion, while young men ditched their cloth caps in favour of Teddy Boy suits. A new teenage culture arrived along with coffee bars and rock 'n' roll. To a background of grisly murders and organised crime, often shrouded in fog, London lurched into the unknown. It was loud, brash and chaotic, yet also sophisticated.

The artistic journey taken by his compatriot trailblazer Sidney Nolan must have been an inspiration to Angove. Nolan has been described as a restless explorer, known for his inventiveness and willingness to experiment, traits that also marked Angove's career.[ccxv]

Fifteen years before the Albany-born ex-serviceman took the plunge in London, Nolan and a mate, "like many aspiring artists … turned their talents towards visiting Europe. Their idea was all about seeing art and being real bohemians." This quotation from Nancy Underhill's 2015 Nolan biography[ccxvi] could almost have been describing Bill Angove's ambitions.

Nolan had other interests which paralleled Angove's. He pursued photography, using a new Rolliecord camera for example in 1952 to shoot the effects of drought on Wave Hill station and the Barkly stock route in Australia's Northern Territory.[ccxvii] Later, he owned a Polaroid and used it prolifically, at times manipulating images to contrive abstract landscapes.[ccxviii]

The Contemporary Art Society to which Nolan belonged in Melbourne was pitched to all those 'open-minded to genuine creative expression.' Sound familiar?

Underhill says Nolan, Albert Tucker and Arthur Boyd, a third Australian painter Angove came to know personally in his early London days, gained a reputation as Melbourne's three artistic musketeers.[ccxix]

Nolan had yet another talent that Angove could admire. By the early 1940s he had won applause for his set and costume designs for the original Ballet Russes. Over the next few decades, Nolan's appetite for large-scale work, including theatre design and film, was apparent. He did a Helpmann ballet in 1963 after a Covent Garden production the previous year.[ccxx]

The connections Angove kindled through former Perth friends with dancers in the Festival Ballet, the Marquis de Cuevas Ballet and the Royal Ballet gave him a toehold in the world of theatrical and stage photography as well as set design for which he had done additional studies as previously mentioned.

Years later, back in Perth, Angove produced a set of slides featuring a pair of embracing lovers for a Mozart production by the WA Ballet, according to Robin Haig. He did other set design as well, including for the Old Mill Theatre in South Perth, the suburb where he lived in the 1970s.

Five years in London in the mid-1950s seemed to satisfy Angove's tastes and ambitions on numerous levels. In each of the three studios in which he worked, fashion was a hallmark pursuit and enlarged his repertoire with models. His advertising contracts paid the bills and gave him the scope to exploit his art and design background and to undertake travel. His stage work delivered perhaps his strongest personal rewards.

He loved his time behind the scenes of a number of London theatres, including the Festival Hall, Covent Garden and the Old Vic.[ccxxi] Among his well-known subjects were the young film and stage actress Claire Bloom and the Australian-born dancer, actor, director and choreographer Robert Helpmann, whom he photographed shortly before they took *Romeo and Juliet* to Broadway in 1957.

He was particularly fond of the Festival Ballet, a young company established just a few years earlier. Because of its "large percentage of Australians in the company"[ccxxii] Angove came to know and photograph many of its dancers including its Russian-trained founders Anton Dolin and Alicia Markova. His lens also captured the troupe's principal dancer John Gilpin, a virtuoso and lyrical performer who often appeared with Australians Marilyn Burr and Lucette Aldous and who later married into the Monaco royal family, patrons of several dance companies. Gilpin had spent some time in Australia as a teenager with a touring dance group.[ccxxiii]

Angove's "action shots from the wings … pleased him very much," a contemporary writer observed.[ccxxiv]

Another Australian in the Festival company who became a good friend was Jeffrey Kovel who married a Spanish dancer, Stella Nova, after they all met and worked in London. By the time Angove began his triennium in Sydney, the Kovels were appearing there on stage in a J C Williamson musical called *Grab me a Gondola*.[ccxxv] They then joined a ballet company headed by Czech-born Edouard Borovansky, toured with small dance troupes around the country and eventually rejoined the Festival Ballet in London, by which time Angove, too, had renewed his ties with that company. Their mutual interests and overlapping work locations brought Angove and the Kovels close.

Angove's passion for the ballet also took him to continental Europe. Here he used his connections with the Grand Ballet du Marquis de Cuevas, a ballet company founded by

Marquis George de Cuevas in 1947. Initially based in Monaco, within a few years the company left Monte Carlo for France, where it toured frequently between mainstay seasons in Paris. It was with this troupe that Rudolf Nureyev made his first appearance with a Western company, dancing in a new production of *The Sleeping Beauty*. [ccxxvi] This company also boasted numerous Australians in its ranks, including the Perth-raised Julie Webster, another friend of Bill's. A decade later in London, Nureyev was among the stars of ballet Angove photographed in performance.

Angove's picture of Rudolf Nureyev

He first shot pictures of members of the Marquis de Cuevas company at Ostend, across the English Channel, during the ballet's tour of Belgium, again plying his Australian links.

On another occasion Angove was able to photograph a number of the French dancers in action during a trip to Paris.

According to the aforementioned writer[ccxxvii], all of Angove's Paris subjects were "dancers well known throughout Europe, the most famous being Ludmilla Tcherina," a French prima ballerina, sculptor, film actress, painter, choreographer and author.[ccxxviii]

In late 1958, the Marquis de Cuevas troupe was performing at Covent Garden in London. Robin Haig secured a free ticket for Angove to attend in the dress circle one night and this quickly opened the way for him to resume his contacts with the company and enjoy photographic access backstage for subsequent matinee and evening performances.

"The 'old hands' all remembered me," he wrote in a letter home. [ccxxix] This reconnection led to a highlight of Angove's embrace of ballet. A famous Russian, Leonid Massine, described by Britannica as "one of the most important figures in 20th-century dance",[ccxxx] was reprising his pioneering and seminal choreographical work from 20 years earlier, *Gaîté Parisienne*, set to music by Jacques Offenbach.

"I never ever thought I would see Massine dance," said Angove, no doubt reflecting on the fact that the man was over 60 years of age by this stage.[ccxxxi]

One of Angove's favourite pictures of Leonid Massine performing

"I watched him from the wings and photographed like mad. I even got him to pose for a couple of shots. He was really wonderful to watch and amazingly acrobatic for one not so young anymore."

While capturing ballet performances were part of Bill Angove's stock in trade, he seemed to prefer these opportunities he negotiated to photograph off-stage. This perspective, evident in the examples displayed, gave him much more scope to be creative. Here you can see the photographer's artistic talent complementing that of the dancers.

The Burr sisters in the wings and the on-stage action

In his portrayal of the pair awaiting their cue in the wings, Angove succeeds on multiple levels. He imbues the image with a sense of anticipation and also appreciation as they look on. He uses the stage light to pick out their facial expressions and the waist-high camera angle highlights their figures and engaged pose. He also takes our eye to the floorboards and back view of scenery to establish a mood.

In the second picture, shot from the wings, we are offered a side-on view of the movement on the set. The slow shutter speed nails that sense of moving bodies while the faces of a male and female dancer are still discernible enough to the viewer. There's a beautiful flow of legs, arms and costumes in motion.

The two photographs testify to the way Angove was able to apply his inventive, interpretive style. It is an example of what, in skilful hands and creative minds, can transform photographs from a documentary genre to visual art. These richly rewarding pictures suggest that Angove may well have aimed to portray his dance subjects in a similar fashion to a sculptor.

Photographer included in contact sheet for rail assignment

Crossways

His four years in London in the 1950s immersed Bill Angove in a world of bright lights, daring creativity and an enduring stream of thrill seekers. For a thirty-something, art-trained ex-serviceman from the sedate south-west Western Australia, it must have constituted a kind of bohemian existence in which his experiences were constantly shaped by restless energy, openness and taste for adventure.

He seemed to develop a successful way of blending his visiting friends, his resident Australian contacts and his burgeoning London network. And this mastery was reflected in the diversity of his photographic output.

While a staunch devotee of colour and contrivance in his fashion and commercial work, he retained a sensitive and soulful ability to capture life on the streets throughout the United Kingdom. For example, this picture (right) demonstrates a gentle yet haunting capacity to depict the struggles of many in the post-war nation. Using Ilford's FP4 low ISO film and a Pentax camera with a 28mm lens, Angove created this striking photograph in a slum area of the famous Yorkshire city of Leeds.

Post-war street scene in Britain

It is a powerful picture and illustrates a range of attributes Angove demonstrated in his documentary work. It is not hard to discern the influence of the legendary French photographer, Henri Cartier-Bresson, one of the co-founders in 1947 of the co-operative enterprise known as Magnum. Famous for his portrayal of "the decisive moment" in street photography, immortalised in a 1952 book originally called *Images à la Sauvette* (Images on the Run), Cartier-Bresson "explored his notion of photography as a candid medium".[ccxxxii]

"To take a photograph means to recognise, simultaneously and within a fraction of a second, both the fact itself and the rigorous organisation of visually perceived forms that give it meaning," Cartier-Bresson wrote.[ccxxxiii]

This notion is strikingly embodied in Angove's slum image which initially conveys a touch of drama and animation through the little boy caught in mid-stride. More potency is injected by the photographer's brilliantly pre-visualised vantage point in an upstairs window containing four panes of mostly broken glass. The prime figure is placed in the lower left panel with the least glass and therefore offering the sharpest view. Yet this clarity is strongly juxtaposed with the depiction of the motion blur generated by the running boy. The other elements in the picture, principally the hazy views of the cobbled street in the lower right and what appears to be scenes of a cemetery in the two upper panels, convey a sense of grimness and pathos. This is reinforced by the evidence of paint drips and gloomy skies.

The viewer is challenged to ponder the boy's story. Is he hoping to run away from his depressed environment or is any prospect of escape in such a forlorn environment entirely fanciful? Angove's inclusion of much of the window frame suggests he wanted the heavy black border to reinforce the deprivation of the place and the child's fate. There's a statement being made here that you can run but you can't get away. That graveyard is destined to entomb you.

Cartier-Bresson had a wide interest in art in general and in painting in particular.[ccxxxiv] Angove surely ranked as a kindred spirit in this respect. He always cherished opportunities to paint, whether it be in the studio or on the streets, as shown on the next page.

His urban street scenes entrench his subjects' day-to-day preoccupations with their own hint of challenge. He briefly engages the subject in each of these examples, the man with the walking stick in Barcelona, the watchman in Soho and the market stall operator elsewhere in London, probably at Covent Garden. Although the contact with the photographer appears fleeting, the pictures illuminate the humanity of the men within the grind of city life.

Paintbrush in hand ... Angove in a studio and on the streets

Angove's take of humanity on the streets

In the engrossing photograph of three young boys playing cops and robbers in the street (below), Angove again shares with the viewer an impression of life in a dour setting, possibly Leeds. He handles the lighting superbly and uses it and his vantage point to position the subjects skilfully in an environment that echoes a theatrical set. His most rewarding strategy is to shoot from very low to the ground. He's at no more than the boys' knee height, enabling him to contain almost all the background buildings within his frame. The respective 'action poses' of each of the boys are central to the narrative success of the image. The sense of perspective, the uncluttered thoroughfare and the simplicity of a single lamp post underscore the picture's impact.

Boys at play

His supremely lit pre-dusk photograph (next page) of the banks of the Thames approaching the Battersea power station, close to where the American painter James Whistler once lived and created his famous paintings of nocturnal London, is masterful. It epitomises the way a photograph can be constructed using the approach inherent in painting, whereby the artist chooses the elements to be included. This, of course, is typically far more challenging for a photographer because they can't readily control what exists in the setting in which they're creating an image. Consider how Angove has "assembled" the key elements that harmonise so effectively in this picture. There's the leading line of the riverbank and promenade wall, guiding the viewer's eye into the scene, aided by the perspective of the two receding lamp posts and ultimately the chimney stacks of the powerhouse. He includes three vessels on the water which is not quite still but with a surface shimmer, from the tide or light breeze, that resembles a watercolour's surface. The gloomy atmosphere, created by a combination of cloud, smoke and shrinking daylight, is reinforced by the reflection of the sun on the river. The wet, cobbled walkway presents its own pattern of small odd-shaped reflections. Then to top it off, Angove includes a barely-visible couple, strolling hand-in-hand, in the lower right quadrant. The photograph is perfectly designed to maximise the composition and viewpoint. Furthermore, the separation of all the key elements is deftly handled through a sublime tonal range.

Battersea Walk

In these examples from his portfolio, it's clear Angove was finding fulfilment within his adopted environment.

But there were also societal boundaries he encountered in those early London years. When his old friend from technical college in Perth, illustrator Les Chiew, came to England in the spring of 1958, Angove was forced to confront some undesirable prevailing attitudes in the community.

He told the story of Chiew's arrival on the doorstep at Lancaster Gate.

"Actually, one day, he came up to Woburn [Studios] where I was working at the time," he recalled.[ccxxxv]

"[Because] I was just on my way out to deliver some shots to a client, I said to Les 'come with me'. I led him a merry chase across London. I don't think he knew what was happening, hopping on and off the bus, diving through the underground, taking short cuts. Maybe I was showing off a bit."

After the frantic introduction to London, Chiew faced a familiar obstacle.

"He had this problem everywhere he went looking for accommodation," confided Angove.

"'Sorry, no coloureds', they'd say."

Back in Perth where he was born to parents of Singaporean Chinese origin in 1928, Chiew had never been considered 'coloured'.

Les Chiew (July 1959)

Angove spoke to his and Palmer's landlady.

"Although she liked black men herself, she said I'd have to talk to the doctor, a Jewish man, who owned the building. But just for the time being, she said [Les] could sleep on our floor if he liked. So we snuck Les in and, in the end, he got his own room.

"He became absorbed as part of the community and was as much accepted as anybody as he should have been."

Chiew, described in the shipping log as a commercial artist, was a loyal friend for many years.

He accompanied Angove on the visit to Paris for the encounters with the Marquis de Cuevas ballet company. Chiew later returned to Perth and, when Bill did likewise in 1970, they formed a design and publishing partnership with George Palmer in Wickham Street, East Perth.

Angove enjoyed the stream of regular drop-ins at Lancaster Gate with a few exceptions who "made more of a feast of it" than he preferred.

Craig McDonald, a descendant of Norman Chester, the man who gave Angove his first camera as a kid, was among those who travelled to London and spent time with his second cousin. Looking back, he describes Angove as the life of the party.[ccxxxvi]

"I'd say he was 'out there', an extrovert but not brash. I remember his infectious laugh and good sense of humour," McDonald added.

Angove confided years later: "When Craig and his mate came over, they used my floor on and off for about six months. I didn't mind Craig so much but his mate … that's another story."

Despite those occasional misgivings, Angove summarised the welcome mat at Lancaster Gate with joy: "We had a lot of interesting people around us all the time. Often, we'd go as groups to promenade concerts right up the top, where we'd get in cheap. Up in the gods it was. When we saw *My Fair Lady,* it cost us seven shillings and sixpence a head but we saw all the right people in it."

The visitors helped Angove retain and revive his friendships from his years of study at Perth Technical College. Among them was a young art student, Lois Robertson. As an indication of how well he had settled into his working environment in London, Angove managed to secure a job for Robertson at Woburn Studios doing colour processing.

"She turned out to be very adept at [operating] a new process called flexi-chrome. She could hardly ever get away from the place. They wanted to keep her all the time [even though] she wanted to travel."[ccxxxvii]

Lois Robertson did eventually get to see Europe and wound up being hired by a designer in Amsterdam. There she crossed paths with a young man who fell quite ill. She took up caring for him and "something developed between them". He recovered and they married and raised a family. He became the top designer for the Amsterdam city council.

Angove took heart from such events because he enjoyed seeing fellow ex-pats succeed and, in Lois Robertson's case, he saw reflected his strong interest in the world of design, artistic, commercial and industrial. He later gained credit for this pursuit.

Angove was a music and arts lover

Being a photog in London in the second half of the 60's is the nearest thing to having been a family in Paris in the 1880-1890s. My little studio flat in Queensway was in its way an ideal set-up for avoiding unattached photo — from there I was able to go in + out of the west end to see my clients, get to any railway to go across England for location subjects + & close to the air terminals for overseas assignments. But the really interesting things happened in the studio. I was a popular photographer for girls from a couple of model agencies who specialised in nudes. This led to my meeting some pretty way out characters as well as some really delightful...

Angove writes of Paris resonance

Thoughts of home

By around the middle of 1958, Bill Angove seemed to sense some of the tide going out on his London experiences, not professionally, but socially. Having surrounded himself with an engaging band of ex-pat friends, their gradual departure to other shores left him also feeling footloose again.

He later wrote about the litany of the revolving door in his life in London.

"The Weedons married, the Faciuses married, [another close friend and young haematologist] Robin Gow goes home to Sydney," he scrawled.[ccxxxviii]

"Lois goes to Amsterdam and marries. George [Palmer] and Barry Carter trip to Europe. Les goes home after a time in Amsterdam."

So after "often postponing" it, Angove himself decides to return to Australia. He remained close to his family, especially his mother, Marjorie, to whom he wrote a letter every week, addressing it at times to other family members too.

Ten weeks before his departure from London, he'd still not told his employer, Ken Wells, of his plans.

"Must do it very soon," he berated himself in a letter home.[ccxxxix] He said he wanted to be paid out in lieu of holidays, part of a strategy to fund his travel. He also decided to trade his camera for a new one when leaving "and make a profit of £10 to £15 at the very least and get a new camera into the bargain".[ccxl]

By the start of September, he'd taken the essential steps to leave.

"I've burnt my boats," he confided in correspondence. "Told Ken at work I want to sail on 6 November. [It was] a bit of a shock to him, but as he said, it was not unexpected and was bound to come someday.[ccxli]

"He offered, all being well, to pay my fare back [to Britain] in about six or nine months, once I have tasted Australia again and may not find it to my liking."

Angove reflected: "It's nice to know my efforts have not gone unappreciated."

Seemingly always alert to managing his finances carefully, if not frugally at times, Angove did a deal with the P&O Line to help defray some of his forthcoming travel expenses.

"I shall be able to recover some of my fare outlay eventually from [supplying] colour photographs on the voyage out," he told his mother.[ccxlii] He calculated he'd earn or save about £50 from the arrangement.

"It should be rather fun."

He was pleased to be given an 'access all areas' pass to go anywhere on the ship, the 10-year-old *S S Himalaya*, including crossing over from tourist to first class at whim.

SS Himalaya at Fremantle (1962) (Fremantle Port Authority picture)

While a Perth reunion was his initial priority, his correspondence[ccxliii] from early September onwards indicates that he was also keen on building his career success abroad by having a crack at Australia's biggest commercial, if not cultural, market, namely Sydney.

His liaison with the public relations officer at P&O provided another fillip for his prospects. The P&O man supplied a couple of contacts to follow up in Sydney, personal friends working in the same field, PR. Angove described this link as "always hand in glove with the advertising field … that's a start anyway." [ccxliv]

In the meantime, he had been receiving another leg up from a family source.

For at least the previous 12 months, Marjorie's brother, Burchell Butcher, who lived in NSW, had been holding a candle for Angove in Sydney advertising and photographic circles.

Butcher wrote to his nephew in glowing terms in August 1957.

"Although your imaginative work most certainly deserves the success and recognition it has brought you, it is not given to everyone with ability to achieve a niche so soon," he wrote. [ccxlv]

"The fact that you have done so is to your own credit entirely and for that I extend my hand to you in the sincere gesture of congratulations."

Butcher, then the Sydney advertising manager of the Perth afternoon newspaper *The Daily News*, goes on to describe the *Women's Weekly* spread as a "cracker" and the Pfizer advertisements as "gems of creative art".

"In fact, they are creative in the very best traditions," he continued, "but how you were able to achieve the results photographically would only be known to you."[ccxlvi]

Butcher (in caricature below) saw parallels between Angove's work and the painted abstracts of Matisse, praising both for their harmony and use of brilliant colour.

Caricature of Burchell Butcher

Burchell Butcher was himself a painter. It was a hobby that generated an average of three pictures a week, according to brief profile in *The Daily Telegraph* in 1947.[ccxlvii] The article described how he'd come home from work every day, don his artist's smock, and paint until dinner time. He was never keen to sell his work and regularly turfed it out. According to his son Terry, he did exhibit once and then decided it was "not for me".[ccxlviii]

Nevertheless, the father did enjoy connections in the art world. Triple Archibald Prize winner William Dobell was a close friend.

Burchell and his wife Frances professed to being strong admirers of Angove's creativity, matched by his ability to "keep [his] feet on the ground … skill and hard yakka."

Butcher played a kind of John the Baptist role in Sydney on behalf of Angove in the year or so before the latter's move back to Australia.

"I have shown the pages from the British Medical Journal to two of our leading advertising men in this city," Butcher wrote, "and they were considerably impressed, as I was, by the fertility of Bill's mind and his techniques."[ccxlix]

"One of the men, who is advertising manager for Phillips Industries, said he had never seen American or continental work of a similar type any better. In fact, he decided before our discussion terminated that it was the best he had seen."

While conceding there was no great demand for work of this nature, Butcher insisted that "when it is required, it needs to be of a very high degree of creative ability to produce appropriate stuff [sic]."[ccl]

Told by his nephew that the work was the result of "almost entirely a photographic process", Butcher apparently told his contacts that he was "more than ever amazed at Bill's handling of the medium". [ccli]

Angove's reputation was gaining recognition back in Western Australia too.

One of the local newspapers in Perth carried an article in 1958 headed *Cameraman Takes a Trick*. It exuded hometown pride in Angove's achievements in London. Describing him as a one-time familiar figure on city streets, the article talked of him "winning fame in England as the creator of an unusual art form". This was a reference to his "trick colour" work and "surrealist effects" showcased in his output for the major drug companies.

The paper also interviewed his mother, Marjorie, to whom he remained close.

"He hasn't set the Thames on fire," Mrs Angove said, "but he's started a few sparks."[cclii]

"When he left here in 1955 to study art, his camera was a means to an end. Now it's his whole life."

It's a memorable quotation and an apt appraisal of Angove's progress to this point. The Thames was set to see much more of him but not before making his mark on the eastern seaboard of Australia.

In the weeks leading up to his departure from London, Angove's correspondence reflected on his personal circumstances after almost four years there.

"Not being too social these days," he confided, "costs money."[ccliii] One exception was a night on the town farewelling another pair of friends as they were also leaving for other shores. He was fond of the National Film Theatre which screened Polish documentaries and experimental films he labelled "pretty good stuff". The latter category particularly appealed because they featured a high quotient of abstract footage.[ccliv]

Angove possessed an extensive collection of classical music records, many of which he acquired at half price through a mate and something called the Navy Export Scheme. His choice of composers and, in some cases, performers was likely influenced by his regular concert-going. Curiously, though, he didn't have a record player of his own, so he relied on visiting friends with radiograms, as they were called. He often wrote of his love of music and ballet and the many opportunities he had to immerse himself in both on London stages.

As he prepared to leave for home, he asked his family to stop sending copies of the *Daily News* from Perth and speculated about where he might live upon his return. He said he'd received an offer from his old mate Ken Knox to stay with him for a while at Manning, an inner southern suburb of Perth.

"He will probably feel hurt if I don't," he admitted.[cclv]

Perhaps hinting at some entrenched insecurity he was feeling, he added: "Anyway, I don't feel as though I will be homeless when I arrive and it will be good to have a place to call my own. What would you suggest?"

He went on to lower expectations of family members that he'd be bringing back gifts even though Christmas was on the horizon.

Again, there was a hint of insecurity and trepidation in his observation: "I'm going to be fairly okay unless I suddenly do something rash."[cclvi]

He seemed anxious about his pecuniary situation, citing ways of raising funds from work, his bank, other transactions and friends. His sensitivity about money even extended to a regret that his 13-guinea new suit bought a year earlier" was on its last legs".[cclvii]

Angove devoted some pages of his weekly letters home to detailing his precarious finances ("hope to have a bit of money … at least I can draw on unemployment benefit to find a bit of cash for such needs as food and bed"), his reformed dietary habits ("you will notice me eating a lot of things I formerly shunned … like tomatoes, onions, carrots and mushrooms") and his adoption of a beard ("everyone says leave the beard on … that will be the only difference you see in me").

However, his personal foibles did not appear to puncture his professional confidence and enterprise. A month before his departure, he went to the markets in the Portabello Road district, "something I have not done for quite a while".[cclviii]

He said he encountered "lots of junk barrows and weird people" which he appreciated as subjects to photograph.

An important feature of Angove's return to Perth was a plan for him to exhibit in the city at the Kodak Gallery. It was to be his inaugural solo exhibition and he was frantically conjuring work for the show right up to his final days in England.

The street market photo shoot produced "one or two good 'uns", according to his last letter home.

"Trying madly to get stuff for the exhibition at Kodak," he admitted.[cclix]

"Had hoped to have it all organised and set before I arrive but it looks like I'll be bringing the prints with me."

He was clearly giving earnest attention to every detail of this seminal event.

"Planning the layout and selecting negs and deciding on the size to enlarge them to takes a bit of thinking before I even get printing.

"I don't want to have any prints on the walls. [I want] an island of prints hanging from the ceiling in the centre so that you walk around and look through and can see people on the other side."[cclx]

He resolved that it might be better to wait until he was on the ground in Perth so he "could make sure it's the way I want."

Within just over four weeks remaining before he boarded the ship, Angove committed himself to "doing the rounds and seeing people before I go home", conceding there were fewer of them due to their own recent departures.

"I have begun to get that suspended feeling others have described before going home, that you really don't belong here. Have another quick look around at everything and go."[cclxi]

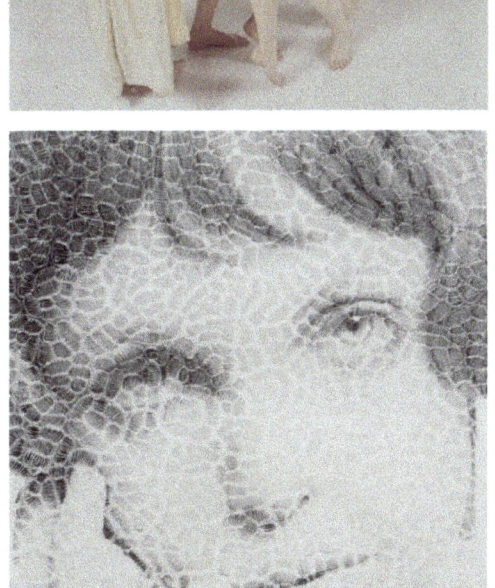

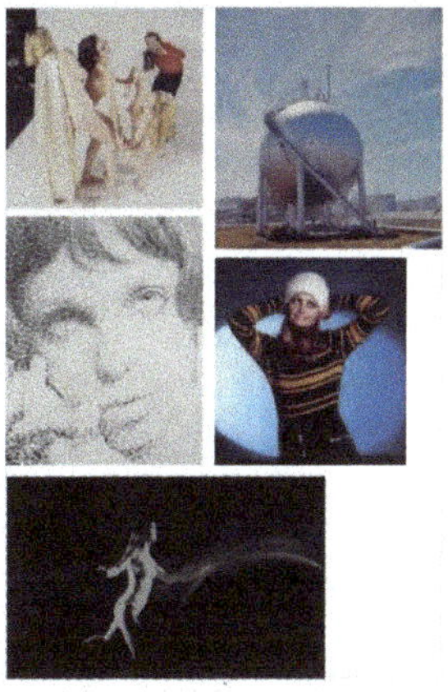

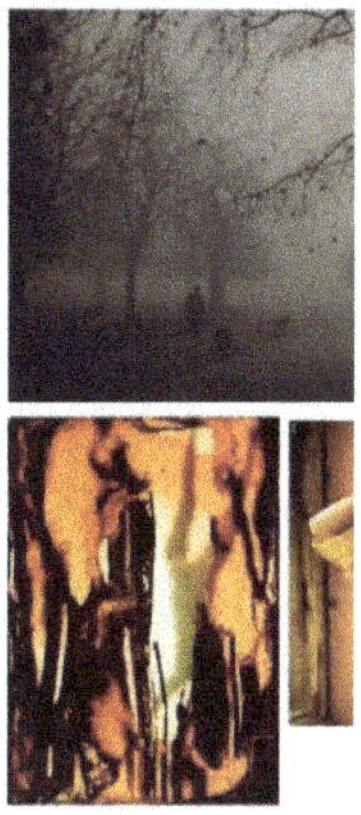

Picture Supplement Pages   Captions

P119 Clockwise from top left - Casino advertisement; Street scene, Portobello Rd; Transcontinental train, 1950s; Bristol Street 1950s; Ballet Dancers (undated)

P120 Portrait at Portobello Rd; Silhouette in studio; Guitar player; Model in window frame.

P121 Love at Wynyard Station (1961); Barcelona bar (1962)

P122 Circular Quay, Sydney (1960); Ferry Ride (1961

P123 Abstract (undated); Darlinghurst Rd, Sydney (1961)

P124 Model with antiques, Portobello Rd; People in same location

P125 Photographer with studio models; Tank, Sydney; Model with wool garments; Dancer with light motion; Abstract treatment of model

P126 London park fog; Woman in yellow; Abstract through burning

P127 Model on tram; Dean St, Soho, London (1962)

P128 Outside Salvos' Hostel, London (1960s); Studio set-up with Still Life objects and model; Model with Umbrella; The Cellist (1960s)

129

Pfizer ad 2 in British Medical Journal

Ambitions in Australia

Bill Angove enjoyed three notable experiences upon his return to Perth.

Emotionally his reunion with his family would have warmed his heart. He appears to have spent most of the summer with Marjorie, Gwenda and her family.

The other two experiences produced foundations for later creative expression and successes.

The extent to which he disclosed his hopes to break into the Sydney scene is hard to determine all these years later. Perth had its own temptation. He received an offer to diversify into film and television from a prominent businessman called Ron Armstrong who ran a photographic and film operation in Bennett Street, Perth.

According to an old friend of Angove's, clinical scientist and photographer, Ted Edkins, Armstrong's studio did most, if not all, of the film development for what was then Perth's only television station, TVW7, just starting up in 1959.

"I used to do the analytical work on their Kodak developer to keep it up to specs for the colour negative film shot by the Channel 7 crew," Edkins recalls.[cclxii]

Armstrong's outfit also did photographic printing for the commercial requirements of the TV station and media customers.

Another contemporary photojournalist Roger Garwood believes Armstrong's lab processed all the 16mm film footage for Channel Seven, which led the TV station to eventually take over the business.[cclxiii] As well as the cine work, Garwood recalls Armstrong introduced a system of producing very large photographic murals on canvas, at least one of which survives as part of the décor of His Majesty's theatre in Hay Street.

But in 1959, fresh back from the bright lights of London, Angove did not feel inclined to accept Armstrong's overture. Years later, he wondered out loud whether he had made a mistake in turning down the offer to enter the film and television sector because it remained an area of interest to the extent that he later took up part-time studies in the field at the WA Institute of Technology (WAIT) in the 1970s.

The second event highlighting Angove's journey was the aforementioned photographic exhibition exclusively featuring his work at the Kodak Gallery in Perth. It was his first 'one-man' show. It later toured to the Paxton's in Sydney, helpfully giving him a profile in the city that became his new professional base.

The Kodak Gallery was located in the basement of the company's film shop and processing darkrooms in Hay Street, next to Plaza Arcade. It was a major venue for photographic exhibitions over several decades. Staff were known to be closely engaged with the local photographic community, professional and amateur, and played a part in the establishment of more camera clubs in the state.

Three pictures from Angove's first solo exhibition in Perth and Sydney

The exhibition was called *Away from Home*. It featured an eclectic sampling from the entire range of Angove's portfolio to that stage in his career. In many ways, it was a giant calling card for the then 35-year-old returned to home shores. The prints included his ground-breaking abstracts for Pfizer's pharmaceuticals, ballet images, a lot of what the trade would refer to as 'stock images' for advertising purposes, theatrical and performance pictures, street images, portraits, documentary work, a few nudes, whimsical studio shots and a smattering of experimental art studies.

Record cover

It also included a cropped version of the original frame of a picture featuring a couple in a romantic embrace (above) which Coronet Records had commissioned or selected for a record sleeve. *Sentimental Journey*, which featured Doris Day's first big hit, was a best-selling seven-inch Extended Play (EP) by a well-known orchestra often referred to on stage and radio as *Les Brown and his Band of Renown*. Brown was an American jazz musician. Coronet's edition was produced for the Australian market with Angove's photography on the cover in 1959.[cclxiv] The band and their other record companies had scores of releases of the same suite of tunes in many countries over the decades.

The exhibition's intention seemed to be to showcase the diversity of his repertoire and how he had developed his skills and reach while abroad. The introductory display panel called him a Western Australian artist photographer back from four years overseas. It described how he "concentrated on advertising photography, to which his creative talents were most suited".cclxv

The exhibition was a useful forerunner for the artist in a new market, namely Sydney.

After returning home, Angove, apparently already determined not to hang about in his native state, readily let it be known that there was "not enough work for me to stay in Perth" cclxvi and, as foreshadowed, headed to Sydney with introductions to a couple of big advertising agencies.

Burchell Butcher was by this time convinced that Angove had chosen freelancing as the best course forward.

"I'm glad," he noted. "It's the only way he would make any money. And I imagine now that he has taken this step, he should make plenty. Not that money is important, but I believe that he will be better known by freelancing and will probably widen the scope for his work. The money will no doubt be useful all the same."

Angove made the move to Sydney around February 1959.

Angove had recommendations to try two advertising agencies in Sydney. One was called Berry Currie, established by Bill Currie and Hugh Berry in the late 1950s, a company that gave the later famous ad guru John Singleton his first break as a 20-year-old. Among its major clients in Australia was Kodak so the agency was deeply immersed in the world of photography at this stage.

His other referral was to a business named Times Advertising run by Doug and June Pollard. He armed himself with his portfolio from the three studios in which he'd worked in London. He didn't crack any opportunities initially. But his luck soon changed in an encounter with another agency, Lintas, established more than half a century earlier as the advertising arm of Lever Brothers, the American soap manufacturer. The then creative director of Lintas was none other than Bruce Harris, older brother of Rolf – Angove's great mate. Bruce Harris had also spent time in London in the early 1950s, yet another example of the tradition of Australian creatives plying their trade and talent there.

The Harris brothers' connection, you would think, opened doors for Angove in Sydney. The Lintas management sent him to Bruce Minette Limited who hired him.

Bruce Minette appears to have run a mixed studio supplying photography to commercial outlets and advertising agencies across Sydney, similar to the businesses Angove had worked for in the UK. Minette himself is known to have produced fashion pictures but Angove's main briefs centred on food photography. For a year he worked out of the studio's basement in the YWCA building.

Angove's arrival in Sydney in early 1959 generated quite a deal of interest. The monthly trade magazine, *Advertising*, ran a full-page story about his success with English advertisers through the use of abstract imagery. The likely hand of Burchell Butcher may well have triggered the coverage. The journal picked up the spirit of the *Women's Weekly* spread of 1955 dubbing Angove's innovative work "crazy".[cclxvii]

Angove told the magazine that, during his London years, he had found a steady stream of demand for his photographic abstracts. He explained that these were created by various distortion techniques.

Angove at Minette Studios (March 1959)

"I found they could prove the answer to the cry of some advertisers for 'something different, something not done before'. The method is used to sell … [an] idea or experience connected with a product.

"People either like it or decry it but one way or the other, it gets a lot of attention."[cclxviii]

He cited the way pharmaceutical manufacturers had effectively used startling examples in medical publications and direct mailers to doctors.

He recalled some of the radical techniques he had used in the Pfizer campaign materials, aimed at stimulating horror at the prospect of dying from flu. In one instance, he used "a reverse white on black head of a man 20 generations from the original negative".[cclxix]

"The result was a ghostly effect with nose and mouth accentuated in white."

He detailed how, in another advertisement, bleached out photographs of a girl's head, a male torso and a girl's hand were deployed with "only vague resemblances but … to introduce the human element in some way."

The magazine article drew a confession from Angove that crazy photography was a welcome relief from more mundane assignments.

"While many London advertising agents were keen to use abstract photography, most advertisers wanted something more down to earth.

"The current theme in London is more to extremism in reality than to abstracts. It is generally recognised that photography has more impact than artwork. People still adhere to the idea that the camera cannot lie – whereas, really, the camera is the most subtle liar of all.

"In London, advertisers are using the photograph a lot more than they do in Australia. The best advertisements feature a photograph blown up as big as possible with a minimum amount of copy."

As the story continued, it was clear Angove was revelling in the opportunity to help educate the Australian advertising industry on trends and developments overseas and, in the process, perhaps promote his own credentials.

The magazine story added: "Agents in London had often called on him to solve such photographic problems as the illustration of stickiness of Cellotape for the Monsanto Chemical Company.

"Angove said he was called upon when several other types of illustration had failed to satisfy the customer.

"He went to a London butterfly farm for a large moth and imprisoned it in a large cobweb of cellotape. The resultant photograph made the grade for an important chemical and plastics trade journal."

The article concluded with Angove extolling the virtues of high key and bleached half-tone photography for generating popular effects.

Eight months after Angove took up residence in Sydney, Paxton's, a major camera store at busy Wynyard in George Street, Sydney, hosted his solo exhibition in its dedicated gallery. The show comprised 70 prints.

An optician named E J Paxton opened his business there in 1908, diversifying into cameras just two years before Angove's show was used as part of building its reputation among NSW photographers. Paxton's operated as an independent photographic retailer with seven metropolitan outlets for more than 50 years. [cclxx]

The reviewer for *The Sydney Morning Herald* began: "It is always pleasing to see a young photographer with sufficient courage to stage a one-man show in a city gallery".

The more high-brow broadsheet called him William Angove and described him as a newcomer to Sydney. The popular tabloid, *The Daily Telegraph*, called him Bill and claimed him as a Sydney professional.

The *Herald* referred to Angove's overseas wanderings with his Rolliecord camera in hand, as providing most of the content for the exhibition.

"[The] pictures … represent a wide range of subjects which include some fine ballet shots", the critic wrote, adding that the show also included fine human-interest studies and excellent examples of advertising photography.[cclxxi]

The exhibition was opened by a former Royal Academy artist from London, Weaver Hawkins, a Sulman, Wynne and Archibald Prize finalist who had made his home in Mona Vale, NSW, since 1935. A leading printmaker in Sydney and a non-conformist in personal style, Hawkins' work may have resonated with Angove because they shared an artistic interest in "depictions of everyday working life and leisure". [cclxxii]

The Telegraph reproduced one of the exhibition's most striking images, *Diagramme*, a picture featuring a "leaping dancer" in the Marquis de Cuevas ballet company taken in the Alhambra Theatre in Paris and enlarged to five feet in width for the Sydney show.[cclxxiii]

Years later, Angove reflected on the impact of his solo exhibition, comforted by the fact that it "was well received by the press in Perth and Sydney",[cclxxiv] and no doubt enhancing his profile as he settled into his new city. He went on to have two other solo exhibitions in Perth in the early 1970s.

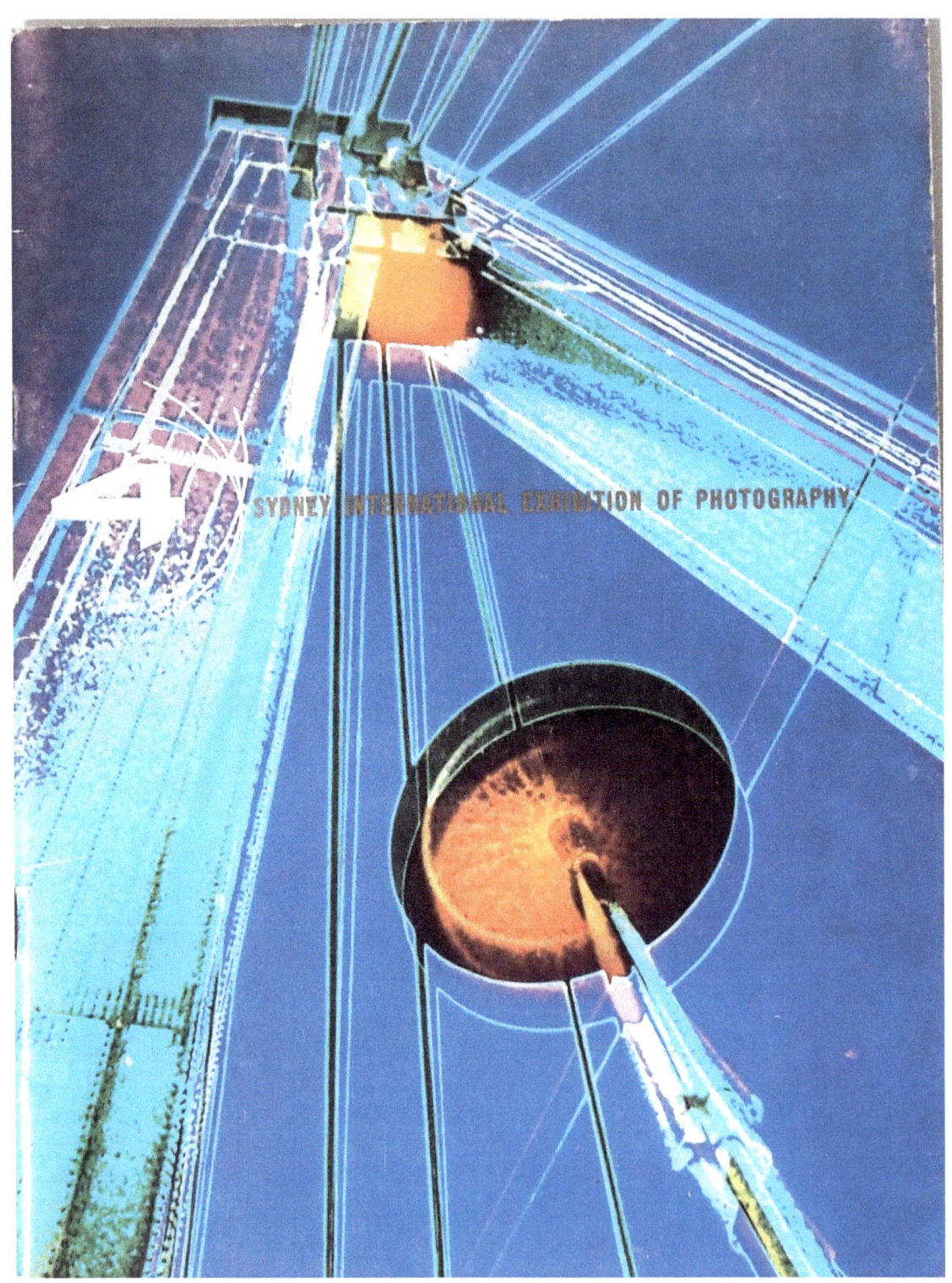

Sydney exhibition program

The Sydney Years

As 1959 progressed, Angove refreshed his social network in his newly adopted home which included friends from the London years. His medical pal, Robin Gow, was an early reconnection, coinciding with her marriage to a young obstetrician and gynaecologist, Rod Macdonald, who later achieved acclaim for his role in helping revolutionise childbirth in Australia.

He also met a woman named Pam who lived in Neutral Bay but about whom little is now known. They developed a love interest but I have been unable to establish any detailed information about this romantic coupling. Angove's cousin Terry Butcher maintains Bill "was very protective of Pam".[cclxxv]

Bill and Pam (October 1961)

"Pam and I became close," Angove later wrote, "and even talked of marriage."
But it was not to be and eventually played a part in him leaving Sydney.
Angove moved into a flat in adjoining Kirribilli. One of his neighbours on the north shore was a man named Bill Pownall who, in his youth in the 1950s, studied at the National Art School in Sydney.

It's unclear whether a friendship between Pownall and Angove began socially or professionally. It may have started as a neighbourly connection or, according to Pownall's hazy memory, it more likely derived from his role as print production manager with George Pattersons advertising agency,[cclxxvi] one of the biggest in town.

This agency was one of a handful that engaged Angove's services over his three years in Sydney for one of its major accounts. He produced images for the adhesive manufacturing business, Behr-Manning Pty Ltd of Lidcombe, which made and marketed cellulose tapes under the Bear brand.

It appears to have been a highly prized contract at the time because Bear Tape's press and magazine advertisements featured photography by Max Dupain's studio as illustrated below.[cclxxvii] Angove had had previous experience in London facing the challenge of illustrating the stickiness of adhesive tapes, as described earlier. He considered "creative industrial" photography one of his strengths.[cclxxviii]

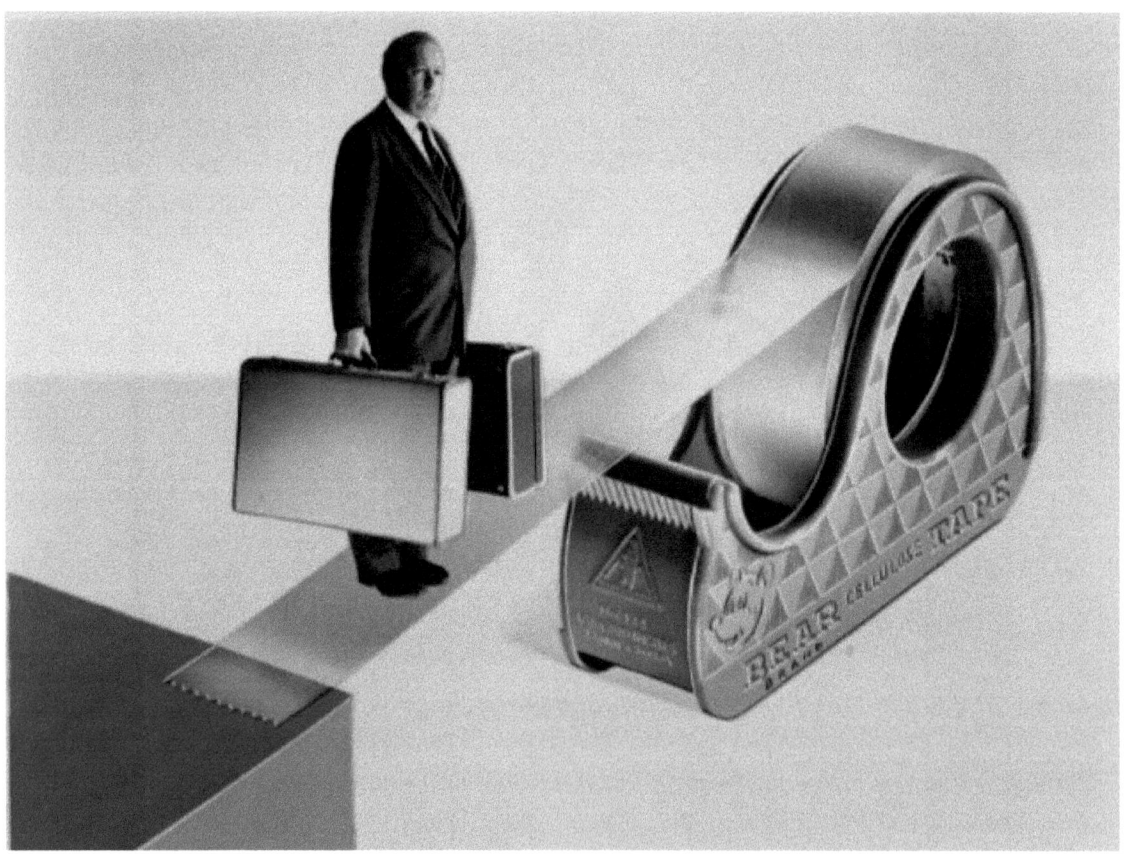

Bear Tape advertisement by Max Dupain Studios (1957) (NSW State Library)

So the ad agency account for Behr-Manning may well have played a part in Angove's relationship with Pownall who oversaw all the company's colour work.

Multi-talented Pownall had studied music as well as art and later performed as a professional jazz musician. Angove's friendship circle included Pownall who would play the double bass at parties they ran or attended.

Bill Pownall playing double bass with Bill Angove and girlfriend Pam in background (1961)

At the start of their friendship, Pownall worked as a musician at night after a day doing his agency work.

He recalls Angove inviting him to his flat "where we sipped Cyprus sherry and nibbled Feta cheese, quite a good combination and perhaps a harbinger of my future in Greece."[cclxxix]

Pownall continues: "Bill was a good friend to me. During these visits we talked a lot about art, photography of course, music and life in general. Conversation did not flag.

"At the time I was very involved with jazz, less so with classical music. Bill played me a couple of Brandenburg concertos by Bach and remarked that they 'swung' just as much as any jazz, if in a slightly different way.

"He was right, of course, and these concertos remain favourites of mine until this day.

"After a tasty meal of savoury rice, Bill told me how he learned to cook rice from a Chinese flatmate," a reference no doubt to Les Chiew.

"Bill told me how. It was simple and effective and I am still cooking rice this way fifty years later."

Their conversations often returned to art. Pownall was fascinated by Angove's collection of postcards depicting the work of various painters.

"I already had a strong feeling for visual art and we would discuss the different styles and periods," Pownall said.[cclxxx]

"One evening, with his customary modesty, he produced a painting of his own, a small, lively colourful abstract with a hint of [Jackson] Pollock about it. The title was *A Taxi Driver Surprised While Driving Down a One-Way Street*.

Angove's Pollock-inspired abstract

"Another time he introduced me to his splashographs, images produced by using photographic chemicals on the appropriate paper … unique in my experience."

Pownall, best known in later years for his unique landscape art, moved to Greece the year after Angove returned to Europe. Pownall established himself in a network of Australians on the island of Hydra, a group garnered by writers George Johnston and Charmian Clift and that, for a time, included Sid Nolan. These were among the cultural figures who, at various points, had an influence on Angove's life and outlook.

Pownall considered himself primarily an abstract painter so he and Angove shared those artistic tastes.

While generating commercial output at Minette Studios, Angove made his mark in the world of art photography. In that regard, Sydney was a propitious place to be.

In 1958, as Angove was plotting his move back to Australia, a prominent camera club in Sydney, established 15 years earlier and known as the YMCA Camera Circle, decided to embark on a significant venture, an annual exhibition of photography from around the world.

By the time this large-scale event entered its fourth year in 1961, the Sydney International Exhibition of Photography staged at the Sydney Town Hall, claimed in its catalogue that it had "become the most notable event in the Australian photographic year".[cclxxxi]

It had big ambitions and high ideals as the show's foreword stated: "Through its good relations with the leading photographers of every major exhibiting country throughout the whole world, [the exhibition] has become a clearing house for the exchange of ideas that must contribute to better international understanding. By their support, the exhibitors have established this as one of the world's leading exhibitions."[cclxxxii]

The organisers boasted of showing "the world's best pictures … and raising local standards".

A year earlier, Bill Angove had entered the third iteration of the Sydney International and won a major award for what he described as "experimental photography",[cclxxxiii] no doubt deriving from his penchant for the crazy and abstract where he'd left a trail of success.

By the fourth year, as a result of his previous success and established reputation as an Australian international practitioner, Angove was enlisted for the exhibition's selection panel and invited to judge the colour slides section of the show, enhancing his standing in the right circles. Other well-known photographers who also judged the Sydney International alongside Angove in this era included David Moore, Max Dupain, Laurie Le Guay and fellow West Australian Hal Missingham[cclxxxiv] who Angove knew from their mutual connections with Gibbney's Studio back in Perth.

Angove judged the pictorial slides category in 1961. The top three images came from California, Melbourne and Finland. As a judge, he obviously wasn't allowed to enter the slides competition but it was the practice of the organisers to invite judges to exhibit their work nevertheless in a separate facet of the show. Angove exhibited a group of three slides, which were listed as untitled.

But he was allowed to enter the print section and two of his submissions were displayed, *Bargain Hunter* and *Three Graces*[cclxxxv], the latter earning a certificate of merit.

Photography was making significant advances in Australian art and culture at the time, an advance that would have no doubt pleased Angove five years after he had exhorted the camera club members back in Perth to embrace its place in the artistic constellation.

The vision and energy of a colleague at that time would have won Angove's applause. The Sydney International's chair was a man named Bert Andrews, who earned a reputation not only for helping to found the exhibition but also for proposing the establishment of the Australian Photographic Society. By the early 1960s, Andrews' ambition came to fruition with a membership consisting of affiliated state photographic federations, local camera clubs, other organisations and private individuals. This was a seminal development in photographic practice in this country that Angove witnessed closely.

Before the end of 1959, buoyed by the success of his exhibition at Paxton's, Angove left Minette Studios.

"[The exhibition] stimulated work," he observed.[cclxxxvi] He embarked upon a period of freelancing, initially working on fashion and advertising assignments from studios in Jamison Street, a small enclave in inner Sydney not far from the Rocks. The area was considered at the time a bohemian part of town occupied by artists' studios and the rooms of the Poetry Society.[cclxxxvii]

A business flyer devised by Angove during his Sydney freelance period

Angove seemed to be drawn to such places as his experiences in various London localities, occupied by creative types, demonstrated. Family and friends I have spoken to in the course of writing this biography willingly ascribe the word bohemian to Bill Angove's lifestyle. He kept albums of photographs of lively parties and gatherings of young friends, often captioned in amusing ways. Those boarding houses and flats in London and Sydney must have rocked to the rafters.

Angove loved his dress-up gatherings

A long-time friend, Bill Weedon, says it was never an effort for Angove to mix with people, such was his personality.[cclxxxviii] Physically he also displayed dynamism.

"He would move all the time," Weedon recalls, "he could never sit still."[cclxxxix]

Around early 1960, Angove entered into some sort of partnership arrangement at the invitation of a former freelance photo-journalist, Brian Chirlian, who was well travelled and worked in London for a time but before Angove's stint there. Chirlian had a strong profile as a photographer in Sydney and beyond alongside the likes of Max Dupain and others. By the mid-50s, he had established a business called Ajax Films. Ajax operated as a production company and studio, moving in 1959-60 into the old bond store in the Argyle Cut at the Rocks.[ccxc]

Chirlian set up Ajax primarily to make TV commercials for the British-Australasian Tobacco Company.[ccxci] It was described as a subsidiary of the cigarette firm by 1967 and turned into a prominent and prolific production house over two decades, strongly participating in the burgeoning Australian feature film industry.

Chirlian was by now a producer and director. Angove managed the stills studio at Ajax in 1960-61.

With the advent of its famous Grange Hermitage in 1951, Penfolds Wines emerged over the next decade as a pre-eminent producer of high-quality fortified and table wines in Australia. When the company's board authorised winemaker Max Schubert to scale up the Grange output in 1960, Bill Angove was assigned work on the Penfold account by advertising agency Berry Currie. Across town, Max Dupain's studio was also shooting work for the prestigious advertiser.

In that era, the major wine producers like Penfolds boasted their fortifieds, such as sherry and port, as their market leaders. Table wines, of which Grange long reigned as the country's most revered label, were still to win over a majority of consumers. By the end of the 1960s, reinforced by the tastes of European migrants, this ranking changed. Angove's sherry-drinking gentleman was soon to be considered passe as red table wines, alongside sweet whites, largely took over the market.

Other contracts Angove worked on included CIG Industrial Gases, Unilever Foods and the aforementioned electrical giant Phillips Industries.

Angove's Penfolds sherry advertisement 1960 (Model and Women's Weekly publication)

Racy magazine cover, Australia

Vogue and variations

Impressively Angove secured assignments to shoot fashion for Vogue magazine. Working for this masthead earned accolades in the photography world. His timing was perfect because Vogue launched its Australian edition in the very year of Angove's move to Sydney.[ccxcii] Publisher Conde Naste's magazine, founded in New York around the end of the 19th century and extended to London in 1920, was and remains a by-word in fashion pictorials.

Throughout the 20th century, Vogue commissioned work from many of the world's leading fashion photographers. Among them was Edward Steichen, a Luxembourgish American photographer, painter, and curator, "renowned as one of the most prolific and influential figures in the history of photography."[ccxciii] Steichen is considered to have helped elevate photography into "one of the fine arts",[ccxciv] an echo of Angove's conviction enunciated in his Perth camera club address of 1953.

A pioneer of fashion photography, from 1938 Steichen was chief photographer for Vogue while also working for many advertising agencies.[ccxcv] A stable of Australian-reared and based photographers also rode the Vogue wave of leading-edge fashion imagery. They included the German-born pair of Helmut Newton and Henry Talbot who worked in Melbourne. Newton, who cut his professional teeth in Australia and became a friend of Angove's, later based himself in Paris.

According to the author of a profile of Talbot from the National Gallery of Victoria (NGV),[ccxcvi] for "fashion photographers working in Australia, magazine work allowed greater creative independence than other commercial work did."

"'Editorial' fashion shoots enabled photographers to collaborate with fashion editors and stylists, and to create photographs in series rather than single images, as was more often the case in advertising work. Magazine commissions, particularly with Vogue Australia, were highly sought after."

Talbot welcomed such work because it gave photographers a free hand with collections.[ccxcvii]

It is clear that the introduction of Vogue's local edition was hugely valued by the Australian fashion industry and its photographic exponents. Its first covers were shot by Norman Parkinson and Lord Snowden. For Angove to land assignments with Vogue, apparently beginning with a double-page spread in the mid-winter edition of 1961, meant he could deploy his talent more freely and earn his career significant credit. His record of work with clothing designers and models in the London years now paid off at a new level.

One of Angove's subsequent Vogue commissions featured "eight of the most delectable [examples] from the advance swimwear collections" from designers and manufacturers such as Jantzen, Lastex, Rose Marie Reid and Ada of California.ccxcviii

From a four-page spread of swimwear fashion photographed by Angove for Vogue

Angove must have loved undertaking this assignment for the Spring 1961 edition of the magazine because it's clear the gig had him either devising one of his signature inventive staging ideas or collaborating with a zany art director or a particularly creative designer. The shoot entailed monochrome studio shots of the swimsuit models, a couple using props such as bathing caps and a parasol, posed and then cropped in a way that suggested they were immersed in a huge fish tank. The accompanying text bleated: "Up to their necks in water." The copy then drew a parallel with the famous American comic film producer Mack Sennett's Bathing Beauties from the silent movies era updated to a 1961 flavour.

Angove enjoyed working with female models who came to feature in both his professional output and in personal projects across three decades. This was an era when the pin-up girl was a regular and ubiquitous photographic feature of many publications. Initially, he found the theatre world was the best source of sexy young women for photographing.

"There were a lot of girls in the theatre world wanting to do nude," he recalled. [ccxcix] He had even more stories of such encounters in a later stage of his career which came to feature a strong engagement with the female form.

The few years back in Australia produced another landmark in Angove's artistic career.

Innovative gallery space in Melbourne, hosting a global exhibition

In 1959, a group of leading Australian photographers decided to establish an annual international exhibition called Photovision, concentrating on documentary photography. For its first five years, the event was hosted by the Museum of Modern Art Australia located in a lane off Flinders Street in Melbourne. The venue was managed by the prominent art editor, patron and co-founder of the famous art retreat Heide, John Reed, a man whose inner circle included Sid Nolan, Albert Tucker and Arthur Boyd. The organising group included industrial photographer John Crook, Melbourne painter, photographer and press artist George Bell and Angove's Western Australian contemporary Richard Woldendorp. They were imbued with an appreciation of international trends and pioneering talents in the documentary photographic sphere such as Lewis Hine, Bill Brandt, Henri Cartier-Bresson, Roy Stryker, Dorothea Lange, Walker Evans, Werner Bischoff and Eugene Smith.[ccc]

According to blogger John McArdle, the event's "reach into the Australian photographic community was considerable". [ccci]

Among the exhibitors were Nigel Buesst (*Newsreel* cameraman and industrial photographer), Keast Burke (Sydney professional and writer on photography), Gordon De Lisle (high ranking member of the Melbourne Camera Club), Max Dupain, Margaret 'Maggie' Fraser (American advertising photographer), Laurence Le Guay, Zillah Lee, David Moore, Wolfgang Sievers, Marc Strizic, Bob Whitaker and Bill Angove.

Angove was an enthusiastic and notable contributor to both the 1961 and 1962 editions of Photovision. His participation was testimony to his versatility and breadth of ability. In accord with the founders' philosophy, Photovision was dedicated to the "use of 'straight' or unmanipulated photography as a means of expression".[cccii] As we have seen, this genre did not always rank as Angove's preferred style. After all, he was in large part an abstract artist and a spirited experimenter. But, as his ballet and street images demonstrated, he also excelled in documentary mode.

The promoters and competitors in the Photovision exhibitions had an enduring influence on the National Gallery of Victoria which came to recognise and celebrate the contribution of 1960s Australian documentary photographers, including successful commercial practitioners and emerging artists of the time.[ccciii]

In the catalogue for its 2004-2006 retrospective exhibition *Flashback*, paying homage to Photovision, the NGV stated: "It [1960s] was a decade in which documentary photography flourished and this is reflected in the range of early acquisitions of the [gallery's fledgling] Department of Photography."

The catalogue authors continued: "Following the high glamour of fashion photography in the 1950s, studios made the transition to a particularly expansive and youth-oriented era, creating images with an exciting, contemporary edge. Contemporary culture was a rich subject for documentary photographers

"Indeed, many of the best-known commercial practitioners of the 1950s went on to consolidate their reputations both locally and internationally in the 1960s. The emerging artists of the decade forged the way for subsequent generations of photographers. The now better-charted period of the 1970s has its origins in the artistic practice of the preceding decade."[ccciv]

The Photovision exhibitions were most successful, according to historian Philip Bentley.[cccv] The same gallery exhibited work by Angove's London friends, Tucker and Boyd, in 1960 and 1964 so the West Australian must have felt in good company. The photographic exhibits were given rare treatment: large, bold prints mostly suspended in the gallery space. It was novel for Australian audiences used to viewing pictures in frames.

Angove exhibited a print in the 1961 iteration called *In a Small Country Torn By War*. I have not yet been able to trace the picture or establish its origins.

He had a second entry which soared into the prize category. *Twelve Variations for Camera and Guitar* was Angove's audio-visual work, essentially a set of slides accompanied by music.

It was a collaboration with his friend Bill Pownall who recalled its complex creation: "Bill took some colour slides of Lulu, a curvy model who didn't mind posing nude. He worked over the images with a razor blade, adding an abstract quality." cccvi

Angove then said to Pownall: "What I need is some music. How about it?"

Pownall responded: "By this time, I think I had become a full-time musician, and I worked out 12 short guitar pieces I could play to try to match Lulu's charms and Bill's skill."cccvii

Bill Angove and Bill Pownall in Sydney

The audio-visual entries at Photovision were projected in the gallery each night at eight o'clock for visitors to the show which ran to 9.30pm each of the 17 days of the event.

David Moore, who did not exhibit that year, was instead a member of the selection panel for the displays and a judge of the entries. In the exhibition's catalogue, Moore devoted most of his commentary to the three works in the section called Slides with Soundtracks.

Here is Moore's critique of Angove's contribution: "*Twelve Variations* was perhaps the most ambitious entry in the whole exhibition. Twelve variations played on a guitar were linked with twelve variations of photographs of a nude figure with abstract handwork added to the transparencies.

"The handwork was vital and complex which, coupled with an intelligent use of colour, helped to increase the impact and magic of the visual message.

"However, some of the nude figures seemed unnecessarily obvious and the guitar music seemed poorly suited to such active visual statements.

"Despite the foregoing this was a bold attempt to do something with the audio-visual treatment."[cccviii]

The organising committee also reflected: "This year has seen the audio-visual section start to come of age."[cccix]

Bill Angove won the Museum of Modern Art award for *Twelve Variations*.

The Age newspaper's arts columnist was rapturous, describing *Twelve Variations* as "the star piece of the Photovision audio-visuals".[cccx]

"You would barely know they were nudes; you can just sense it," the paper continued. "Then he scratched out some of the outlines. Some were left clear and others he dyed, though they were coloured to begin with. The guitar plays a slight, haunting accompaniment, which helps to create a good feeling."[cccxi]

The writer then quoted organiser John Crook suggesting that after viewing Angove's winning work, people will tend to regard orthodox slide shows as a bit boring.

"When the entry won," Bill Pownall recalls, "we decided to drive to Melbourne to see the resulting exhibition. It was quite an amusing trip. While in Melbourne we visited a friend of Bill's, the painter Albert Tucker. It was an interesting meeting for me."[cccxii] Pownall is probably implying that Tucker would have loomed in his mind then as a towering and inspiring figure in world art.

While preparing to depart for the UK again, Angove entered a series of prints to Photovision the following year alongside work included in a joint submission.

Back to Britain

Angove considered his three years in Sydney "quite a success".cccxiii Nevertheless, he said he still hankered for the British capital.

"The lure of London was still there," wrote Allanah McDonald cccxiv who interviewed Angove some years later for a magazine about Australian creatives shining in the UK.

Another factor in his decision, as previously noted, was the breakdown of his relationship with his lover, Pam. In a batch of handwritten notes, all Angove mentions is Pam being struck by an illness, coupled with a reference to "her rejection of me".cccxv He added that this harsh turn of events influenced his decision to go back to London.

Curiously, however, his mate Bill Pownall remains vague about Pam's status.

"When we were friends and neighbours in Sydney, Bill did not have any significant relationship with any woman, though he liked them!" Pownall divulged.cccxvi

"I do recall that he was quite taken with a lissome young lady whom he saw from time to time on the ferry we sometimes took to work. Her name was Oriel Sanleville, perhaps in her late teens or early twenties … attractive, off-beat, enigmatic, as I remember.

"I well understood his enthusiasm for her.

"Bill organised a meeting with her, myself and another girl – an amusing afternoon which did not lead anywhere as far as I knew."

Despite relationships that might or might not have encouraged him to stay there, Angove no doubt felt that he could build on his Sydney achievements and reconnect with his former working environment on the other side of the world before ties withered.

Again, in 1962, Angove travelled by sea. His passage from Sydney was on the *SS Stratheden*, a P&O company wartime troop carrier converted to a single-class passenger liner in 1961. cccxvii This time, though, he did not sail all the way to the vessel's destination, Tilbury Dock, as he had seven years previously. Instead, he disembarked in Barcelona on the north-east coast of Spain.

He was immediately rejoining his adventures from the 1950s. In Barcelona, he met up with the Festival Ballet company, which sounds too much of a coincidence but which he insisted was "quite a surprise".cccxviii He had deep friendships within this company, as previously outlined, and dined daily with members of the group during those Spanish nights.

Shortly afterwards, he travelled with the Festival dancers overland to Paris and eventually on to London, skiting that he still beat the *Stratheden* to port.cccxix

It was the middle of 1962 and, back on the streets where he had built his international career, Angove was offered a couple of job prospects. He turned them down in favour of familiar territory. He resumed at Mayflower Studio at the invitation of Howard Byrne. Byrne's business partner Lee Israel had died in the interim, as previously recounted.

The studio had moved to new premises at Colquhoun House on Broadwich Street, about a kilometre north-east of its original address but still in Soho. Byrne had continued to expand the business with fervour. He positioned the studio as an international picture provider to the editorial and advertising industries. Mayflower's picture library supplied clients across continental Europe, Africa and Scandinavia. It did a deal to supply its clients with exclusive access to images from a major US stock photo library, Ewing Galloway.

Byrne also branched out into the design world, starting a graphic design partnership with Lawrence Marshall. This allied business offered adjunct services to photography clients such as packaging and product design, exhibition stands, leaflets and anything that constituted a sales promotion tool.

While Mayflower hired models and actors from leading London agencies, in a folksy way it still maintained the feel of a family business. Byrne, who was married to an artist, used his then three-year-old daughter in children's clothing photographs and created a granny picture enlisting his ironing lady sitting in a rocking chair with her nine-year-old daughter holding her knitting wool.

Angove's friends were recruited to the studio too. His Australian friend Marilyn Burr, the dancer from the Festival Ballet, posed so the business could boast that it offered authentic and accurate ballet shots.

Bill Angove was appointed studio manager at Mayflower. The company played up his background in studying art and his drive to "always ... push back camera frontiers".[cccxx] Blaming his 1958 departure on homesickness, the studio was excited to regain his services, telling its clients Angove "has fallen in love with London twice, and now its [sic] for keeps".[cccxxi]

"When his nostalgia for Europe regained ascendency, he returned to London and rejoined Mayflower."[cccxxii]

The studio clearly welcomed him back and promoted him as a unique asset, describing him as "a photographic impressionist who produces colour photographs that look like modern paintings.

"He likes to work in abstract or to take on assignments for clients who want something off-beat. He experiments ceaselessly and has even boiled colour transparencies and printed three colour negatives on top of one another in his striving for a new image."[cccxxiii]

The Byrne team delighted in parading Angove's edginess, disclosing that some of his most original effects were executed by painting on the back of his transparencies. This catalogue blurb was accompanied by a picture of Angove in which he resembled a magician.

Mayflower depicted Angove as a magician

The versatility of Angove cemented his appeal to the photographic market. His imagination stoked his creative output. His professional path was typical of many successful peers during this period. Most photographers who earned a living from their work combined commercial assignments - in fields such as architecture, industrial, lifestyle and press - with their 'purer' output in art photography where their creative souls could soar.

Angove's initial return to Mayflower saw him contributing to the studio's massive photo library which at the time boasted more than 5000 images on both negative and slide film. The business cultivated its connections with the theatre and film industries, appealing to Angove's interests and engaging character actors as models to create more convincing pictures, especially for "people who can't be photographed in real life"[cccxxiv] such as judges, clergy, soldiers, doctors and police officers.

The studio's catalogue was issued for a fee to clients as a loose-leaf binder with sheets of thumbnail images regularly updated.

Angove also chased assignments with his former clients, one of whom was Burt Greene who by now was running his own company, Childs-Greene Associates. He was also aided by David Davies, another former ad agency colleague, who provided Angove with a studio for one of his first jobs back in town in 1962. Various agencies, established and start-ups, commissioned work from Angove who was living in Cheyne Walk, Chelsea. He later moved to the Fulham Road area, down the road from Earls Court and opposite Battersea Power Station. He also renewed his Australian connections like Robyn and Ross Haig.

A new love interest appeared on the scene. He was introduced to 17-year-old Jeanne Johnson-Flint. The relationship triggered mixed emotions. Angove, then aged 38 or 39, recognised the age gap between the two but described the friendship as "grand passion". cccxxv He added: "[I] was not popular with her father."cccxxvi

Despite objections and the 20 years between them, Angove and Johnson-Flint hit it off. Notwithstanding her father's view, he met her family and also managed to get a job for her in another studio, run by friend and artist Kingsley 'Hoppy' Hopkins, as a junior retoucher. After hours, they enjoyed a string of regular haunts including playhouses, restaurants and the advertising club off Piccadilly.

During this period, Angove moved on from Mayflower and forged a partnership with a man named Andre Hettena, running a small studio called AdLib, again concentrating on fashion and advertising commissions.

Two business setbacks then altered the course of Angove's professional and personal lives. After 12 months, he and Henetta split because the "partnership … did not work very well for me".cccxxvii

Around the same time, Hopkins closed his business and Angove decided to employ Johnson-Flint directly on a part-time basis. He moved to a residential building at 44 Inverness Terrace in Bayswater with the intention of freelancing. It was a humble start though, with minimal equipment at his disposal. He recorded that he only had a Rollei camera and three Malham photographic lights.cccxxviii But his reliable clients continued to give him plenty of work and, as he puts it, "always backed me up".cccxxix He used fast service labs for his regular large volume of colour work.

It was now the mid-60s, a decade after leaving Western Australia, and Angove was thriving. His clients were all industry leaders, Trafalgar Tours, the National Coal Board, NCR Computers, the British Iron and Steel Federation and Agfa Cameras. His advertising assignments for this stable of companies found him travelling constantly, both within the UK and around Europe.

Trafalgar was a household name in holiday touring, offering sightseeing coach travel, meals and accommodation within the British Isles and particularly on the Continent but also extending into Russia, Scandinavia and Turkey. Its Globetrotter Tours were cheap and pitched at the under-30s as "Swinging Holidays". Angove was enlisted to shoot hundreds of images for the company's high-volume catalogues (below), at one level surely a commercial photographer's dream job.

Trafalgar catalogue pages shot by Angove

The briefs Angove received continued to demand the inventive flair on which he had built his reputation.

An English magazine, *Photography*, carried an extensive article in about 1965 called Creating the Mood which looked at "the exciting work of Bill Angove, colour photographer extraordinary"[cccxxx].

"How can one illustrate an idea - photographically? Or an attitude of mind … or instil one idea of a new product or service from one mind to another? This is the problem which I am constantly up against as a creative photographer in colour, my work used mainly in advertising," the opening paragraph quoted Angove.

The writer, known only as EWS, observed "his ideas racing ahead of him as he talks in staccato bursts".[cccxxxi]

"Indeed, he so cackles with vitality and ideas that one wonders how he manages to discipline his abounding energies so tightly in the studio – as obviously he does, often involving multiple exposure and printing or other complicated technical tricks of the trade."

The magazine discusses various approaches advertisers and their agencies took to planning and executing colour print advertisements. The aim of using photography was to attract attention or enhance the appeal of a product, and sometimes merely to illustrate.

"Bill Angove likes assignments in the first category," it continues.[cccxxxii]

"Here, imagination can let rip. Angove finds that pure, saturate colour is the best attention-getter; and plenty of it. But his multiple exposure shots (as for Hohner mouth-organs below) where vivid colour crosses vivid colour, and challenging, bold patterns fairly demand attention, are stoppers too."

Mouth organ advertising picture

Angove had a deep understanding of the power and psychology of individual colours. He extolled the ways human nature responds to certain colours and how this nexus could be applied to generate perceived characteristics of certain products and moods for their reception.

It was his penchant for abstraction - in images and in thinking - that often helped him excel. A good example of this was a brief to market a new electric watch from manufacturer Bulova. It was a watch that hummed rather than ticked, a relatively new concept at the time.

Having consulted the assignment's art director, Angove "returned to his studio to consider how it was possible to illustrate 'hum', and settled for double-exposure techniques on a single half-plate sheet of Ektachrome-B."

The answer was to feature a hand holding a tuning fork to mimic the generation of waves (below).

Bulova watch advertisement

The interview with Angove threw more light on what we would today describe as his workflow. He'd spend a long time devising a tricky system of various exposures and printing techniques.

"His special effect satisfactorily obtained for the particular creative problem at hand, Angove may never again precisely duplicate the methods used to achieve the result he planned. Therefore 'how to' explanations or the keeping of elaborate records of data have small purpose. He believes the creative photographer must - having mastered the basic chemical and optical techniques - develop his own style via methods suitable to him."

The author found it amusing that "this highly skilled and original worker made excellent capital of certain early failures". But to harness mistakes is far more difficult than might be supposed. Angove insisted he never resorted to stunts for their own sake.

"He carefully considers the selling problem his photograph has to solve: then, the effect which will most forcefully get his picture across."

There was also an aspect of Angove's output, reflecting the social and cultural values of the time, that tolerated the exploitation of young women's sexuality. In the chauvinistic world of the 1960s, the ethics of the pin-up was scarcely a subject for debate. His old camera club back in Perth even offered the pin-up as a topic for a monthly competition a decade earlier. Angove contributed to a science fiction fantasy and glamour magazine called *Zeta*. He also shot models for the Annie Walker Agency, one of London's biggest suppliers of 'the female form' for photography.

Years later, Frank Evans, photography columnist for Perth's *Sunday Times* newspaper, found another way of spinning Angove's work in this field: "One job which called for nerve and gallantry, as well as photographic skill, was for an avant-garde magazine featuring nude models leaping about the landscape."[cccxxxiii]

The same article mentions glamour shots supplied to *Playboy* magazine but I think this may have been an exaggeration or misunderstanding. Angove shot some pictures of a pair of London models, identical twin sisters Mary and Madeline Collins, in 1969. His photographs were sent to *Playboy* publisher Hugh Hefner who subsequently contracted them for a centrefold feature in late 1970, a first for the magazine.

Cousin Terry Butcher says Angove's mother Marjorie was quite religious and maintained some propriety.

"She didn't always approve of what he did in later years," Butcher claims.[cccxxxiv]

*Twins Mary and Madeline Collins,
photographed by Angove and then hired by Hugh Hefner*

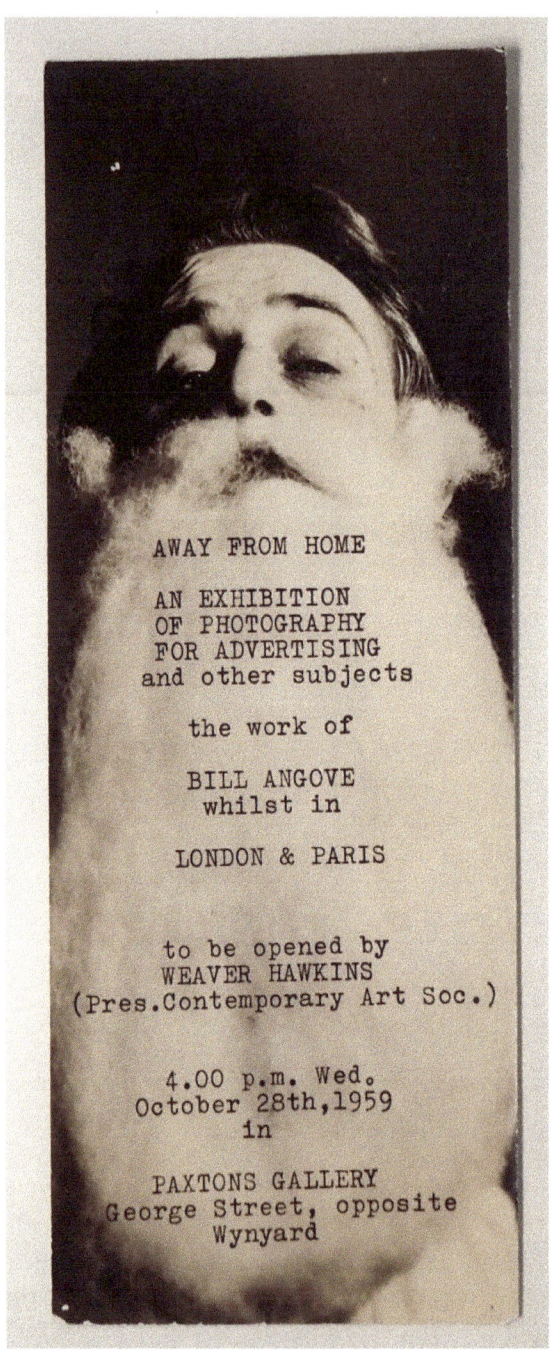

Flyer to promote Sydney exhibition

Australians and the Swinging Sixties

It is no exaggeration to say that for the many Australians with creative instincts who ventured there, the London of the 1960s must have been intoxicating.

"Being a photographer in London in the second half of the 60s is the nearest thing to having been a painter in the Paris of the 1880s and 90s," Bill Angove wrote with jubilation about what he considered a new Belle Epoque, a period of elevated artistic and cultural advancement.

The era was all about new possibilities and freedoms especially on social and cultural dimensions. London was at the heart of these changes and creatives in all branches of the arts were the prime beneficiaries.

The design firm Spacestor is among the many British trend recorders of cultural waves. It declares: "The 1960s brought us Swinging London and a flourishing of art and design and rock'n'roll that made the city the coolest place in the world." [cccxxxv]

"Post-war doom and gloom was gone forever, replaced with a wave of optimism from the young creatives flooding the capital. Everything was happening at once. On a Saturday afternoon, you could go down to the King's Road and mix with the Rolling Stones, Terence Conran opened the first Habitat store on the nearby Fulham Road in 1964, and Bridget Riley became the star of the op art movement with paintings of repeating patterns and optical illusions."

Reviewing even just a handful of books and articles that set out to describe this era seems to unearth an endless parade of name-dropping.

The Australian comedy actress, Noeline Brown, reflected that in the 1960s "Australia seemed a long way from the rest of the world", she wrote.[cccxxxvi]

"Artists I knew longed to be able to see a genuine old master, rather than a photograph of one, so they took off overseas, among them John Olsen, Colin Lanceley, Leonard French and Charles Blackman.

"They were only able to do so because they had won major competitions or travelling scholarships, or had received help from their wives. Robert Hughes went overseas … Germaine Greer left for the University of Cambridge, comedian Barry Humphries and yet to be discovered Clive James took off. We waved goodbye to the creators of *Oz* [magazine]."

British academic Simon Pierse has extensively researched creative Australians in 60s London. He relates stories such as the painter South Australian-born Lawrence Daws remembering an Indian summer, "everyone in shirt sleeves, windows open and … popular Cliff Richard's song *Living Doll* pouring out everywhere".[cccxxxvii]

Artist Charles Blackman reportedly recalled the exciting time as marked by [the TV spoof show] *That Was The Week That Was,* [satire anchor and interviewer] David Frost and the Profumo scandal. cccxxxviii

Pierse says the ex-patriate community of Australian artists formed a loose-knit group of friends and associates in inner London districts. Painter Brett Whitely had a house in Ladbroke Grove, a locality familiar to Angove from his earlier years in the city. Arthur Boyd, soon to become Angove's friend, had arrived in 1960 and enjoyed instant success. His exhibition sales enabled him to buy a house in Highgate. He and his wife "never forgot earlier hard times and were always willing to offer a bed or at least space on the floor to friends and fellow artists from Australia."cccxxxix

"There was a mateship not only in the sense that ex-patriate Australians tended to stick together ... meeting at parties, in favourite pubs or at the theatre as well as the regular exhibition openings, but contacts could also be made and introductions given," writes Pierse.

Arthur Boyd at work, photographed by Angove

Rolf Harris and the Easybeats, photographed by Angove

James, Greer, Humphries and Hughes all became immersed in the lively cultural scene and made connections with their fine art associates such as Boyd, Blackman, Nolan, Tucker, Whitely and John Perceval.

Using these four acute observers of society as examples, film-maker Howard Jacobson believes the native Australian sense of having been culturally deprived rapidly disappeared.[cccxl]

The impact of the Australians in London brought many European ideas of intellectualism and sophistication, he claimed. So, it was a two-way interaction. They lapped up the glitz and high jinks. They delighted in the cultural milieu. They paraded their new ideas and fresh ways.

The Australians' ascent was visible in many spheres. On the music front, the Easybeats made a sparkling debut on the BBC's Top of the Pops. Actors like Keith Michell and Leo McKern, who both worked with Angove, won roles on screen and stage. On the heels of Sid Nolan's Ned Kelly exhibition at the Whitechapel Gallery, London art critics gained "a sense of the power and originality of Australian painting", according to Boyd's biographer.[cccxli] And Angove's original Perth mate, Rolf Harris, enjoyed success in every field he tackled. Incidentally, their influence on each other was two-way. When Harris returned to Australia for a period in 1958, he bought a Rolleiflex camera at a Middle Eastern duty-free port and "started my lifelong love of photography".[cccxlii]

Another Australian who enjoyed a breakthrough in this cultural mecca was Angove's friend Bill Pownall who had moved to Greece and taken up painting as a full-time occupation.

Pownall recalls the events of the time: "The junta, the Greek military dictatorship, came into power. My wife and I left for London where I was able to have my first exhibition."[cccxliii]

"Bill was in London … so we took up our friendship again. He took photos of my paintings for the invitation. I couldn't afford to pay him for this at the time and I regret it still," he said sixty years later in a letter to me in 2021.[cccxliv]

"When I returned to Greece after the collapse of the colonels' rule, we lost touch … rather a pity, largely my fault. Living on a Greek island rather took over my life and old friends got neglected."

Meanwhile, a breakout fashion industry – with its accompanying dependence on photography to propagate and elevate its popularity - boomed in London and drew photographers such as Helmut Newton, who had spent two decades working in Australia.

London also led a charge to enhance the status of photography during these years. A doyen of British art, Sir Kenneth Clark, went on TV declaring that he agreed with growing opinion that photography can be art. Major galleries began running exhibitions to demonstrate photography's place in the fine arts.

Photography historian and collector Helmut Gernsheim wrote in 1960: "Even if these exhibitions were only a first, though important, step in the direction of a serious and sustained effort for the widest possible acceptance of fine photography as fine art, they came as a revelation to art critics and public alike and laid the foundation for the furtherance of a better appreciation of photography."[cccxlv]

Bill Angove could not imagine a more stimulating place to live and work. He loved to play and party. He cherished his artistic Australian links and he frequented many of the haunts Pierse describes to sustain those ties.

One of his favourites was a Greek restaurant called Kalamaras, just around the corner from his bachelor pad. This was a London institution, frequented by the likes of Peter Sellers, Mick Jagger, the Beatles and Dusty Springfield,[cccxlvi]

Angove befriended the founding owner, Stelios Platonos, who was one of the first restaurateurs to bring quality Greek food to London. [cccxlvii] One of his well-known photographic colleagues, the Earl of Lichfield, was another regular and is said to have rated Kalamaras as one of the best restaurants in the world. Aristotle Onassis ate there when in London and Noël Coward was an early customer.

Angove wrote that he was thrilled when he discovered Kalamaras. He described it as "a source of gastronomic delight". Despite the humble diet of his early years in London in the previous decade, he had clearly stepped up in taste, style and expense on the epicurean front. In fact, a decade later back in Perth, Angove frequented restaurants in notable Northbridge and was especially fond of one called Casa Latina, according to his friends.

Angove dances with restaurant owner Stelios Platonos

One old mate, Ernie Laidlaw, recalled: "Bill had very sophisticated tastes by Western Australian standards" for the 1970s. There was one occasion when Angove, dissatisfied with the dishes his party had ordered, later returned to the restaurant with a cook book in hand to prove to the unfortunate chef that he had not done the meal well.[cccxlviii]

Angove's London archives include several folders of photographs from nights at places like Kalamaras and from parties at his nearby flat. He lived a playboy lifestyle in many respects, constantly surrounded by female friends. His social life seemed richly blessed with good company from which he assembled travel groups from time to time. There were skiing trips to Switzerland and holidays in France, Austria and Spain, sometimes spun-off from work assignments.

His next-door neighbours in Bayswater were also Australians, an actor and radio announcer from Perth, Dibbs Mather and his wife Meg. Dibbs was a family nickname that replaced his Fremantle birth names of Donald Allan Mather-Brown. Mather graduated from the National Institute of Dramatic Arts (NIDA) in 1960 alongside Robyn Nevin.

"Like many of his generation, he soon headed for London and found some work as an actor but made his name as a broadcaster for the BBC World Service", according to his obituary, penned by Milton Cockburn in 2010.[cccxlix]

He claimed "the posh accent and posh name" had helped him to win the job. Cockburn's article mentions that Dibbs did one of the earliest radio interviews with the Beatles in 1963 and scored a notable interview with Rudolf Nureyev, shortly after his defection from the Soviet Union and soon to be a prized subject of Angove's ballet photography.

Dibbs pioneered a journal in 1966 called *Australarts*. Testimony to the number and range of Australians working in creative fields in London during the era, the subscription-only magazine proclaimed in its first edition that its purpose was "to promote the interests of Australians involved in the arts and communications in both England and Australia".[cccl]

"The traffic in our people between Australia and England increases every year," wrote Mather.[cccli]

Ever the patriot, but with a measure of jaundice about Australia's aforementioned cultural cringe, Mather had strong views about this phenomenon and the detriment it could cause his homeland.

"It is wasteful, at this time in Australia's history," he wrote,[ccclii] "that such a number of our expert artists and communicators should be enriching societies other than our own, and while those who are working in these fields in Australia deserve all the praise one can give them, they cannot do the job alone. They need the stimulus of the returning majority.

"The question of 'returning to Australia' is a physical and economic impossibility for many. Either they have been away for too long and become firmly rooted in the society they have enriched, or, though making valuable contributions in their fields, they just haven't enough money to go home and work there. It's very hard to save money in England.

"Then there are those who have experienced, possibly for the first time in their careers, the satisfaction of being accepted as an adult making an important contribution to an adult society. It's hard for any man, particularly an artist, to give that up, to return and work hard in a country where respect for the individual gift, no matter how out of context with local conformity, has only just started to flower."

Angove was profiled in the inaugural edition of *Australarts* alongside his friends Arthur Boyd and Robin Haig, as well as many others including author Morris West, composer Malcolm Williamson and actor Diane Cilento.

You can imagine the conversations he and Mather would have had over drinks about the lack of recognition that loomed for antipodean returnees. It was a topic that would come to haunt Angove.

In his interview in the magazine, Angove reflected on the creative challenges of his advertising work. The author, Allanah McDonald, observed: "His work is attracting a great deal of attention here, not only in the hard-costing world of advertising, but also among theatre people who need photographs with just that much to say about them. And while he supplies these demands, this wiry, bearded, restless man is assured of work in England for years to come."[cccliii]

But while he progressed professionally, his personal life did not go as smoothly.

Independent studio

Over the Christmas-New Year period of 1966-67, Angove made a quick trip home to Australia to catch up with family. Among the topics of conversation that summer was likely his romantic attachment to Jeanne Johnson-Flint, the most impassioned of his dalliances since the break-up with Pam back in Sydney. His records don't identify the duration of his relationship with Jeanne but there are undated clues to its depth. Among them is a home-made illustrated greeting card from Jeanne when she was in Paris.

"My sweet darling Bill," she wrote.[cccliv] It oozes affection.

"I will always love you; please never change. Just as you are now is how I shall remember you. My deepest love from yours forever."

While Angove was away for the six weeks in Australia, he had left Jeanne to look after his studio at his flat. It was apparently during this time that she met a man named Keith Davis. He may have been a mutual associate of the pair but I've been unable to find out any detail about him.

Angove was rocked by what had occurred during his brief absence.

"When I returned, everything had changed," he wrote later.[ccclv]

"Eventually [Jeanne and Keith] marry and [cause] much heartache to me."

Curiously Angove's contact with the pair survives. They are listed in a succession of his address books for the years that follow, suggesting he was still regularly in touch.

In an undated letter from Stratford-on-Avon, Jeanne writes to her former lover: "My dear Billy," she begins, "Here I am darling as I promised. How are things at the studio?[ccclvi]

"Please forgive me and my foolishness. I didn't realise the damage I was doing to you. I thought of you and wished their [sic] was something which I could do to repair the situation."

The letter finishes with an exhortation: "Please dear Billy, take care of yourself. My thoughts are with you. All my love, kisses and friendship. Thanks for everything! No regrets? No regrets!"[ccclvii]

Jeanne as photographic subject (from left), as Angove's girlfriend and with one-time employer Kingsley Hopkins

The fact that Angove maintained ongoing contact with Jeanne and Keith Davis might suggest that she remained his muse. His photographic library contains many pictures of Jeanne although most carry no dates. He caught up with them (below) on return visits to London.

Angove with Jeanne and Keith Davis

Angove tackled most branches of photography during these ebullient London times including press work, shooting fashion for *The Evening Standard* newspaper, and assignments to support the public relations office of the Church of England.

His business and personal connections continued to flourish. He struck up a productive association with the owners of a major photographic library called Colorific, Terry and Shirley LeGoubin. LeGoubin prints still sell today. Terry (pictured on next page) was a distinguished practitioner who had enjoyed an impressive international career in photography.

Terry LeGoubin at work and later in life

"Terry ... photographed some of the most iconic people and events of the twentieth century including Sir Winston Churchill's funeral," wrote an admirer years later. ccclviii LeGoubin's other subjects included French film star Brigid Bardot and Pope Paul VI.

Colorific rated among the most polished and prolific of Britain's photo syndication agencies during its time. It was a valuable business outlet for Angove. A decade later, back in Australia, he was still supplying educational and editorial images to LeGoubin's agency.

He worked with Australian Tony Vuletich, an illustrator who apparently ran his own design studio. They likely met earlier in Sydney. Vuletich was later known as a film producer too, a contact likely to have encouraged Angove's interest in moving pictures.

During a productive period for Angove, operating his own independent studio, he found himself undertaking a great deal of travel both in the UK and in Europe on behalf of his stable of clients. Among those commissioning work from him was advertising executive Ken Done, later to become one of Australia's best-known artists.

Done and Angove became friends. Done lived in nearby Chelsea, working with the global advertising company J Walter Thompson from 1964 to 1969. He understood the prevailing creative ethos in the UK, as Angove did, summarising it thus: "There was this sort of class system operating in England but being Australian, you had to be accepted for what you could do ... for your ability."ccclix

He commissioned a number of jobs from Angove through these years and has fond memories of their shared experiences.

"I remember I took him to Wales on one occasion," Done recalled in an interview in 2021.[ccclx]

"The Wales Steel Company was our client. We were standing on a cold Welsh hillside in sleet and rain. Bill was about 200 to 300 metres away walking into a field making noises to try to draw sheep towards him. It was an Aussie thing, attracting the sheep.

"Another story I recall was one time when Bill had a bad back. He visited a Mews house with one of those double stable doors. Bill was bent over and of course he was short in stature. He told me later that the bloke who answered the call only opened the top door and couldn't see anyone."[ccclxi]

The pair spent quite a lot of time together, according to Done.

"He was a lovely bloke. Bill took the pictures at our wedding. Judy Walker and I were married in Cranford in 1965 and Bill was our photographer. I remember standing at the altar listening to the marriage vows when I heard a crash in the church. It was Bill falling over something. He was a bit clumsy."

In a mischievous vein, Done also recalls with hilarity Angove's ability to exploit his stature to make out with women.

"He had a certain skill," Done chuckles.[ccclxii]

"He knew how to get the stain out of everything. He was the best stain remover I ever knew. As I said, Bill was very short. When he was chatting up a girl, he'd put his beer on what looked like a shelf slightly above him but it would then often spill over the girl. He'd then offer to clean up her clothes!"

After Jeanne's marriage and Angove's crushed emotions, Angove moved onto a string of casual relationships with women in a manner seemingly befitting the freedoms of the era.

"I took out dolly birds," he said.[ccclxiii]

"The swinging sixties were well under way and I had some success with birds but nothing steady."

For a time, Angove enjoyed an exciting cross-over between his professional life and his social life. He considered his studio flat an ideal set-up for "an unattached photographer".

"I was able to go in and out of the West End to see my clients, get to any railway to go across England and be close to the air terminals for overseas assignments.[ccclxiv]

"But the really interesting things happened in the studio. I was a popular photographer for a couple of model agencies who specialised in nudes.

"This led to my meeting some pretty way-out characters as well as some really delightful young ladies, but the things they told me about their personal lives were pretty hair-raising.

"Some of them became my good friends and used to just drop in for cuppas or lunch."

The Kalamaras restaurant was a focus for similar encounters after dark.

"I gained a tremor boy reputation … as a result of the companions I'd take there for dinner."

In his notes from years later, Angove mentioned four of these young women in detail, "Sammy", Maria, Helga and Lena, while acknowledging there were others as well, almost all fond of posing without clothes whether for a camera session or a social encounter.

"I lost count of the number of girls who stripped for my cameras," he confessed. "Mostly they asked me and offered to pay as well.

"For quite a few it was the first time for them nude in front of a camera and I found they were awkward at first."

Angove protected the privacy of the models he worked with and deflected requests for their contact details from external parties by referring inquirers back to their agencies. His caution was in part motivated by the news of an abduction of another UK model for three days.

This was a time in Europe when a raft of leading photographers was producing highly commercial glamour and fashion work, among the most prominent being David Hamilton, Helmut Newton, David Bailey and Sam Haskins. Newton's work was characterised by his crisp exposures and bold compositions. Hamilton was fond of highlighting black-and-white grain and exploiting soft focus designed to showcase a sensual look. Haskins and Bailey, who Angove knew and seemingly admired, created racy, provocative images of models and celebrities. Many pictures of women during this era were clearly erotically-charged, intended to both stoke and reflect the hedonistic flavour of the Swinging Sixties, in the same way its popular music often did.

Angove referred to this field of photography as "kinky work" but qualified the interest in the genre by declaring that "even top fashion models are doing nude work in London".[ccclxv]

Today this work divides opinions because many people argue that its practitioners were sexist and voyeuristic. In the name of freedom of art, it certainly pushed the boundaries of taste in some people's minds. In its mix of what hindsight might describe as anarchy, misogyny and vulgarity, it's not surprising that few in the mainstream of 21st century culture would feel comfortable with this style of photography especially viewed through contemporary feminist and societal standards.

In the years after leaving London, Angove observed that he kept seeing many of his models on book jackets, record covers and in the pinup sections of various magazines. He took pride in their success and in his own ability to develop a marketable niche.

"To be a successful photographer," he related in a later magazine article,[ccclxvi] "you need a spark of imagination, a ton of enthusiasm, some recklessness and a bit of luck."

One of Angove's models from the heady, perhaps seedy, London days was Gilly Grant who was interviewed by *Practical Photography* magazine in the late 1960s on the subject of her favourite photographer.[ccclxvii]

"I choose Bill Angove," was Grant's quote, "because he is easy to work with and his pictures would enhance any model's portfolio."

"A photographer who can keep up an interesting conversation keeps the atmosphere informal and he gets the best pictures."

Angove featured in other articles in *Practical Photography* during the 1960s. In one story on colour portraiture, he discussed what amateur photographers often saw as the high cost of shooting colour.

Vicky Owen (left) and Holly Allsop

Emphasising that the well-established professional was in a different position, he said "this is where new thinking is needed. You'll never get anywhere until you can persuade yourself that using a lot of colour material is not necessarily wasting it. Cost must be related to effective, pleasure-giving output in this context."[ccclxviii]

Producing specimen files of aspiring models in what the magazine called 'help your neighbour' sessions, Angove admitted, allowed him to introduce experimental techniques to his work, a hallmark of his output for more than a decade at this stage of his career.

One of the images dissected in the magazine was cited as an example of the photographer's innovation.

"In the picture of [model] Vicky [Owen] (left), Angove deliberately mixed his light sources, thus defying rule number one in every colour textbook."

The application of both daylight from the window and domestic tungsten from inside the room was not particularly elaborate but as an experimental set-up it did make it hard to estimate the required exposure.

A second portrait, featuring model Holly Allsop, (previous page right), was photographed through a slit in a sheet of coloured cellophane held close to the lens of Angove's Mamiyaflex.

The author concluded: "If you feel your … work is humdrum and long to emulate the photographers whose pictures you admire in the glossies, throw your preconceptions to the winds and be willing to break the rules."[ccclxix] It's certainly an apt way of describing Angove's approach.

Working World

Scrutinising a person's photographic collection spanning three critical decades of their life is a revealing means of gauging their interests, challenges and achievements. In Angove's photographic archive, there's strong evidence of a drive to produce art from whatever subjects were in front of his camera. From his early days in Western Australia to his extensive European travels and back home again, there's a consistency in how he applied his talent and a discernible absorption of styles from other art forms. He used his painting skills, his love of dance, music and other performance arts and his ease with human subjects to create images that bear unique characteristics.

Consider three pictures from the mid-1950s. He captured his closest friends in Perth, Ken and Thelma Knox, on a city bus ride (below). It shows the pair unaware or unengaged with the photographer's presence, absorbed as they are in reading an item of interest in the newspaper. The three faces portrayed each contribute to a narrative, as a curiosity imbues the whole scene. Its composition is precise and faultless, right down to the fact that the seat in front of the couple is not occupied and therefore allows its cushioning to be visible and delicately lit. Aided by the 35mm colour transparency film, Angove's photograph has a wonderful cinematic feel and mood. I may have a bias because, almost 60 years later, Ken Knox became a revered friend of mine but judged by any empirical criteria, this picture soars.

On the Bus (circa 1954)

The second photograph worthy of commentary also features two people integral to Angove's life journey. As outlined earlier, Michael and Peggy Barrington-Martin were instrumental in persuading him to venture to London the first time, and they supported him throughout many of his early months there. Michael had strong show-biz connections, initially derived from working around his father's portrait studio and later enriched by his own similar pursuits. In the picture (below) Angove has presented a suave and elegant couple setting off on a sea voyage that already has a flavour of the high life. Just take note of the warm, pale light in the background, the romantic pose of the couple, the dual framing from the solidity of the ship's bulkhead and the blur of the traditional streamers marking embarkation. The eyes both perform a connection with the camera - and therefore the viewer - but also convey a bond of affection between them.

The Barrington-Martins shipboard

The third example of Angove's lifestyle portraiture (page 181) is particularly poignant. He's captured a young man who was instrumental in his success in Britain, advertising art director Burt Greene, of the aforementioned agency Napper Stinton and Woolley. Greene's admiration for Angove's highly inventive abstract work - exemplified in the commissioned Pfizer medical magazine plates – opened channels for the Australian.

Burt Greene

As environmental portraits go, this works wondrously. The composition exploits the dynamic pose and excels for its framing of all the elements in the office scene. The structure of the image is flawless, the exposure perfect and the mood resonant of a cinematic take. It speaks unambiguously of the flashy and sophisticated world of advertising executives. Angove owed Greene a lot and he seems determined to honour his friend lavishly in this outstanding portrait. Greene was there again for Angove when he returned to the UK in the 1960s after his Sydney stint.

A decade of growth and experience in these two creative and commercial art hubs set Angove up for new heights of satisfaction and success. The 1960s found him combining extensive travel with rewarding photographic assignments, a playboy way of life and a diverse artistic output.

He developed his own take on bullfighting in Barcelona, ballet in Belgium, beach life in Italy, cabarets in Paris, butchering in Hong Kong, nightlife in Soho and fun fairs in Battersea. His days of virtual confinement to studio spaces were superseded as he became a cosmopolitan traveller on several continents.

He never lost his love of street photography. He had that Australian knack for connecting with people. Variety was an essential and innate hallmark of his photography.

Images from Portobello Markets, Hyde Park and Barcelona

"Bill was often called out at short notice by a travel agency," Frank Evans wrote on the eve of Angove's next exhibition in Perth, "to pose models against a backdrop of famous buildings in Europe or to shoot tourists at famous resorts."[ccclxx] Here are a few examples (below).

Skiing couple in Italy, BEA terminal in London and ship passengers on deck

Talent and skill awarded Angove with acknowledgement and on occasions admiration. However, he never acquired fame. During his second longer stint in London, he only entered several minor group exhibitions.

In a 1960s profile published in his hometown weekend newspaper, author Cyril Casellas wrote that Angove's photography was "described as the work of a genius in photographic magazines both in Britain and in America". [ccclxxi]

Casellas added: "[His] work is not seen and appreciated by the general public."

At his peak, Angove was considered successful and well-paid. His commercial work could bring in more than $4000 a day in today's money but it was hard earned. He cited one example of shooting in eight different locations around the country in three days.

Alas the output of a typical advertising photographer is rarely accredited and often serves specialist publications in fields like industry and technology. Thus was Angove's livelihood.

"Angove's touch of genius is in his wildly creative productions that ensure he gets plum jobs at the drop of a hat," the article continued. [ccclxxii]

"His work has been sought in faraway places [such as] South Africa, Greece, Germany and other distant horizons."

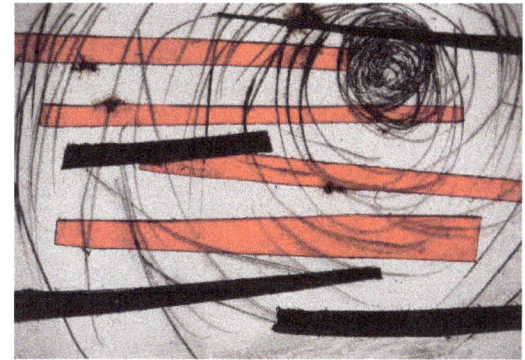

More examples of Angove's abstract imagery which combined art techniques with photography

Angove's abstract work, referred to as a combination of art, science and trickery, involved the deployment of multiple exposures and complicated printing techniques.[ccclxxiii]

"He's been known to paint on the back of his transparencies, pour developer and fixer on exposed photographic paper or print three colour transparencies simultaneously, striving for that 'different effect'," fellow Perth lensman Barry Baker once observed in a specialist article.[ccclxxiv]

Angove's passion, curiosity and scope for travel allowed him to produce other work which retained merit and earned personal rewards.

Casellas wrote: "Angove could not resist the unlimited potential of shots for his personal album, which typifies his photographic zeal."[ccclxxv]

He loved nothing better than getting away on his own in the many parts of the world which he scoured for photographic opportunities, some close to home and some exotic.

Residential buildings on the Left Bank in Paris, fisherman in Sri Lanka,

the harbour at Marseilles and Snowdonia in North Wales

Angove enjoyed a love affair with London.

"The high-class films, the theatre, concerts, exhibitions are very stimulating," he reflected. ccclxxvi

"There is so much going on in all creative fields here that the atmosphere suits me. I guess I'm a bit of a highbrow. I'm accused of being a musical snob. To be highbrow in Perth seems a little suspect."

And alongside his exhilaration sat his ambition.

"The ceiling here is so high, it's almost impossible to see it."

Theatre held a special place in his heart.

"I enjoy the theatre," he wrote in later years.ccclxxvii

"Fortunately, my camera takes me into the company of theatre people, whose company I enjoy."

Angove became a forceful advocate for what he called the art of theatre photography. He worried at times about it becoming a neglected art to the detriment of the theatre.

He criticised producers who, on the one hand, clamoured for slick PR images of their shows but expected photographers to confront avoidable difficulties in executing the pictures.

"The photographer can get grab shots, of course, but often the costumes and sets are incomplete, the lighting isn't properly adjusted and some performers are wearing full make-up while others aren't made up at all," he told journalist Ray Ellinson on one occasion.ccclxxviii

"The photographer is expected to come up with the goods under these conditions and is blamed if the results are less than perfect."

Ellinson described Angove as "the complete master of his medium" with a capacity to convey "every nuance he can squeeze out of a given situation."ccclxxix

Angove subscribed to the view that theatre photographers who generated work of a high standard needed "an interest in and knowledge of dance, opera or drama" and an appreciation of the producers' challenges as well.

Over the years, he worked with all types of theatrical people from children trying out street theatre to stars of stage and screen. At one time he involved himself in an organisation called Inter-Action.

Inter-Action was the brainchild of American-born British activist and playwright Edward Berman who set out to create a range of performance activities to bring the arts closer to the community. ccclxxx

According to a website recording the history of alternative theatre in Britain, Inter-Action's enterprises "ranged from producing new writing and experimental plays to taking performance directly onto the streets to organising workshops and performances for community participants."[ccclxxxi]

As an umbrella organisation, Inter-Action was responsible for the formation of several fringe companies, including the Ambiance Lunch Hour Theatre Club, and a publishing branch and film company.

Angove connected with Berman's ambitious venture when the latter became playwright-in-residence at the Mercury Theatre in Notting Hill and subsequently provided his photography services to help promote the organisation. Berman's theatres gave playwrights the opportunity to nurture one-act plays, among them rising and famous names like Tom Stoppard, Henry Livings, Mike Scott, Edward Bond and John Antrobus. Angove shot all the stills for a 1968 Antrobus work called *Why Bournmouth* launched in a lunchtime theatre restaurant in Soho. Projects like these were intended to test new works on audiences.

Although Berman's company was notably avant-garde, if not risque in its choice of material, its patrons included leading names in British theatre such as Dame Peggy Ashcroft, Vanessa Redgrave and Peter Sellers.[ccclxxxii]

Angove's role as official photographer is recorded in a typed program for an "experimental literary" performance entitled *The Nudist Campers Grow and Grow*, one of a sextet of plays "on an erotic theme" under the collective title of *Kiss My* ....[ccclxxxiii]

It appears that his involvement with Berman's string of operations extended to engaging with his experimental film group. Angove played various roles with this outfit, ranging from stills photographer and camera operator to lighting director.

Angove also produced and helped publish photographs of children experimenting with street performances and mock films in various parts of inner London.

In this work and his many other engagements with the press, Angove acquired intimate knowledge of editorial requirements.

"Editors hate too much black in pictures," he reported, "because the ink shows through the page."[ccclxxxiv]

"Big dark areas are anathema to picture editors."

Of course, his work with performers had a long history. For example, he photographed a young Rex Harrison acting in *Blythe Spirit* in 1956, the cast of the musical *Oliver* in 1963, Australian opera diva Dame Joan Sutherland and shot hundreds of "audition" pictures for aspiring young performers - dancers, musicians, actors - as part of the services offered by Mayflower Studios who would advertise such a line of business. Mayflower invited people off the street to avail themselves of this 'service'. While the vast majority of his theatrical images were straight production scenes or portrait stills, Angove was always willing to apply his experimental style to performance photography such as in the captivating picture (below) from an unidentified opera or dance production.

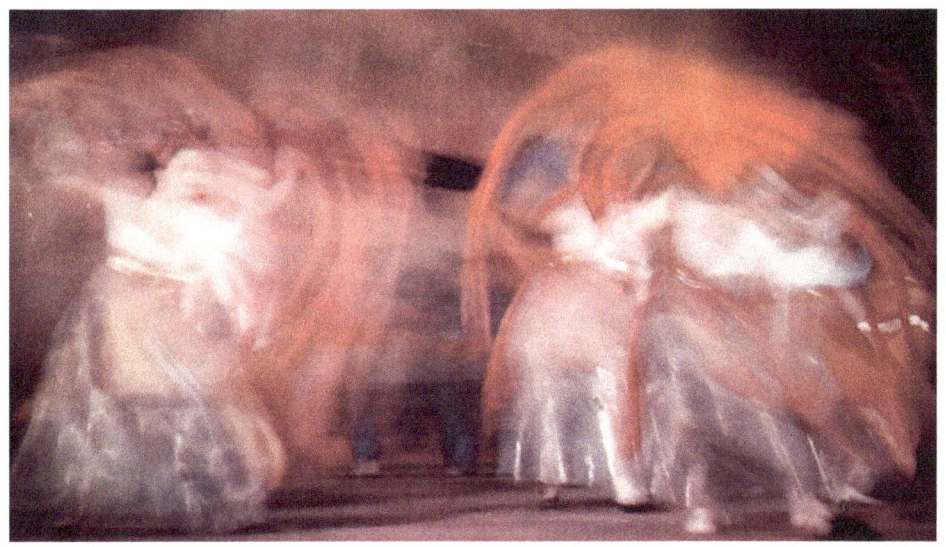

Motion blur on a grand scale in this example of Angove's stage photography;

Joan Sutherland centre stage at Covent Garden.

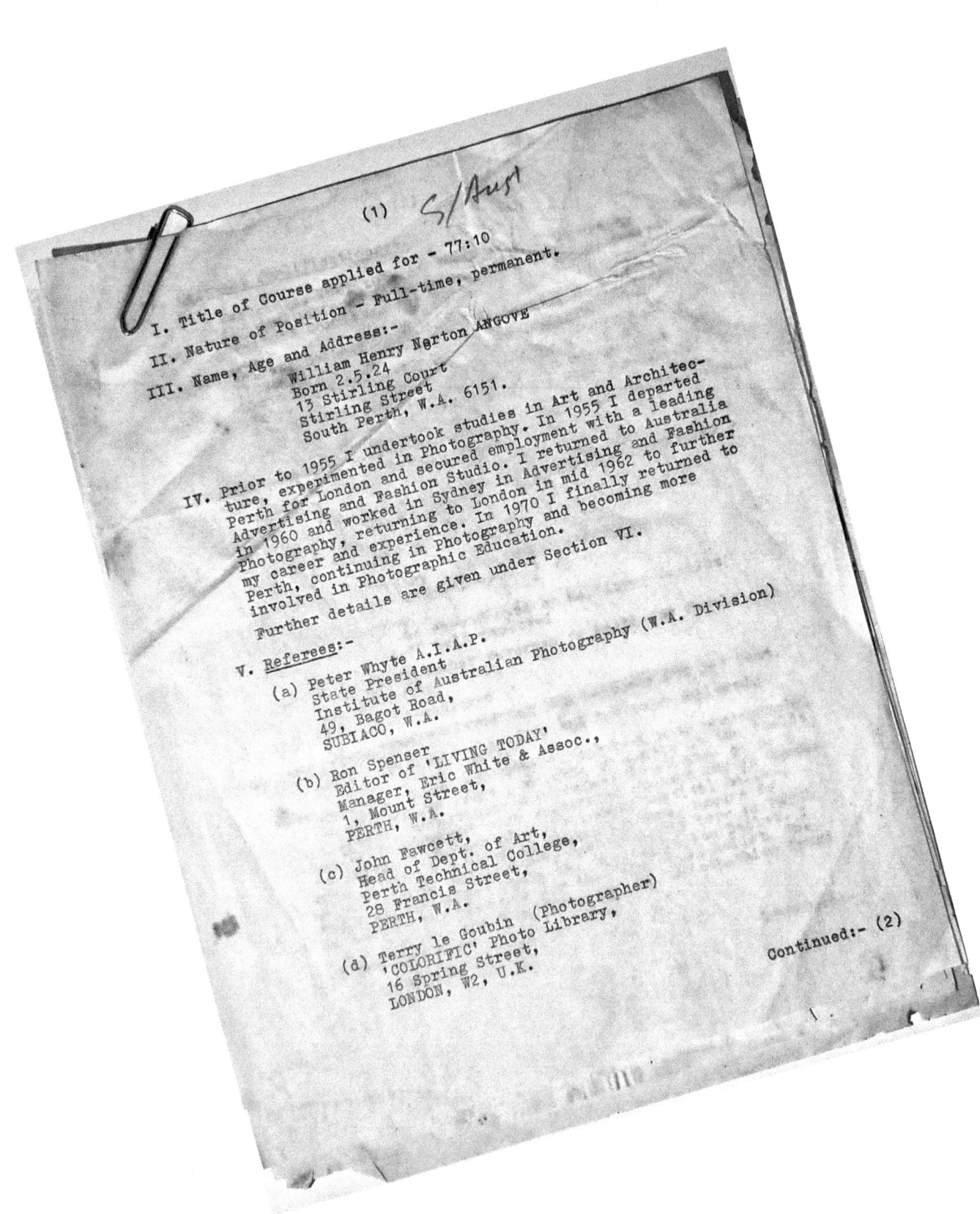

Job application as lecturer

Home to new directions

During the year of 1970, Angove started to feel that his time was running out in his London base. It was his sixteenth year working there and in Sydney. He'd been away from his roots for more than half his adult life.

"Work was generally dropping off," he wrote, ccclxxxv while also complaining of rapid inflation in the British economy, presumably making the cost of living more challenging. He also cited family reasons, likely to be his mother's deteriorating health, according to niece Beverley Angove.ccclxxxvi

In September he "pulled out" – his expression - and returned to Perth.

His old friend Les Chiew offered him the previously mentioned partnership in a design and publishing venture with their mate George Palmer in East Perth. In making this choice, Angove, as he'd done a decade earlier, knocked back an offer from Ron Armstrong who was still running a burgeoning photographic lab and studio.

The Chiew-Palmer business struggled during 1971 as a result of high overheads and insufficient income. Angove felt he had to step away from these problems and decided to reactivate his freelancing, this time from his flat in South Perth.

Despite the business setback and some harsh realities his mind had to grapple with, other factors aided Angove as he settled back into Western Australia. He was given opportunities to participate in several exhibitions, renewing his artistic reputation back on home turf.

The first exhibition was at the Octagon Theatre, opened in 1969 at the University of Western Australia's Crawley campus. It was a radically-designed building, conceived by architects who consulted with one of Britain's most original theatrical trail-blazers, the director Tyrone Guthrie. Angove would have felt an affinity with the experimental philosophy that Guthrie brought to performance spaces.

The second show was at another newly-opened premises, a camera and photographic supplies store known as Herbert Smalls, which had moved into a new outlet in 1971-72 in City Arcade featuring some exhibition space. Smalls, founded in Melbourne in 1860, was a revered institution among the photographic community across Australia and had been operating in central Perth since the 1930s.

It is unclear what work of Angove's was displayed in these two exhibitions but it's likely to have had an emphasis on his ballet catalogue, perhaps samples from his European portfolio and a smattering of his hallmark abstract output.

He teamed up regularly with the Western Australian Ballet Company, for which he was the official photographer, to conduct three separate exhibitions of his dance pictures during 1971, and again in 1973. He held similar roles with the Western Australian Opera, the Elizabethan Trust at the Playhouse Theatre, the WA Gilbert and Sullivan Society and the Old Mill Theatre around the corner from his base in South Perth. When national companies, such as the Australian Ballet and Australian Opera, toured to Perth for performance seasons, Angove created the pictorial records.

His immersion in exhibitions also accompanied his active involvement in the Institute of Australian Photographers (IAP) which he joined in 1971 as a WA divisional councillor. The IAP ran major annual exhibitions in which Angove was regularly represented.

"Exhibiting … in shows … has been a means of self-expression," he observed.[ccclxxxvii]

In one such exhibition of 157 works, Angove was one of nine members of what seems to have been designated as the IAP's Colour Group and the show's catalogue described them as "photographic artists".[ccclxxxviii] They included the aforementioned Garwood and Woldendorp.

His work also featured in and sold pictures through stock photo collections in Perth, which mainly handled wall art and décor imagery, and at least two photo libraries in London, Pictor International Ltd and the aforementioned Colorific run by his old friend Terry LeGoubin.

Angove valued his participation in the IAP and contributed extensively to the association.

"I've taken part in a great deal of the social, official and backroom organising," he reflected in 1976. "I believe my efforts have been appreciated."[ccclxxxix]

When he became eligible in 1973, he applied for an associateship within the IAP. It was the first time such applications were evaluated on an Australia-wide level by a national honours committee. He was duly awarded the status.

Angove supported WA state presidents Brian Stevenson and Peter Whyte in running successful professional workshops for members in the mid-1970s. The organisation used to run a national convention each year, called a *Hypo* and, from 1977, these events included a judged print exhibition of members' entries. Angove attended the Hypo in Canberra where the fellowship and quest for professional standards particularly appealed to him as a member who had done most of his best work abroad.

Having shot advertising photographs for a wide range of global manufacturing and service brands for a decade and a half, Angove found Perth quite restrictive. Western Australia is not a home to many consumer products. A decade earlier in Sydney, Angove was shooting for products such as Stripe toothpaste (below) owned by the giant Unilever.

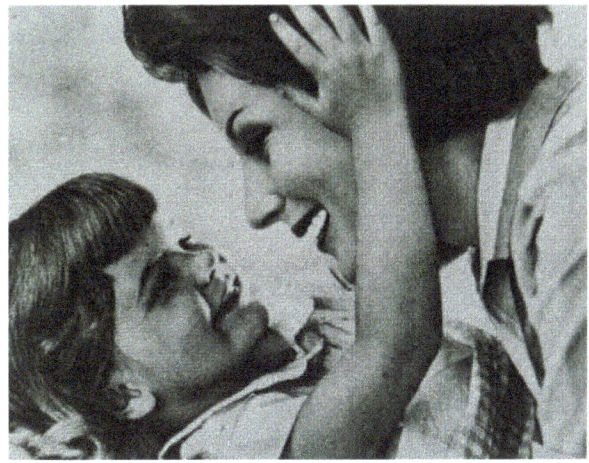 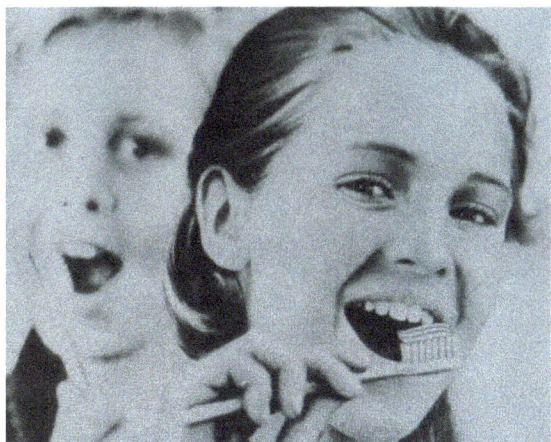

1960s Toothpaste advertising pictures by Angove

Because Perth generally produced fewer and more basic consumer items, this branch of work seemed a dead end for Angove.

"Product photography gave me little creative scope in Perth," he complained.[cccxc]

Fortunately, his old contact at the Perth Technical College from nearly 20 years earlier, John Fawcett, came to his rescue, offering him a part-time job teaching photography to the graphic art and design students. Although he lacked a university degree, Angove's credentials at the time included membership of the Royal Photographic Society in London. He had also been appointed as a Fellow of the Royal Society of Arts in recognition of his industry record and his service to photography.

It was the start of a fruitful involvement with the college. His roles there expanded throughout the 1970s.

"My actual work with the art and design students is not so much to make them photographers," he wrote a few years into the job, "but [to make them] aware [of] what photography can achieve for design."

This work tapped into a reservoir of experience and passion for Angove because his versatility and quest for inventiveness had seen him embrace design in its many applications.

"We do give our students a lot of practical work," he said, "and from first to third year, they really do achieve quite a high standard."[cccxci]

He was proud of the fact that some of the class eventually obtained employment in photography.

Having gained the confidence of the staff and students, as he put it, Angove secured an appointment to a full-time lecturing position in mid-1976.

This role operated alongside Angove's years of initiating and running two night classes for advanced amateur and young rising professional photographers at the technical college.

"I have shared in the very rapid upgrading of standards in that time," he reflected, accrediting the improvement to more modern equipment and better encouragement afforded to the students.[cccxcii]

His non-vocational evening classes essentially amounted to creative workshops. Some of its students were enrolled in a largely technically-based program at Mount Lawley College, and they yearned for a more "creative outlet", as Angove described it, which they chose to pursue in their own time. Its enrolment level was high, and the drop-out rate low.

"We are practical and not involved with excessive theory," he said. The goal was to encourage students creatively.

Perth Technical College seems to have been a satisfying place for Bill Angove.

"I am really very happy at James Street," he confided.

Among the staff, there were old friends and colleagues from the Perth pre-1955 cultural and media landscape such as John Lunghi, the painter and advertising studio art director, and Cedric Baxter, a Burma-born artist who worked in Perth as a newspaper political cartoonist, illustrator, art critic, designer and lecturer. Baxter actually enrolled in the graphic design course in which Angove taught the photography unit.

The students, too, were a source of pleasure to Angove.

"I can honestly claim that I get on well with my students," he wrote, referring to a wide demographic range, which he described as "from fifteen to beyond retirement age".[cccxciii]

"All seem to mingle well," he added. "I don't feel the late teens and early twenties are a race apart."

He was proud of the fact that former students considered him a friend and continued to consult him when they faced photographic problems.

Angove's commitment to photographic education tapped into his sense of belonging and worth.

"I am now well known throughout the photographic world here in Perth," he wrote.[cccxciv]

"I have a good knowledge of other photographers - their types of work, needs for the future and have some ideas about how students of photography should be educated into the business, having seen the work and workings of the schools in the UK such as the London School of Printing and Regent Street Polytechnic and the high standards they attain."

Angove felt his experience as a creative photographer balanced the more technical aspects of the existing teaching approaches in Western Australia.

While he possessed solid technical knowledge and a wealth of experience in business operations, such as hiring models, finding locations and securing props, he believed his greatest strength was his understanding and execution of creative photography.

Incidentally, he once tried to research a definition of creative photography but came to the conclusion that no author was prepared to make a definitive statement as to its characteristics.[cccxcv]

"Photography is all things to all men," he wrote, "a marriage of science and art."

"I am more than a little reluctant to take the plunge [into defining creative photography]."

"One's concept also changes. It's more than 'trick' photography although often the same techniques are used.

"Creative photography should be relatively simple but examples exist of very complex images which are also successful."

He revealed much about himself when he additionally noted that "creative photography can be a medium of expression to a person who is an artist".

"Conversely," he continued, "the camera has released many who are creative, whose drawing ability is basic, to true aesthetic fulfilment."

Angove's value to his students was his mantra that photography "should be above the straight record, the humdrum".

He stressed that creative photographers should possess a sound technical knowledge but not be afraid of mistakes because out of such errors "new creative techniques can be evolved".

Helpfully, he did lay down the criteria he considered made a good photograph: visual impact, personal style (he called it "the individual touch"), expressive qualities (by which he said he meant meaning or character), good composition and design and finally continual interest.

Expanding on the last requirement, he said a good picture needed to hold a viewer's interest beyond the first impact through a harmony of shapes, forms, colours and textures and the absence of distractions.

Ultimately, Angove staked out his territory in the art form in this summary: "Perhaps creative photography is more aligned to subjective expression of an idea or ideas than the literal rendering of the subject. This is why those whose ideal is to only render technically the object are confused by grain, soft focus, double exposure interpretations - which they have been taught are 'wrong' and manufacturers strive to eliminate."[cccxcvi]

Angove exemplified the true educator because, while he imparted knowledge through his teaching, he also set about exploring new horizons through further studies of his own. In this pursuit, he embraced a fine art form known as seriography, a blend of photography and silkscreen printing, sometimes also referred to as serigraphy. [cccxcvii]

Seriography is a means of making numerous prints of a picture using silk mesh. Although it was a method devised half a century earlier, "it came into its own in the 1960s with the advent of Pop Art and Op Art".[cccxcviii] Among its best-known exponents was Andy Warhol who created his celebrated series of portraits of Marilyn Monroe using the technique. Other famous practitioners included American Pop Art figures Roy Lichtenstein and Jasper Johns.

Angove chose recent works of his as well as some from his back catalogue for his experimentation with seriography. He even appeared naked in one of his own pictures alongside a female model – both with backs to the camera – to conjure an image about escape on a beach (next page, centre). He also dabbled in photo etching in a series of investigations with the technical college's printmaking department. Many of his silkscreen prints survive (next page, right with niece Meredyth McLarty).

He took some pride in his seriographical skills.

"I have been able to put [them] to good use, designing posters for AIP workshops," he wrote. [cccxcix]

Examples of Angove's seriography

A portrait of Sam Haskins found in Angove's photographic archives

Angove's contact books

Staying global

His combined teaching work, freelance assignments and library sales provided sufficient means for Angove to fund several return trips to the UK during the 1970s.

The first, which he said was "to do some private business",cd was during the Australian summer of 1973-74 for 10 weeks. He used his travels to connect and reconnect with a string of big names and places.

Among them was the London College of Printing, established in the late 19th century and renowned by the 1950s, "across the globe for the strength of its teaching and resources".cdi

Students from around the world studied subjects ranging from photography to lithographic drawing. It had a good parallel syllabus for the work Angove and his colleagues were doing back in Perth. He also ventured back to the Regent Street Polytechnic where he'd studied studio and set design a decade earlier. According to Angove, both institutions had "highly regarded schools of photography".

He visited a range of photography hubs of which he had fond memories or connections, including the Vogue studios in Hanover Square on the top floor of Vogue House. This was a setting where many of the biggest names in fashion photography, like David Bailey and Norman Parkinson, worked in the 1960s and 70s.

It was on this trip that he first met photographer Sam Haskins, a graduate of London's Printing College, a man of similar age and background. Haskins hailed from South Africa and began work as an advertising photographer around the same time as Angove. He moved to London in 1968 and made a living from commissions from corporate clients and brand manufacturers, like travel firms and alcoholic beverages, similar to Angove's. At the time they first met, Haskins had also successfully branched out into publishing.cdii

Angove and Haskins shared much. They both trained initially as painters. They both exhibited acclaimed work using projected slides synchronised to a musical backing. They had a fascination for the nude female figure and they both took on roles in education and training.

Their relationship was cemented when Haskins visited Australia in 1976 as a guest of the IAP. He was a workshop presenter at its Canberra convention that year, attended by Angove who arranged some models for him to work with while in the country.

Angove was delighted at Haskins' willingness to sit down with him on that return trip to London and talk at leisure about their interests in photography and education. It was a friendship on which Angove was to build later.

He had hoped for a similar experience with the internationally renowned fashion photographer Patrick Lichfield, but the doyen was abroad at the time and his return to London to meet up with Angove was delayed past the latter's travel times. But there was more to that link still to come too.

Another valuable liaison Angove established during the British winter visit of 1973-74 was with Professor Margaret Harker, one of the country's leaders in photographic education. She started as a budding art student in Lancashire and then, inspired by her father's interest in photography, soon pursued a career path that brought her keen recognition as a photographer and photographic historian.[cdiii] At various times she headed the School of Photography as Regent Street Polytechnic and presided at the Royal Photographic Society, two affiliations relevant to and admired by Angove, as was Harker's historic track record in architectural photography.

A week before Christmas in the following year, 1976, Angove made another trip to London, with a similar mission to his previous journey. He told a local paper he was off to catch up with the latest overseas photographic developments and ideas, including looking over photographic education facilities.

"You're never too old to learn," he said.[cdiv]

He clearly craved his British associations and was determined to grow them in order to maintain and improve the standing of his work in Perth.

"I feel it is time to give my wide experience back to photography," he said,[cdv] adding that he aspired for better recognition as well. This hints at an underlying issue he wrestled with for the whole decade back in Australia.

Still jet-lagged, he met with old friends within 48 hours of reaching London this time. They included Terry LeGoubin and Ron Facius and their wives. He caught up with Stellios at Kalamaras and called Sam Haskins to arrange a catch-up session for drinks. He also got lost on the train, a reminder that he was a bit out of touch with his previous cab-driver standard of knowledge of London's geography. He made contact with Margaret Harker again too.

He met up with Haskins on numerous occasions during the trip, the gatherings being both social and professional. The latter included a discussion about new Polaroids and training materials. He attended a Haskins' exhibition at the Pentax Gallery based on the photographic artist's latest calendar for the camera company. Some of the work was done in Japan.

"The master can produce haunting and sensual landscapes," Angove wrote in his travelling notebook.[cdvi]

Another English photographer who Angove admired was German-born Bill Brandt, a one-time apprentice to the American Man Ray in Paris. It's not known if Angove ever met Brandt, who was a generation older, but he became very familiar with his work and, it could be argued, felt inspired by his style. There are certainly similarities in the choice of subjects and treatments of the two.

Angove referred to Brandt as "the grand old man of photography"[cdvii] and commented on Brandt's later work with collages of "beautifully arranged objects like driftwood, seaweed, shells, feathers, small bones and flotsam ropes".

"Although physically frail, he shows it's possible to be creative quite late in life," Angove observed, somewhat portentously.

New York's Museum of Modern Art, which has Brandt represented in its collection, talks about his "published pictures exemplifying his technical skill and his interest in building visual narratives" and also refers to his later "long exploration of the female nude, transforming the body through the angle and frame of the camera lens".[cdviii] It's not hard to see why Angove considered Brandt a source of influence.

On this return trip to the UK, Angove was armed with a folio of his latest slide work ready to pitch to advertising agencies and especially stock picture libraries. He had a long list of the latter and personal contacts with many.

He collected ideas wherever he went. His notebook from the trip includes illustrations of lighting effects gleaned from Haskins' studio (relevant extract left), sketches of new styles of gallery mounts for exhibitions and introductions to people like British photojournalist Ian Berry. Berry had just been elected chairman of Magnum Photos to which Cartier-Bresson had signed him up in the wake of Berry's exclusive coverage of the Sharpeville massacre in South Africa.[cdix]

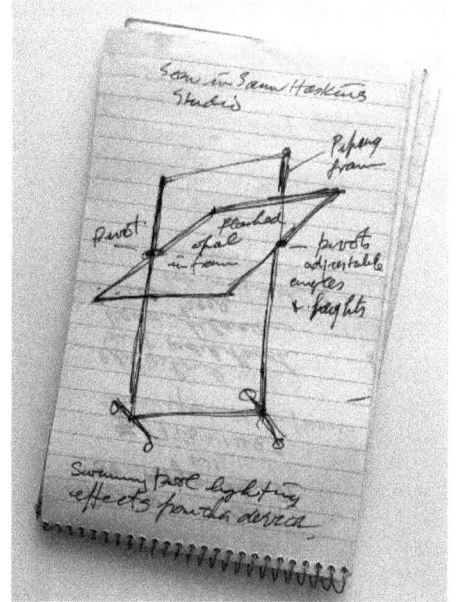

Extract from Angove's London notebook illustrating a lighting setup of Haskins

Angove's itinerary included the *Pompeii AD79* exhibition at the Royal Academy of the Arts, the most comprehensive display of the relics of ancient Pompeii ever seen outside Italy.

He had a reunion with the Barrington-Martins and chased up Patrick Lichfield again on behalf of the IAP who wanted to secure him as a future workshop presenter in Sydney. Lichfield was perennially booked well ahead, and it seemed he was going to be in California not Australia on the initial desired dates, although he expected to be Down Under in 1977 and 1978. Angove also put out feelers to the Paris-based Helmut Newton, to try to arrange a return visit to Australia for such an event.

A visit to the Central London Polytechnic had Angove's eyes watering at a new building to house its media school. The darkrooms, studios, library, theatres and TV control rooms impressed him.

"They've spared no expense," he observed. [cdx]

Another facility he encountered was called the Camera Club, a venue off Charing Cross Road that provided darkrooms, studios and a register of models for visiting amateur and professional photographers from overseas for a small fee.

Angove caught up with an old friend from Perth, John Lunghi, painter, former Society of Artists president and former art director at Gibbneys Studio, who had retired the previous year and returned to London after living in WA for more than 35 years.

Aligning a number of Angove's tastes was another exhibition he attended – and rated as "fantastic" - called *Nomad and the City*, a pictorial record of parts of Old Cairo painstakingly captured by an Australian architect, Ron Lewcock, who shared with Angove a passion for the architecture of Colombo.[cdxi]

Touring various galleries, Angove was keen to check out prevailing fees and commissions for photographic print sales around London. He concluded that "big names" could earn "top prices" in the market.

He collected a hefty payment for pictures he'd sold through Barnaby's Picture Library, which began as a photographic studio in 1934 supplying photographs to Fleet Street and then started to acquire collections and represent individual photographers' work, such as his, from the mid-1950s.[cdxii] Now owned by Mary Evans Picture Library, this business still has a catalogue of almost a hundred Angove photographs on its books, now digitised and viewable online. Among them are rare images of celebrities such as Woody Allen alongside Dusty Springfield and several of his friend, Australian painter Arthur Boyd.

Angove investigated other photo agencies, some of which specialised in particular genres. These included a wildlife picture agency called Ardea run by ornithologist John Gooders and his wife, Su. The pair also ran a successful tour company, taking hundreds of people around the world in search of birds.[cdxiii] Another such outlet was wildlife photographer Bruce Coleman's animal and bird agency established in 1960, enabling photographers to earn a living from their archival images.

Angove also tracked down London Features International, an agency run by John Halsall specialising in pictures of the rock music scene, as well as Picture Point Ltd, a photographic unit headed up by Ken Gibson concentrating on the recording and TV industries.

Clearly, Bill Angove made strenuous efforts to nurture connections with leading practitioners in their shared fields of interest. He saw it as a means of enriching his own experiences and enlarging his capacity to contribute to the world of photography and those who immersed themselves in it.

His contact books from the 1960s and 70s testify to his appetite for building relationships with allies and associates and seeking out prime sources of photographic wisdom and success. Their pages list big names from the photographic profession including the previously mentioned Newton, Busselle and Lichfield. There are others like Gus Wylie, a photographic educator at the London College of Fashion, and an author best known for his book *The Complete Photographer* and several volumes of photographs depicting the changing life on the Hebrides Islands off Scotland.

Angove also cultivated ties with some of the best-known Australian photographers of the era, among them David Moore, Max Dupain and Clive Kane, a fellow specialist in fashion, advertising and industrial photography.[cdxiv]

"I know a number of [these] big names … and they have not forgotten me I'm glad to say," he wrote in what turned out to be the twilight of his life in the late 1970s.

In his final trip to London, Angove achieved another milestone. Conscious of a need to develop his qualifications and credentials in the art and educational spheres, he applied for membership in the Society of Industrial Artists and Designers (SIAD), an accredited professional body founded in 1930 to represent and support new and established practitioners in all creative disciplines.[cdxv]

He was required to make a formal submission to join SIAD's photography chapter so he caught up with one of his former employers, Ken Wells, and used his studio facilities to prepare his paperwork and photography lodgments. The pair also chatted at length about the state of the photographic business in London.

Extraordinarily, the society appears to have assessed Angove's submission within a 48-hour period and awarded him entry, unexpectedly and unrequested above the level of member, at the more senior level of Fellow.

Angove was elated because he was thinking about applying for teaching roles back home in higher education institutions, notably the colleges of advanced education or institutes of technology then prevalent across the country. He saw the fellowship of SIAD as a distinct fillip to this ambition.

Later that year confirmation was forthcoming. The head of art and design at the Western Australian Institute of Technology, A K Russell, wrote to Angove about the standing of SIAD ranks, explaining that the professional competence of applicants was always examined "by a rigorous assessment panel". [cdxvi] Being admitted as a member, he wrote, would be a qualification favourably viewed for teaching positions.

He added: "The senior category, Fellow, is much more rare and is only awarded to distinguished practitioners whose work is judged to be of an exceptionally high standard.

"The award is recognised as a distinction within the profession and we would similarly regard this as a high qualification in terms of academic appointment.

"I note with pleasure that you have been elected to that category particularly because to my knowledge there have been very few Fellows made in your special field. I would regard this as adding distinction to your very high professional degree of skill and qualification."[cdxvii]

What a glowing endorsement this was of Angove's standing. Alas, it failed to secure him a higher academic posting before illness struck him down. He made at least one application to the Newcastle College of Advanced Education as late as 1979.

Bill Angove.

THE ROYAL SOCIETY *for the encouragement*
OF ARTS *Manufactures and Commerce*

JOHN ADAM STREET · ADELPHI · LONDON WC2N 6EZ · TEL: 01-839 2366 · TELEGR: PRAXITELES LONDON WC2

7th November, 1978.

Dear Sir,

I have pleasure in informing you that at the last meeting of the Council you were duly elected a Fellow of the Royal Society of Arts. A form of declaration for your signature is enclosed.

The subscriptions of Fellows date from the quarter-day nearest to their election, and I shall therefore be obliged if you will kindly remit the sum of £15, to cover the Registration Fee of £5 and your first subscription of £10, if you wish to become an annual subscriber, or for £125 (to include the Registration Fee) should you prefer to compound as a Life Fellow.

On receipt of your remittance a Diploma of Fellowship will be issued to you and your name officially entered in the List of Fellows, in accordance with the Bye-Laws, a copy of which is also enclosed.

The Council of the Society and the Privy Council are particularly concerned about the use of designatory letters. I have been asked therefore to draw your particular attention to the attached leaflet on the use of the letters 'FRSA'. If further clarification is needed, please do not hesitate to get in touch with me.

Yours faithfully,
CHRISTOPHER LUCAS
Secretary.

William H.M. Angove Esq., F.S.I.A.D.

original signed
G. Brennan
6.12.78

*Angove's business stationery over the years
Angove's rate card, Perth, and
friend Rolf Harris writes to Angove in 1970s*

Showtime

Throughout the 1970s back in his home state, Angove continued to operate his freelance photography business from his South Perth flat. It was not necessarily a pretty place, according to his friend, researcher and photographer Ted Edkins who recalls the flat being full of developed films, drying on clothes hangers throughout the home.[cdxviii]

"You'd have to walk through them like one of those strip door hangings designed to keep out insects," he says.[cdxix]

Edkins and Roger Garwood insist Angove wasn't very tidy when it came to his desk, likening it to Einstein's, and he was often tardy or lazy about sending out accounts for work he had done.

The mainstays of Angove's output remained theatre, fashion and glamour. He supplied pictures to his beloved WA Ballet Company and various theatrical troupes previously cited.

He earned his income principally through advertising and promotional assignments. His list of clients was varied, essentially in the service sector because, as he had previously stated, Perth was not a market flush with manufactured product. The slate included major companies like Wesfarmers, which owned Masters Dairy, Plunkett Homes, the Parmelia Hotel and Chrysler vehicle dealership Halberts, fashion outlet Sportslane, tourism business the Geographe Bay Motor Inn, and entertainment outlets such as radio station 6PM and the Wanneroo Park speed car raceway.

Among his non-commercial clients were the Greek Consulate, the National Trust of Australia and the Australian Wool Corporation.

He even appeared on the other side of the camera. His name and face headlined an advertising campaign for a photographic supplier called Camera Craft, which traded on Angove's endorsement and reputation. Its advertisements for a discount membership for weekend photographers and enthusiasts, branded *Hobbycard*, featured a description of Angove as a "photographer of world renown, photographic lecturer and camera wizz."[cdxx]

Angove was particularly proud of his first assignment back in Perth. His commission for a new office block in the heart of the Perth CBD required innovation. After the building developer described its challenge, Angove proposed a helicopter shoot of the cityscape (next page) and added a zoom effect later in darkroom processing. The advertisement won an award in a national exhibition for the local agency, Parks Clemenger.

City skyscraper shot for press advertisement

While it offered little scope to apply his inventive and artistic magic, he was a regular contributor to a free weekly newspaper called *Living Today* which published a steady diet of images of young women featured in events such as beach girl contests and fashion launches and others posing for 'lifestyle' pictures. It also ran advertorial content, some of which he supplied.

The newspaper also ushered in a return to Angove's fledgling years as a photographer on the streets of Perth. On one occasion, it ran a double-page spread of new candid pictures he took around the city, all of them depicting aspects of love and tender moments.

His local connection with the fashion industry is perhaps best exemplified by the work he did with innovative designer Anne Somoff who immigrated to Australia as the daughter of a German family renowned for producing high quality leather shoes.[cdxxi] Anne set up a leather fashion business, Dreske-Somoff, in 1967. It became a national brand for which Angove produced its advertising and catalogue output.

Angove built a reliable stable of models with whom he worked during this decade. Some, like beauty queens and actors Cheryl Rixon, Jane Priest and Karen Pini, became very well-known nationally and beyond while others, such as Cheryl Morin, were among the cream of the Western Australian modelling scene.

Rixon recalls that at the time she met Angove, he was one of just a handful of photographers running their own businesses in Perth. The rest were press photographers.

£500 REWARD
FOR THE APPREHENSION

William Angove

WHEREAS

A Man known by the name of **WILL** has unlawfully, rebelliously, and traitorously levied and arrayed Armed Men at Ballaarat, in the Colony of Victoria, with the view of making war against Our Sovereign Lady the QUEEN:

NOTICE IS HEREBY GIVEN

That whoever will give such information as may lead to the Apprehension of the said **WILL** shall receive

A REWARD OF £500

being the Reward offered by SIR ROBERT NICKLE.

By His Excellency's Command,

JOHN FOSTER.

DESCRIPTION

SYDNEY'S MOST WANTED

PHOTOGRAPHER

"Bill was involved in a lot of things," she recalls.cdxxii

"I became very fond of him. He even got to know my family to the extent that my mum and sister featured in some of his shots."

Hired through an agency, Rixon says her first modelling job was for a seasonal retail campaign shot by Angove who had her wrapped in Christmas paper.

The pair regularly worked together producing advertisements for what was then Western Australia's biggest local chain of supermarkets, Charlie Carters.

"I would regularly go over to his place in South Perth," says Rixon, adding that he and her family grew quite close. Her mother, an artist, shared interests and tastes with Angove and was happy for her daughter to work with him.cdxxiii

"She knew I'd always be safe. He was never predatory.

"Sometimes we'd go over to the Old Mill near his place for afternoon tea. I remember occasionally I'd be looking after our neighbour's child while she was at work so she would come with me. Bill actually worked the child into the Carter ads so I'd be depicted as shopping with a bub.

Two of the advertising campaigns featuring Cheryl Rixon, shot by Angove

"We had fun too. I'd bring over wigs and hair extensions and clothes and we could spend all day playing with different ideas.

"He was fabulous. I think Bill shot many of what were my favourite pictures, the most beautiful pictures I ever had."

Another model who has fond memories of Angove is Jennifer Tyrie.

Hailing from Kilmarnock in Scotland, Jennifer was just out of her teens when she migrated to Australia with her parents in 1974. She had a short stint with them in Melbourne, but after they returned to the UK when her sister died, Jennifer made her way to Perth, living initially in Fremantle. She had worked as a sign-writer in Melbourne after previously doing window dressing in Scotland.

The family had lived in London during her teens and she recalls a photographer chasing her to see if she was interested in modelling for him.

"He could have been a child molester of course," she laughs, "but he gave me his card and suggested I bring along my sister and her mother-in-law."[cdxxiv]

By the late 1970s in Perth, Jennifer says she realised she was photogenic and began taking on assignments through an agency. That was when she met Bill Angove.

"He found me through City Models and Mannequins in City Arcade in Perth," she says. "He booked me and we did a few jobs."

One was for the cover of a magazine produced by Charlie Carters. Another one was a picture to illustrate a story about stockings for Myer.

Jennifer Tyrie - 1979 and 2020

"Bill was a gentleman, a nice man. Some [photographers] were a bit lecherous but I was comfortable working with Bill. He was always very professional. He knew his stuff and put you at ease."[cdxxv]

"Bill was well regarded in the business."

Angove also worked on occasions with novices such as a bunch of glamorous university students recruited as extras for appearing in a rather extraordinary documentary film shot in the state about the Dutch East Indies ship *Batavia*, wrecked on a coral reef off the coast of Western Australia in 1629 during its maiden voyage.[cdxxvi]

It's speculated that the ship's rich cargo, which included silver coins, jewels and wines, may have seeded the idea of a mutiny by the crew. The leading plotter was Jeronimus Cornelisz, recorded in later history as a sort of 17th-century Charles Manson figure and "considered one of history's first documented psychopaths".[cdxxvii] Before the mutiny had taken place, poor navigation resulted in the ship hitting a reef on Beacon Island, one of the Abrolhos Island group off the coast of WA.

The film, depicting the story of a hippie-style colony of survivors led by Cornelisz, was made by Reg Grundy Enterprises, one of Australia's best-known television production companies. The documentary, with a heavy emphasis on re-enactment back on the Abrolhos, was directed by no less a talent than Bruce Beresford, fresh from making the infamous hit, *The Adventures of Barry McKenzie*. Beresford had lived in London at the same time as Angove.

Angove was hired to shoot the stills and the publicity pictures.

The filming encountered a string of logistical challenges and mishaps, including Beresford being knocked unconscious in a locational accident involving a tent pole.

The film portrayed "one of the most grisly episodes in Australia's early history" in which Cornelisz conducted a reign of terror that saw 125 men, women and children killed.[cdxxviii]

"Box office success is what the documentary makers are hoping for," wrote Hugh Schmitt in a magazine story at the time.

"When a film features bloody murder, rape and full-frontal nudity, you could say it smacks of box office."[cdxxix]

Other scenes were shot in Perth and on Rottnest Island, where a skinny-dipping frolic was to be included, subject to it passing Australia's then-tough censorship rules.

Angove's folio of photographs from this rare experience survives today. Here's a sample on page 211.

Angove's pictures from the Wreck of the Batavia film production

The year 1979 marked the 150th anniversary of British settlement of the Swan River colony. Major celebrations were conducted throughout the year to honour the sesquicentenary.[cdxxx] They included a yacht race from Plymouth in England to Fremantle and the publication of fourteen volumes of books commemorating Western Australian achievements in various fields of endeavour from literature to agriculture to education.

The occasion prompted a return to Perth by Angove's old friend, performer Rolf Harris, who headlined a New Year's Eve outdoor concert featuring all-local talent and attended by 60,000 people. Later in the year the city hosted the Miss Universe contest, an opportunity for Angove and other photographers to shoot beautiful young women from around the world.

In the lead-up decade to 1979, there was significant growth in the number of fine art galleries in the state. Rose Skinner founded a gallery that quickly earned a national reputation [cdxxxi] and it demonstrated its appeal with exhibitions between 1970 and 1975 featuring, among others, Arthur Boyd, Sidney Nolan and Albert Tucker, no doubt to the delight of Bill Angove who must have been thrilled to have the work of three of his London friends touring to his home state.

Angove got his own chance on the major gallery scene in 1979. A ground-breaking show organised by the Art Gallery of Western Australia was the first in the state to afford photography the recognition it was earning worldwide. It was an exhibition, simply called *Western Australian Photographers*, featuring the work of nine contemporary practitioners, including Angove, the oldest by age, and his regularly-displayed colleagues Garwood and Woldendorp.

It was a sign of photography taking its place in the visual arts constellation which had blossomed during the decade, due in no small part to the election of the Whitlam Government in 1972. As researcher Maria Brown noted: "The promotion of change and innovation in art was seen as a desirable and legitimate use of public resources. The avant-garde was no longer a troublesome, bohemian under-class."[cdxxxii]

The Art Gallery of WA's exhibition included 54 works by Angove and others, among whom were John Ogden, Neil Sullivan, Faye Williams and his friend Will Kohlen. Angove's photographs were all recent, created the year before, although some of the other exhibitors dipped into their back catalogues.

Angove's gallery prints reflected his deep attachment to music and the performing arts. Two were blue-toned silver prints, *The Guitarist*, and *The Cellist*. Two were silver (black and white), *One Second of Ballet (Western Australian Ballet)* and *One Second of Dance Class (Contemporary Dance Centre)*. A fifth was colour, *Rehearsal of the Australian Ballet at the Entertainment Centre*, and the last was a sepia-toned silver print, *Untitled*.

After its debut at the Art Gallery of WA, the exhibition toured around more than 20 senior high schools in the metropolitan area and a dozen town halls and libraries in the Mid-West and Wheatbelt throughout 1979 and 1980.

As he had done in earlier stages of his life and career, Angove used this period to indulge his appetite for learning, traversing new ground and acquiring new skills. He began 1979 with a return to study, this time at the WA Institute of Technology (WAIT) where he enrolled as an extension student in its film and television offering.

Western Australian Photographers Exhibition

This exhibition has been prepared to tour metropolitan and country centres in Western Australia during 1979. The photographers have lent us their work and we wish to express our thanks for their co-operation.

W.S. ELLIS
Director

William Angove
John H. Browne
Roger Garwood
Will J. Kohlen
Jonathan Morris
John W.A. Ogden
Neil W. Sullivan
Faye Williams
Richard L. Woldendorp

William Angove

Born in Albany, Western Australia 1924. Self-taught as a photographer. Travelled to London 1955, employed as a photographer with Mayflower Studios. Returned to Sydney 1959, worked with Bruce Minette Studios. 1962 returned to London for eight years, re-employed by Mayflower Studios, in 1964 began freelance work. Since 1971 he has lived in Perth and has lectured in the Graphic Design School, Perth Technical College since 1972. Official photographer to the Western Australian Ballet Company, Western Australian Opera Company and the Gilbert and Sullivan Society. Associate of The Institute of Australian Photographers, Fellow of The Society of Industrial Artists and Designers (UK), Member of the Royal Photographic Society (London), Fellow of The Royal Society of Arts (UK). Exhibited 1958/59 Kodak's Gallery, Perth and 1959 Paxton's Gallery, Sydney. He exhibits regularly with the Institute of Australian Photographers.

Titles
1. **The Guitarist** 1978
   blue toned silver print
   27.8 x 40.0 cm
2. **The Cellist** 1978
   blue toned silver print
   30.2 x 40.2 cm
3. **One Second of Ballet (Western Australian Ballet)** 1978
   silver print
   30.2 x 40.5 cm
4. **One Second of Dance Class (Contemporary Dance Centre)** 1978
   silver print
   29.7 x 40.3 cm
5. **Rehearsal of the Australian Ballet at the Entertainment Centre** 1978
   colour print
   40.4 x 29.5 cm
6. **Untitled** 1978
   sepia toned silver print
   30.2 x 40.3 cm

Introductory page of 1979 Art Gallery of WA catalogue

He had shown during numerous periods that the moving picture and accompanying audio was a medium of interest. The WAIT course was intended to culminate in a degree. This would have buttressed his quest for credentials at a time when the higher education sector was starting to obsess about such status. Alas, in this instance, Angove was not to live long enough to advance down this path.

Arthur Boyd and Albert Tucker, photographed and befriended by Angove

A premature end

For all its rewards, 1979 turned out to be the last year of Bill Angove's life. Two shadows came to bookend his decade back in Western Australia.

While he tried to extend the professional and artistic achievements of the 1950s and 60s away from home, Angove was gnawed by thoughts that he wasn't as valued back on his original turf.

In a torn, faded typescript discovered in his personal documents and provided to me as part of a huge cache of archives used for compiling this story, Angove went on record as believing he was under-appreciated upon his return to Australia.

He likens himself to the main character, David Meredith, in a book called *Clean Straw for Nothing* by dual Miles Franklin award-winning author George Johnston, a former Australian foreign correspondent who spent years in London and Greece before finally returning home. The 1969 book is considered a memoir of fiction.

"The Australian who moves overseas, establishes himself well in his field and finds when he returns that he can't find a niche to settle into," is a quotation attributed to Angove in this typescript unidentified by an author. He may have written it entirely himself although it's in the third person.[cdxxxiii]

It continues: "He [the Australian] is almost resented."

It then juxtaposes the singular Australian for the collective: "The Australian wants his contemporary to be beaten … to go overseas and try the big smoke … and fail. If he returns beaten and with his tail between his legs, then he will be accepted with open arms. If he succeeds then he is resented."

Angove was friends with Johnston, whether through overlapping associations in London in the 1950s and 60s or through Sid Nolan and others who spent time with Johnston and his wife Charmian Clift on the Greek island of Hydra. That nine-year idyll eventually came to be episodically painful due to lifestyle excesses. Cousin Terry Butcher remembers[cdxxxiv] Angove bringing Johnston and Clift to a party one night in Woolhara when all three were back in Sydney, probably in the summer of 1967 when Angove was holidaying in Australia.

In *Clean Straw for Nothing*, Meredith is confronted by a character who asks him: "Why did you come back to Australia from overseas? You haven't written anything since you came back, have you? Anything worthwhile I mean. Why come back at all if it stops the flow, if it buggers you as a writer?"[cdxxxv]

It's stark to realise that Angove, ever the artist, saw himself on these profound pages.

Former journalist, crime fiction author and literary critic Charles Boag observes that "Meredith counts himself as a failure"[cdxxxvi] although adding that is not how he emerges in *Clean Straw*.

Boag adds: "The book reveals why most people choose to live their lives within the four rigid walls of conformity. It exposes the dangers of trying to escape. But it shows that it can be done – and for an artist, must be done: whether the escape is a physical one or only in the mind."[cdxxxvii]

Johnston's biographer Garry Kinnane speculates that a generation of Australians who came of age after the Great Depression and World War II perceived a "dull and routine" country in which they "saw nothing to look forward to but a quiet life unnoticed by the rest of the world".[cdxxxviii]

He concludes: "Thus many of them ... became expatriates of one sort or another ... both as physical and imaginative exiles, torn in a love/hate relationship with their country of origin."

There's no sign of regret in Angove's story to the extent to which he's contributed to it in his own words. But his frank admission of discerning a parallel with Johnston's character raises the question of whether a touch of bitterness ever saddled his decade back on home shores.

This whole life story establishes why an adventurous and talented son of the Australian bush had to fly to fulfil his ambitions, like so many others. Of course, some never came back and may have been the better for it.

Angove revealed more of his feelings later in the same document. He complained that "the work he used to do just didn't exist in Perth" so "he had to be practical and forget his favourite field of abstract and experimental work".[cdxxxix]

Instead, he "accepted bread and butter stuff just to survive ... and even this was difficult to get."

According to this typescript, "most of the people who knew him said they wouldn't insult him by giving him menial jobs ... and so he missed out both ways."[cdxl]

Little wonder he savoured his trips back to Britain. Here clearly was a man with what would have felt like an unspeakable burden at the time. And, as the decade rolled over, a bigger impediment was to overtake Bill Angove.

As 1979 drew on, he started to experience shoulder pain. As a result of preliminary medical tests, he was sent for treatment to Royal Perth Hospital's rehabilitation annexe in the suburb of Shenton Park.

There he was diagnosed with a cancerous tumour on his spine.

"This was a huge shock," his niece Beverley recalls.[cdxli]

"The prognosis seemed to get worse on each visit," recalls nephew Peter Bolt.[cdxlii]

"Initially [there was] some optimism around curing what was ailing him, to invasive surgery and beyond," he adds.

In the end, the doctors decided to undertake risky surgery.

Beverley says that, in the lead-up to his operation, he was allowed to leave the hospital briefly to have dinner with his close friend and model, Cheryl Morin.

"We were so grateful that he had got out that night," Beverley says, "as it was to be his last time."

The operation was unsuccessful because the tumour was too close to his spinal chord, and Angove was left immobilised.

Peter Bolt remembers conversations about what it would mean for his uncle to be wheelchair-bound.

"We discussed the ability to access his ground floor flat and to work at his photography and teaching," he says.[cdxliii]

"Bill never obtained a driver's licence and never owned a car so transport was discussed and the possible use of mobility taxis to get around Perth. Unfortunately, his condition deteriorated very quickly and it seemed that in such a short time Bill was completely paralysed."

Losing the use of all lower limbs, the only movement he had was his head.

Beverley takes up the story: "I was 22 at the time and had to phone Mum, his sister, and give her the awful news."

Meredyth was also living in Perth and their brother Peter, then a teacher in Geraldton, came down to Perth for the summer holidays with his girlfriend Terry. They all visited Bill in hospital as much as they could.

"Bill asked me to look after his flat," recalls Beverly, "so I moved out of my rental in Claremont and moved to Bill's place in South Perth."

Peter and Terry also stayed there during their visit.

Angove had been living in his two-bedroom flat for about eight years. As mentioned, it was also home to his darkroom and photographic studio. It was on the ground floor and had a courtyard at the rear with a beautiful plane tree, as high as the three-storey building.

The block of flats had been recently strata-titled and, rather than have to move, he had managed to purchase his home.

At the time, Angove had been working on what might be described as a passion project, a book of aesthetic nude photography that he was close to completing when struck down.

Beverley recalls him battling with how he could continue with his work - or indeed do anything – now that he was so paralysed.

"I remember him being in traction for a week or so and experiencing 'phantom limb' movement.

"There was little that could be done to help him. I offered to record some of his stories. He was keen so we recorded two audio tapes, and then he felt too unwell to do anymore.

"Bill had many friends visit him in hospital. This was his greatest pleasure," she says.

Angove's condition was irretrievable. His hospital confinement stretched into many weeks.

One of his closest friends at the time, one-time student of his and model, Cherie Scott, recalls dropping him off at the hospital at the start of his health crisis. She says she visited him every second day for six weeks.

"Lots of photographer friends came to say their goodbyes," she recalls.

"It was tough. They'd ask him how he was. I just wanted to hit them."[cdxliv]

Beverley Angove remembers her uncle getting upset and agitated about his condition.

"The medical staff ended up giving him sedatives, which unfortunately meant he was not able to enjoy his friends' visits so much."[cdxlv]

According to Beverley, the medical staff's advice was confined to the common euphemism urging Bill to 'put his affairs in order'.

"Part of Bill's frustration at this time was that he wasn't really being told that he was dying," she says.

"He didn't have much time to come to terms with his impending death."[cdxlvi]

Beverley had studied 'Death and Dying' in anthropology and was aware of the importance of dignity in dying.

"I had made contact with a professional in this field and had made arrangements to speak with the medical team. Tragically, Bill died before this happened."[cdxlvii]

Peter visited him on what was to be his last night alive, 4 February 1980.

"There were many other visitors that late afternoon," he recalls.[cdxlviii]

"Bill was immobile in bed, his head being supported by a frame and clearly heavily sedated. It was a tragic scene. Visitors stood back from the bed and just outside the room and spoke in hushed tones.

"One by one, one at a time, each visitor approached Bill and spoke their words of comfort.

"Bill called me to his bed in a gruff, low, barely audible voice. I bent down to him and he spoke of his photography collection and where to find it. His last words to me were about his work, his passion, his legacy. I said goodbye to my Uncle Bill.

"Early the next morning Bev took a phone call from the hospital. She was told that Uncle Bill had died. Bev came into Bill's bedroom and told Terry and I the tragic news. It was a shock. A short time later I heard Bev, in the shower, crying at the loss."

Beverley adds: "I had to tell Mum [his sister] the terrible news. I always remember [also] phoning our [paternal] nanna to tell her."[cdxlix]

Another poignant story remains with her: "There was an owl that came and sat in the plane tree in Bill's courtyard and stayed for about a week. I'd never seen it before and never again after that. I'm sure that Bill had taken a photo of it though."

Cherie Scott says she was among those visitors to the bedside in the hours before he died. She describes it as a seminal experience in her life.

The pair had met at the technical college where Scott was enrolled in graphic design. Angove obviously piqued her interest in the photography unit and she became his darkroom assistant.

Darkrooms figured tragically in the Angove's family's suspicions about his contraction of cancer. By the later 1980s, medical evidence was mounting that toxic chemicals used in photographic processing could trigger disease. Inhaling toxic fumes while mixing chemicals, operating and cleaning film processors and disposing of wastes were identified as the cause of severe health complications.[cdl]

It wasn't hard to draw conclusions from Angove's well-documented experiences in poorly ventilated darkrooms throughout his career. And in his case, developer and fixer were chemicals he even used outside the darkroom. He used them to 'paint' images on large sheets of photographic paper as part of his edgy style.

A local newspaper reported in 1972: "Angove, who won acclaim in the world photographic press for his creative photography, has been experimenting with the unusual technique in his Perth studio. The chemicals are poured, splashed, sponged and dripped over the emulsified paper which has been exposed to light, and the end result is a mass of tones which have been shaped into the subject matter. The paintings will be on display at an exhibition held by the Red Cross early next month."[cdli]

Many generous and genuine tributes to Angove were placed on the record in the weeks and months after his death.

"The world of photography has just lost one of the outstanding cameramen of the twentieth century, Bill Angove," his hometown newspaper, *The Albany Advertiser*, wrote, adding: "Artist, craftsman, teacher, Bill Angove combined all these in a rich and varied life that is its own memorial."[cdlii]

...MS I HAVE KNOWN

...clinical, I sometimes wonder how we ever
...hrough the system of worn out, antiquated
...ntilated darkrooms.

...of my friend Michael Barrington Martin, my
... initially venturing to London in 1955
...rcus, behind the old Windmill Theatre -
...hael's stud... ...sed and printed for
... ...he show and all it
... ...room was sort of
... ... advantageous
... studio and was
... studio and provid-

... ...t prints litter-
... ...ng off a peculiar
... to it.

... This was a
... ... used as a
... ...egatives of

I ... ...ertisi... ...negatives.
busy... ...some time, as ... ...nverted corridor,
pre-war fashions were ca...

The enlargers, I would th...
Several printers occupied ...
the space was all in one d...

On a recent visit to the old ...rm, since moved to more spacious
premises, some of the old enlargers were still in use. (they don't
make them like that any more – thank goodness).

A couple of moves later found me in Soho, joining up with a young group
who occupied the upper floors of a building in Wardour Mews. The top
floor being a glass roofed studio, darkrooms next floor down and
below this a prostitute conducted business. I was quite impressed by
the quality of light produced by a light covering of snow on the glass
roof of the studio. The impression didn't last when the snow melted,
dripped into the studio, down the darkroom walls onto the enlargers
and how the lady below plied her trade during such times, I have no
idea, but I imagine an umbrella could have been useful.

We later moved to a basement in Frith Street and partitioned the area
to suit ourselves. Against my advice, the plumber installed a copper
lined wet bench. Residual hypo eventually proved me right. In the
negative darkroom you could quite easily see the end of the bench,
but due to one dark spot we didn't fog any film.

One of the photographers in this group was David Davies who I met on
a later trip to England and was thankful for the use of his darkroom.
His negative darkroom at this time served a dual purpose as negative
processing was done in the toilet.

Until I started to freelance, the positions I held were as a photographer only, and kept me out of darkrooms, and I wasn't sorry. I
still have impressions of dark green, slimy holes, out of which, I
must admit come brilliant sparkling prints. London was not alone in
these black holes, one or two I saw in Sydney come up to the mark quite
well.

Bill Angove f.s.i.a.d. a.i.a.p.

The paper that filled pages with Angove's work, *Living Today*, said his death robbed the Perth photographic scene of one of its outstanding figures.

"Originality, painstaking technical skill and true artistic creativity were hallmarks of a professional," the paper eulogised.[cdliii]

"He induced the camera to produce results of a calibre achieved by few of his contemporaries. During his periods abroad he worked with some of the world's great photographers and all were impressed by his skills."[cdliv]

His fellow photographers held him in high regard.

Ted Edkins, who helped Angove in the studio at the Old Boys School on St George's Terrace after the closure of the James Street college, described him as a placid man able to make friends easily, especially in the arts. They became good friends, dining every Friday night in Northbridge. Edkins drove because Angove never learned to drive.

"He was an even-tempered man," Edkins recalls, [cdlv] "I can only remember one occasion when he lost his temper. It was a minor incident at a restaurant when a waitress thought he had short-changed the bill. A coin had been obscured on the table."

Photographer Roger Garwood considered Angove "a very fine teacher".[cdlvi] He says he was fond of pointing out to his students that if you thought you needed all the latest whizzbangery, it wasn't the case.

"Bill was a master of improvisation. He could design a scene using items such as twigs, a fog machine and polystyrene objects, stuff that cost little or nothing. These days photographers are told they need to invest big in all the gear. Bill just used what was around, anything makeshift would work in his hands. He knew how to capture the essence of a place with very little equipment, just simple gear. In his day, you had to be creative, it was the quick or the dead."

Edkins cites an example: "He was once commissioned by a shipping line to photograph its newest ocean liner. The budget did not run to aerial shots so Bill went out and bought a miniature model of the ship, some glass, shaving cream and shot it in a studio. It became the headline picture for the business."

Garwood says Angove was a performer when it came to teaching, "every bit the extrovert in front of a class".

Both men agree he was a very professional person in the way he worked.

Had he not died prematurely, Roger Garwood believes Angove could have had a far greater impact in the years that followed his cut-short career.

Another international photographer who eventually settled in Perth in the late 1970s, Stephen Smith, came to know Angove well.

He says they first met at a place run by Miles Glenville who was attempting to open Perth's first photographic gallery. Angove was exhibiting there in 1978 but the venture only lasted a few months.

"I ran into Bill at other events and jobs around the town," Smith recalls. [cdlvii]

"I was interested in the performing arts and Bill was principal photographer at the Western Australian Ballet. I'd seen the Bolshoi Ballet perform at the Kremlin years earlier and it sowed a seed in my mind.

"Bill was a most likeable man. He was interested in what you were doing. He was a most encouraging man."

Smith, like others, describes Angove as "a natural teacher".

"He was generous with advice and guidance, never heavy handed."[cdlviii]

The staff and students at the Perth Technical College were generous in their praise.

"A teacher and friend who inspired us to see art through photography," the student guild wrote in a newspaper death notice.[cdlix]

His fellow lecturers referred to him as a "colleague and friend who gave his talents to teaching".[cdlx]

Richard Woldendorp, one of WA's greatest photographers, also reflects on Angove's humanity, describing him simply as "a kind, humble gentleman".[cdlxi]

His niece, Meredyth McLarty, one of the bunch of loyal guardians of Angove's legacy, thinks of him as extroverted and charismatic.

The Institute of Australian Photography inaugurated a memorial award for photography students in honour of Angove's contribution to the art and to education. The award was conferred annually for meritorious prints and was initially presented by Lord Lichfield.

Angove's photographic collection survives as a monument to the man's art, honed by his instincts as a painter, shaped by his livelihood and testifying to his unstinting energy and passion.

The name of William Henry Norton Angove stands among an impressive list of people born or raised in Albany. They include the Australian Broadcasting Corporation's first Washington correspondent Peter Barnett, publisher and editor of *The Bulletin* magazine Trevor Kennedy, pop singer and composer Ross Ryan, educator and university vice chancellor Peter Tannoch, WA state archivist Margaret Medcalf, notorious murderer Frederick Deeming, international surfing champion Jodie Cooper, journalist and later Premier of WA Alan Carpenter and author Tim Winton.

On the map of Australia, beautiful Albany occupies a remote and rugged location.

It has produced, welcomed or farewelled notable adventurers, from the first convoy of troop ships sailing to Gallipoli to writers Henry Lawson and Anthony Trollope, from naturalist Charles Darwin to saint Mary McKillop.

Something in the air surely imbued Bill Angove with a similar enterprising spirit.

Bill Angove, as featured in a Perth camera store advertising

Acknowledgements

Researching and writing this biography of Bill Angove would not have been possible but for the dedication and enthusiasm of the offspring of his late sister, Gwenda. When their mother died in 2014, the four of them were determined to retain the huge store of archival materials and the vast photographic collection she had inherited after his passing in 1980. It was safeguarded for most of the intervening years in the family home in Albany.

Beverley Angove, in particular, held a candle to her uncle's legacy for more than 40 years, with the support and assistance of her siblings Meredyth McLarty, Jenny Bodie-Hall and Peter Bolt. Sharing all these records with me was the key to my work. I am indebted to them for their help, generosity, patience and unstinting involvement in the project.

I would not even have made it to the starting point except for my old late friend Ken Knox (1925-2020). During the eight years of our friendship, he introduced me to his great mate Angove's story, starting with our shared participation in the Western Australian Camera Club. To Ken's daughter Robyn, I owe thanks for helping facilitate my connections with the family and its artistic achievements.

Archivist, author and friend Dr Joanna Sassoon has been a constant and wonderful source of guidance and encouragement to me throughout my work on both the Knox legacy and the Angove biography.

I record my thanks to the string of people who were willing to be interviewed for this project, sharing their recollections of Bill Angove or filling in gaps in the life and times he traversed. Their names feature throughout the story. In particular here I mention Bill Weedon, Cheryl Rixon, Robin Haig, Ken Done, Bill Pownall, Roger Garwood, Paola Anselmi, Stephen Smith, Jennifer Tyrie, Ted Edkins, Howard Grey, Cherie Scott, Craig McDonald, Terry Butcher and Vic Singh.

A range of other kind people have assisted or encouraged me in various ways along the journey and I salute them. They include Christine Froude, Angela Frodsham, Erica Lorimer, Robyn Tsapazi, Virginia White, Gael Newton, Andrew Murray, Bob Charteris, John Wood, Valerie Lawson, Alec O'Halloran, Bernice Barry and publisher Helen Iles.

I also acknowledge the access I have had to information from institutional sources such as the National Library of Australia's Trove database, the Australian War Memorial's records and the City of Albany Library's local history centre.

Richard Goodwin
Wembley Downs, Western Australia © 2024
goodies.ar@iinet.net.au

Index

A

Advertiser's Weekly, 67, 77
Aisbett, Norman, 36, 37
Albany, 1, 11, 15, 18, 20, 21, 40, 49, 61, 83, 97, 220, 223, 224, 225, 232
Aldous, Lucette, 98
Andrews, Bert, 144
Angove, Beverley, 7, 8, 11, 13, 50, 189, 216, 217, 219, 220, 225
Angove, Gwenda, 7, 15, 16, 17, 19, 20, 21, 23, 25, 38, 131, 225, 232
Angove, John Henry (Harry), 9, 11
Angove, Marjorie, iii, 9, 11, 12, 15, 16, 17, 19, 113, 114, 116, 131, 162
Angove, Thomas, 9, 11, 12, 16
Annie Walker Agency, 162
Anselmi, Paola, 42, 225
Armstrong, Ron, 131, 189
Art Gallery of Western Australia, 41, 212
Australian War Memorial, 26, 225
Australian Women's Weekly, 69, 74, 77, 78, 84, 115, 135, 147

B

Baker, Barry, 184
Ballet, Russes, 97
Barnaby's Picture Library, 200
Barrington-Martin, Michael, 49
Barrington-Martin, Peggy, 49, 55, 56, 180, 186
Baxter, Cedric, 192
Beaton, Cecil, 64, 65, 66, 74, 85
Beresford, Bruce, 210
Berman, Edward, 185, 186
Berry Currie, 134, 147
Bird, 21
Bird, Francis and Augusta, 21
Bissett, Win, 69
Blackman, Charles, 165, 166, 167
Boag, Charles, 216
Boans, 41, 49
Bolt, Basil, 83, 232
Bolt, Charlie, 83
Bolt, Peter, 83, 217, 225
Boyd, Arthur, 97, 151, 152, 166, 167, 170, 200, 212

Brandt, Bill, 151, 199
British Iron and Steel, 158
British Medical Journal, 74, 75, 76, 116
British-Australasian Tobacco Company, 147
Brodie-Hall, Jennifer, 13, 15, 20
Brown, Noeline, 165
Bulova, 161
Burchell, William John, 12, 232
Burr, Marilyn, 93, 98, 156
Busselle, Mike, 92, 201
Butcher, Burchell, 114, 115, 134, 135
Butcher, Edward William Norton, 11
Butcher, Terry, 23, 63, 139, 162, 215, 225
Byrne, Howard, 29, 34, 61, 62, 64, 65, 67, 69, 77, 78, 87, 90, 156, 167, 225

C

Cartier-Bresson, Henri, 104, 151, 199
Casellas, Cyril, iii, 28, 30, 183, 184
Channel Seven, 131
Charlie Carters, 208, 209
Chester, Norman, 23, 110
Chiew, Les, 109, 110, 141, 189
Clift, Charmian, 142, 215
Colebatch, Hal, 39, 40
Collie River Irrigation Scheme, 17
Coronet Records, 133
Covent Garden, 58, 97, 98, 99, 104, 187
Curtin, John, 39
Cutts, Len, 30, 31

D

Dakin, William, 39, 40
Davies, David, 92, 157
Dolin, Anton, 98
Done, Ken, 174, 225
Duchesne, Mary, 93
Dufaycolor, 45
Dupain, Max, 39, 140, 143, 146, 147, 152, 201
Dwyer, John J, 40

E

Edkins, Ted, 131, 205, 222, 225
Evans, Frank, 162, 182

F

Facius, Ron, 84, 95, 198
Festival Ballet, 93, 97, 98, 155, 156
Forbes, Captain James, 9, 10
Forrest, Alexander, 11

G

Garwood, Roger, 131, 190, 205, 212, 222, 225
Gibbney, James & Son, 33, 34, 49, 143
Gilpin, John, 98
Goons, 57
Gow, Robyn, 113, 139
Grant, Gilly, 177
Great Southern Railway Line, 11
Greene, Burt, 74, 76, 87, 91, 92, 157, 180, 181
Grey, Howard, 15, 86, 87, 90, 225

H

Hackett, John Winthrop, 33, 40
Haig, 93, 94, 96, 98, 99, 158, 170, 225
Harris, Rolf, 32, 34, 37, 47, 50, 94, 134, 166, 167, 204, 211
Haskins, Sam, 176, 196, 197, 198, 199
Hawkins, Weaver, 137
Hettena, Andre, 158
Hopkins, Kingsley, 158, 172
Hutton, Mike, 96

I

Institute of Australian Photographers, 1, 190
Israel, Leon 'Lee', 61, 62, 63, 66, 69, 78, 156

J

Jimmy the Greek's, 94, 95
Johnson-Flint, Jeane, 158, 171
Johnston, George, 142, 215, 216

K

Kalamaras restaurant, 168, 169, 176, 198
Kanzler, Eric, 20
Kapooka Camp, 1, 25, 26, 28
Kinnane, Garry, 216
Knox, Ken, 5, 6, 7, 8, 31, 32, 33, 37, 38, 41, 42, 45, 46, 117, 179, 225, 232
Kodak Gallery, 43, 117, 131

Kos, Fritz, 41, 45
Kovel, Jeffrey, 98

L

Laidlaw, Ernie, 169
LeGoubin, Terry & Shirley, 173, 174, 190, 198
Lichfield, Patrick, 168, 198, 200, 201, 223
Lorimer, Jack, 47, 225
Lunghi, John, 34, 49, 192, 200

M

Marchant, Leslie, 47
Marquis de Cuevas Ballet, 97
Massine, Leonid, 100
Mather, Dibbs & Meg, 169, 170
Mayflower Studio, 58, 61, 64, 66, 67, 68, 76, 77, 78, 156
Mayflower Studios, 62, 186
McDonald, Allanah, 28, 50, 155, 170
McDonald, Craig, 110, 225
McLarty, Meredyth, 7, 13, 16, 194, 223, 225
Meredith, David in Clean Straw for Nothing, 215, 216
Mills, Thelma, 6, 32, 33, 34
Minette, Bruce, 134, 135, 143, 144
Moore, David, 17, 52, 143, 152, 154, 201
Morin, Cheryl, 206, 217

N

Napper Stinton and Woolley, 74, 180
National Coal Board, 158
National Gallery of Victoria, 149, 152
NCR Computers, 158
Newton, Gael, 52, 225
Newton, Helmut, 85, 149, 167, 168, 176, 200
Nicholas pharmaceutical company, 78
Nolan, Sidney, 52, 95, 96, 97, 142, 151, 167, 212, 215
Nureyev, Rudolf, 99, 169

O

O'Brien, Philippa, 34

P

Palmer. George, 82, 83, 84, 96, 110, 113, 189
Parkinson, Norman, 85, 149, 197

Paxton's, 136, 144
Penfolds Wines, 147
Perth Technical College, 1, 31, 32, 34, 36, 47, 110, 191, 192, 223
Pfizer, 74, 75, 76, 77, 78, 79, 81, 84, 92, 115, 133, 135, 180
Phillips, 51
Phillips, A A, 51
Phillips, Colonel, 40
Phillips', 51
Photography magazine, 177
Photovision '61, 151, 152, 154
Pierse, Simon, 165, 166, 168
Platonos, Stelios, 168
Playboy magazine, 162
Pownall, Bill, 139, 140, 141, 142, 143, 153, 154, 155, 167, 225
Practical Photography, 177

Q

Quant, 85
Quant, Mary, 85, 94

R

Radford, Kevin, 30, 32
Regent Street Polytechnic., 86
Rigby, Paul, 36, 37
Rixon, Cheryl, 206, 208, 225
Robertson, Lois, 110, 111
Roche, Ted, 41, 46
Roelands, 1, 17, 18, 19, 23, 24, 25, 232
Ross, Alexander David, 39
Royal Ballet, 94, 97
Russell, A K, 202

S

S S Iberia, 53
S S Stratheden, 155
Sainsbury, Harold, 29
Schomberg, The, 9, 10
Scott, Cherie, 186, 219, 220, 225
Seriography, 194, 195
Singh, Vic, 64, 66, 67, 225
Smith, Stephen, 222, 225
Soho, 56, 57, 64, 74, 87, 91, 94, 95, 104, 156, 181, 186
Somoff, Anne, 206

State Housing Commission, 31
Steichen, Edward, 85, 149
Sutherland, Joan, 186, 187

T

Talbot, Henry, 149
Tcherina, Ludmilla, 99
Terongie, 15
Trafalgar Tours, 158
Tucker, Albert, 95, 97, 151, 152, 154, 167, 212
Tussaud, Louis, 90
Tyrie, Jennifer, 208, 209, 225

V

Veal, Hayward 'Bill', 50
Vogue magazine, 149
Vuletich, Tony, 174

W

WA Ballet Company, 205
WA Institute of Technology, 131, 212
Wagga Wagga, 1, 25
Watson, Don, 51
Weedon, Bill, 84, 146, 225
Wellington Dam, 18, 19
Wells Studio, 91, 92
Wells, Ken, 91, 113, 201
Western Australian Camera Club, 1, 5, 6, 31, 39, 69, 225
Whitehorn, Katharine, 52
Williams, Fred, 212
Windmill Theatre, 55, 56, 57
Woburn Studios, 84, 85, 86, 87, 89, 90, 110
Wreck of the Batavia, 211
Wright, Hilda Margaret, 41

References

[i] *Australasian Photo-Review* p 380 June 1953 (via Sydney International Exhibition of Photography website)

[ii] ibid

[iii] Interview by author with Kenneth J Knox, January 2013, at Manning, Western Australia

[iv] *The West Australian* 13 May 2020

[v] https://en.wikipedia.org/wiki/Rolleicord

[vi] http://members.iinet.net.au/~thediaryofthomasangove/DIARY%20OF%20THOMAS%20ANGOVE%20new.pdf

[vii] ibid

[viii] http://www.flagstaffhill.com/media/uploads/ShipwreckTrail.pdf

[ix] https://clunes.org/history

[x] *Albany Advertiser*, 14 September 1912, p 3.

[xi] Obituary of William Henry Angove, *Albany Advertiser*, 1912.

[xii] *Western Perspectives of a Nation*, https://slwa.wa.gov.au/wepon/transport/html/railways.html

[xiii] ibid

[xiv] The Cyclopaedia of Tasmania, p. 143

[xvxv] Blog Reel on *Travels in Southern Africa* by W J Burchell, Biodiversity Heritage Library, https://blog.biodiversitylibrary.org/category/bhl-news

[xvi] ibid

[xvii] ibid

[xviii] *The Multi-Skilled Polymath* in South African Journal of Science. On-line version ISSN 1996-7489 Print version ISSN 0038-2353 S. Afr. j. sci. vol.108 n.11-12 Pretoria Jan. 2012 REVIEW ARTICLE William John Burchell: The multi-skilled polymath Roger Stewart; Brian Warner Department of Astronomy, University of Cape Town, Cape Town, South Africa http://www.scielo.org.za/scielo.php?script=sci_arttext&pid=S0038-23532012000600015

[xix] ibid

[xx] Swainson W. *Taxidermy, bibliography and biography*. London: Longman, Orme, Brown, Green & Longmans, 1840; p. 383, cited in *South African Journal of Science*, On-line version ISSN 1996-7489 S. Afr. j. sci. vol.108 n.11-12 Pretoria Jan. 2012

[xxi] J H Angove Military Record, National Archives of Australia

[xxii] International Encyclopaedia of the First World War, *Battles of the Somme,* November 2014, https://encyclopedia.1914-1918-online.net/article/somme_battles_of

[xxiii] ibid

[xxiv] Gwenda and Basil Bolt's Anniversary Album (2013)

[xxv] Email with author, 1 February 2021

[xxvi] ibid

[xxvii] ibid

[xxviii] http://inherit.stateheritage.wa.gov.au/Public/Inventory/PrintSingleRecord/1403632c-30fd-4340-93cf-00b852a52ea7

[xxix] Gwenda and Basil Bolt's Anniversary Album (2013)

[xxx] James A Kane's Letter to Chris Hartley in 1978, *A Brief History of Roelands,* 17 February 2016, Harvey History Online, https://www.harveyhistoryonline.com/?p=2699

[xxxi] ibid

[xxxii] ibid

xxxiii ibid

xxxiv ibid

xxxv http://inherit.stateheritage.wa.gov.au/Public/Inventory/PrintSingleRecord/88cb5aa9-a4a3-4435-bffe-05be94282fcf

xxxvi Op cit xxiv

xxxvii https://en.wikipedia.org/wiki/1930s_in_film

xxxviii *Everyone's* magazine, 11 March 1936 and 6 October 1937, via Trove, NLA.

xxxix Interview with Rose family descendants by the author, Pinjarra, 12 March 2021.

xl Note to author by Jenny Brodie-Hall, 2 March 2022.

xli Gwenda and Basil Bolt's Anniversary Album (2013)

xlii The Old Farm, *Albany Advertiser,* 16 October 1939, p 3

xliii Pioneer Passes, *The West Australian,* 7 September 1946 p 7

xliv Interview with Rose family descendants, op cit

xlv Handwritten notes by Terry Butcher to Peter Bolt, 11 July 2022

xlvi Gwenda and Basil Bolt's Anniversary Album op. cit

xlvii https://www.abc.net.au/news/2020-05-21/kapooka-military-tragedy-remembered-75-years-on/12271288

xlviii Ibid

xlix https://www.mikeeckman.com/photovintage/vintagecameras/recomar18/index.html

l Photograph, Film and Sound Collection, Australian War Memorial, Canberra, Accession No. ARTI02471, supplied to author.

li www.awm.gov.au

lii *Stop Laughing, This Is Serious,* A social history of Australia in cartoons, Jonathon King, 1978, Cassell Australia (Sydney)

liii Daily Advertiser, Wagga, 24 July 1945, p 4, via Trove

liv Army Art Show, *Tribune,* Sydney, 29 June 1944, p 5, via Trove

lv *I'm Really A Frustrated Painter* by Cyril Casellas, *Weekend Magazine, Supplement to Weekend News,* Perth, 4 June 1966.

lvi ibid

lvii Bill Angove, Photographer by Allanah McDonald, *Australarts,* EMPress, Mornington Avenue Mansions, London, England, First Issue, 1966, p 32

lix https://commons.wikimedia.org/wiki/Category:Military_history_of_Australia_during_World_War_II

lx https://en.wikipedia.org/wiki/Speed_Graphic

lxi Casellas, op cit.

lxii Author's interview with Ken Knox, Manning, 6 December 2017

lxiii Casellas, op cit.

lxiv Typed document entitled *Position Applied For 3388 Lecturer B Art (Photographic Design),* undated but likely circa 1979.

lxv *Employment in the Profession,* hand-written notes by Angove, undated, circa later 1970s.

lxvi Interview with Ken Knox by the author, 6 December 2017

lxvii Casellas, op cit.

lxviii ibid

lxix Unidentified magazine clipping, *Through the Lens to London,* undated

lxx Angove's handwritten notes, undated but likely late 1970s

lxxi Email from Robyn Knox to author, 24 February 2021.

lxxii Interview with author, 2014

lxxiii Handwritten notes by Bill Angove, undated.

lxxiv Interview with author, op cit.

lxxv Paul Rigby Obituary, *The Independent,* London, 2 January 2007.

lxxvi ibid

lxxvii Biography by Joan Kerr, 1996, Design and Art Australia Online, https://daao.library.unsw.edu.au/bio/senior-norman-warwick-aisbett/groups/

lxxviii *Studio Group of Six Display Their Art*, *The West Australian*, 15 September 1954, p. 17, via Trove https://trove.nla.gov.au/newspaper/article/49880407?searchTerm=Norman%20Aisbett

lxxix Robyn Knox op cit.

lxxx Interview with Knox, 2017, op cit.

lxxxi Australasian Photo-Review, http://siep.org.au/General/WACC_1940.html

lxxxii Ibid

lxxxiii ibid

lxxxiv https://www.verywellmind.com/lev-vygotsky-biography-2795533

lxxxv Email to author, 2 March 2021

lxxxvi Haptic Aesthetics and Bodily Properties of Ori Gersht's Digital Art: A Behavioural and Eye-Tracking Study, 7 November 2019, https://www.frontiersin.org/articles/10.3389/fpsyg.2019.02520/full

lxxxvii Walter Benjamin: The Art Story, https://www.theartstory.org/influencer/benjamin-walter/

lxxxviii Marks, L. U. (2002). Touch: Sensuous Theory and Multisensory Media. Minneapolis: University of Minnesota Press.

lxxxix Geraldton Guardian newspaper, 22 September 1951, p. 1

xc Australasian Photo-Review, April 1953, p 243 via SIEP website, op cit.

xci Ibid, April 1954, p. 247

xcii AUSTRALASIAN PHOTO REVIEW Vol 61 No 4 1 April 1954 p. 57 via SIEP website, op cit.

xciii ibid, September 1953, p. 524.

xciv Interview with author, December 2017, op cit.

xcv https://en.wikipedia.org/wiki/Dufaycolor

xcvi https://www.uwa.edu.au/news/Article/2020/Uniview/Summer/A-treasure-trove-of-images-finally-finds-its-way

xcvii An Exhibition by CG, *The West Australian*, 4 November 1954

xcviii ibid

xcix Perth Life Class, *The West Australian*, 22 May 1954

c Bill Angove CV, undated, probably 1979.

ci ibid

cii Oral History recorded by Beverley Angove, 1980.

ciii Bill Angove-Photographer, *AustralArts*, London, 1966, p 34

civ Oral History, op.cit

cv National Portrait Gallery of Australia https://www.portrait.gov.au/people/hayward-veal-1913

cvi Ibid, https://www.portrait.gov.au/portraits/2009.100/portrait-of-rolf

cvii Hayward Veal Biography, *Design and Art Australian Online*, https://www.daao.org.au/bio/hayward-veal/biography/

cviii Can You Tell What It Is Yet? My Autobiography, Rolf Harris, Bantam Press, London, 2001, p. 100

cix Handwritten notes by Bill Angove, undated, likely late 1970s.

cx *Strange Country: Why Australian Painting Matters,* Patrick McCaughey, Miegunyah Press, Carlton, 2014, pp.100,104

cxi *Before I Forget – An Early Memoir,* Geoffrey Blainey, Hamish Hamilton, Australia, 2019, p. 88

cxii *Rabbit Syndrome* Don Watson, Quarterly Essay, November 2001, from *Watsonia – A Writing Life* Black Inc, Carlton, Vic, 2020, p. 160

cxiii Ron Radford's Foreword, *Fred Williams – Infinite Horizons,* Deborah Hart, NGA, Canberra, 2011

cxiv McCaughey, op cit. p 163

cxv McCaughey, op cit, pp 175-178

cxvi *Sidney Nolan* by Nancy Underhill (New South Publishing) Sydney, 2015, p. 241

cxvii *David Moore – Australian Photographer,* Sandra Byron, Art Gallery of NSW, Chapter&Verse, McMahon's Point, NSW, 1988, sleeve

cxviii *Breaking News – the Golden Age of Graham Perkin*, Ben Hills, Scribe, Melbourne, 2010, p. 2

cxix Newton, Gael (1980), *Silver and grey : fifty years of Australian photography, 1900–1950*, Angus & Robertson https://www.photo-web.com.au/Silver&Grey/default.htm

cxx Australian Women Photographers 1840-1960, Barbara Hall and Jenni Mather, Greenhouse, Richmond, Vic, 1986, p. 60

cxxi *The Best of Times*, Katharine Whitehorn, The Guardian, 10 October, 2007, from her memoir, *Selective Memory*

cxxii Oral History, op cit.

cxxiii Three-page typed manuscript entitled 'Please Return to BA' undated and of unidentified authorship, possibly 1974

cxxiv Oral History, op cit.

cxxv Oral History, op cit.

cxxvi Oral History, op cit.

cxxvii *Darkrooms I Have Known*, Bill Angove, manuscript held in his personal archives.

cxxviii Oral History, op cit.

cxxix *Photos Reveal Racy Loophole Used Naked Showgirls*, Shari Miller, The Daily Mail, 20 March 2017, https://www.dailymail.co.uk/news/article-4328796/Photos-reveal-racy-loophole-used-naked-showgirls.html

cxxx ibid

cxxxi https://www.photrio.com/forum/threads/michael-barrington-martin.24191/ 1 June 2010

cxxxii ibid

cxxxiii ibid

cxxxiv Benny Hill and the Windmill Theatre in Great Windmill Street, Soho, in a blog called Another Nickel in the Machine, Author Unknown, 31 January 20212, http://www.nickelinthemachine.com/2012/01/benny-hill-and-the-windmill-theatre-in-great-windmill-street-soho/

cxxxv Oral History, op cit.

cxxxvi Ibid

cxxxvii *Peter Sellers: An unpredictable, irrepressible, irreverent mimic*, Zinsser, William K (20 June 1960), Life: 63–70 (see p.66), retrieved 23 August 2010 via Wikipedia https://en.wikipedia.org/wiki/The_Goon_Show#cite_note-Zinsser-30

cxxxviii Oral History, op cit.

cxxxix ibid

cxl ibid

cxli *Darkrooms I Have Known,* op cit.

cxlii ibid

cxliii Job reference from Somers Photo Service, London, 8 June 1955.

cxliv Oral History, op cit.

cxlv The Faces Behind the Names at Mayflower Studios, unknown magazine page, undated.

cxlvi At Random, Howard C Cohen, Pittsburgh Post-Gazette, 28 December 1965, p. 10

cxlvii Faces Behind Names, op cit.

cxlviii https://www.mysticseaport.org/category/mayflower-ii-restoration/

cxlix Faces behind names, Op cit

cl Oral History, op cit

cli ibid

clii Terry Butcher interview with author, 16 March 2022

cliii ibid

cliv https://www.npg.org.uk/whatson/exhibitions/20041/cecil-beaton-portraits.php

clv Email correspondence with author, March 2021.

clvi Oral History, op cit.

clvii ibid

clviii Email correspondence, March 2021
clix Advertisement for Mayflower Studio Library, *Advertiser's Weekly,* London, 6 April 1962.
clx ibid
clxi Oral History, op cit.
clxii ibid
clxiii *Crazy Pictures Won Him London Job,* Australian Women's Weekly, 16 November 1955, pp 18-19.
clxiv ibid
clxv ibid
clxvi Oral History, op cit.
clxvii https://pharmaphorum.com/sales-marketing/a_history_of_pfizer/
clxviii American Chemical Society, https://www.acs.org/content/acs/en/pressroom/newsreleases/2008/june/pfizers-work-on-penicillin-for-world-war-ii-becomes-a-national-historic-chemical-landmark.html
clxix Pharmaphorum, op cit.
clxx Oral History, op cit.
clxxi ibid
clxxii *When Will The Last Patient Die?,* British Medical Journal, undated, circa 1956, copy in Angove's personal archive.
clxxiii https://www.bmj.com/about-bmj/history-of-the-bmj
clxxiv Handwritten note by Bill Angove, undated, circa 1970s.
clxxv Photography in Advertising, *Advertiser's Weekly,* London, 5 October 1956, pp 32-33.
clxxvi Oral History, op cit.
clxxvii Ibid
clxxviii Ibid
clxxix ibid
clxxx https://www.gracesguide.co.uk/Aspro
clxxxi Letter to Marjorie Angove, 30 August 1958, in possession of author
clxxxii Ibid
clxxxiii ibid
clxxxiv Email correspondence to author from Peter Bolt of Albany, 8 March 2022.
clxxxv ibid
clxxxvi Letter to Marjorie, op. cit
clxxxvii ibid
clxxxviii ibid
clxxxix ibid
cxc https://artguide.com.au/the-rise-and-rise-of-mary-quant/
cxci Undated CV, op cit.
cxcii FaceTime interview from London with author, 10 June 2021,
cxciii ibid
cxciv ibid
cxcv https://en.wikipedia.org/wiki/Grattan_plc
cxcvi Google book review of *Mail Order Retailing in Britain: A Business and Social History by* Richard Coopey, Sean O'Connell, Dilwyn Porter
cxcvii Oral History
cxcviii Undated anonymous draft typed manuscript with pencilled heading "Bill Angove"
cxcix ibid
cc Interview from London with author, op cit.
cci Oral History, op. cit.

ccii ibid
cciii ibid
cciv Mike Busselle obituary, *The Daily Telegraph,* London, 6 July 2006, online
ccv Oral History
ccvi ibid
ccvii Phone interview by author with Robin Haig from Melbourne, 24 June 2021.
ccviii Thesis https://ro.ecu.edu.au/cgi/viewcontent.cgi?article=3044&context=theses
ccix Oral History
ccx ibid
ccxi ibid
ccxii From Nolan, a film by Flaming Star Productions, Directed by Sall Aitken, 2019, ABC-TV
ccxiii Haig phone interview, op cit.
ccxiv *Life in London in the 1950s,* Mike Hutton, Amberley Publishing, 2014
ccxv From *Nolan*, a film, op.cit
ccxvi *Sidney Nolan* by Nancy Underhill, New South Publishing, Sydney, 2015, p. 48.
ccxvii Ibid, p. 237
ccxviii From *Nolan*, a film, op.cit.
ccxix Ibid, p79
ccxx Ibid, p. 86
ccxxi Anonymous draft manuscript, op. cit.
ccxxii ibid
ccxxiii John Gilpin (1930-1983) by Cherry Palfrey, http://www.thurb.com/cherry/gilpin.htm
ccxxiv ibid
ccxxv www.theatreheritage.org.au
ccxxvi Grand Ballet du Marquis de Cuevas in *The Oxford Dictionary of Dance* https://www.oxfordreference.com/view/10.1093/oi/authority.20110803095903323
ccxxvii Anonymous manuscript, op. cit.
ccxxviii https://en.wikipedia.org/wiki/Ludmilla_Tch%C3%A9rina
ccxxixccxxix Letter to Marjorie Angove, 14 September 1958, in possession of author.
ccxxx https://www.britannica.com/biography/Leonide-Massine
ccxxxi Letter to Marjorie Angove, op cit
ccxxxii http://www.artnet.com/artists/henri-cartier-bresson/
ccxxxiii ibid
ccxxxiv *Who is Cartier-Bresson?* Amateur Photography, 9 October 1968, p. 13
ccxxxv Oral History, op. cit
ccxxxvi Craig McDonald interview with author, Albany, 14 October 2021 at Middleton Beach Rd
ccxxxvii ibid
ccxxxviii Handwritten notes by Angove, undated
ccxxxix Five letters from Angove to his mother, 30 August – 28 September 1958.
ccxl ibid
ccxli ibid
ccxlii ibid
ccxliii ibid
ccxliv ibid
ccxlv Letter by Burchell Butcher, 2 August 1957
ccxlvi ibid

ccxlvii *A Painter kept his Palette Clean,* Daily Telegraph, 16 November 1947

ccxlviii Terry Butcher interview with author, 16 March 2022

ccxlix Handwritten extract of a letter from Burchell Butcher to Angove, undated

ccl ibid

ccli ibid

cclii *Cameraman takes a trick*, unknown Perth press clipping, 1958

ccliii Five letters, op.cit.

ccliv ibid

cclv ibid

cclvi ibid

cclvii ibid

cclviii ibid

cclix ibid

cclx ibid

cclxi ibid

cclxii Email correspondence with author 20 August 2021

cclxiii Email correspondence with author 21 August 2021

cclxiv https://www.45cat.com/record/kep183

cclxv Display panel in one-man-show exhibition 1959

cclxvi Handwritten notes, op. cit

cclxvii Crazy Photos Sell Product Ideas, *Advertising* magazine, March 1959, Sydney, p 14

cclxviii ibid

cclxix ibid

cclxx https://www.insideimaging.com.au/2016/teds-cameras-purchases-paxtons-stores/

cclxxi One-Man Photography Show, *Sydney Morning Herald,* 23 October 1959

cclxxii Hawkins, Harold Frederick, by Daniel Thomas, Australian Dictionary of Biography, https://adb.anu.edu.au/biography/hawkins-harold-frederick-10457

cclxxiii Caption to photograph of Leaping Dancer, Snapshots column by Allen Pout, *The Daily Telegraph,* Sydney, 23 October 1959.

cclxxiv Typescript by Angove entitled Career Details, undated.

cclxxv Terry Butcher interview, op cit

cclxxvi PLAYING AROUND WITH ORGANISED NOISE by Bill Bottomley, https://www.billbottomley.com.au/wp-content/uploads/2018/05/Apendix-music.pdf, p. 5

cclxxvii State Library of NSW https://digital.sl.nsw.gov.au/delivery/DeliveryManagerServlet?embedded=true&toolbar=false&dps_pid=IE16319426&_ga=2.115447814.1251108423.1633245406-1723759314.1628754743

cclxxviii Handwritten CV by Bill Angove circa 1970s

cclxxix Bill Pownall letter to author, 19 October 2021, from Hydra, Greece

cclxxx ibid

cclxxxi Sydney International Exhibition of Photography, Foreword to Catalogue, August 1961, Sydney

cclxxxii ibid

cclxxxiii Typescript, job application by Angove, circa 1977-78

cclxxxiv https://www.siep.org.au/General/SIEP_History.html

cclxxxv SIEP catalogue, op. cit.

cclxxxvi Handwritten notes, op.cit.

cclxxxvii Lillian Roxon biography

cclxxxviii Bill Weedon interview with author, 15 October 2021, Middleton Beach, Albany
cclxxxix ibid
ccxc https://en.wikipedia.org/wiki/Ajax_Films
ccxci ibid
ccxcii https://en.wikipedia.org/wiki/Vogue_Australia
ccxciii https://www.museoreinasofia.es/en/exhibitions/edward-steichen-lives-photography
ccxciv https://www.nytimes.com/1973/03/26/archives/edward-steichen-is-dead-at-93-made-photography-an-a-rt-form-edward.html
ccxcv https://en.wikipedia.org/wiki/Edward_Steichen
ccxcvi https://www.ngv.vic.gov.au/ebooks/HenryTalbot/index.php?chapter=2
ccxcvii Ibid
ccxcviii *Show-off swimsuits that really take to the water*, Vogue Australia, Spring edition 1961, pp 84-87
ccxcix Oral history, op. cit.
ccc https://www.photo-web.com.au/GroupM/about/00.html by Philip Bentley
ccci https://onthisdateinphotography.com/2018/09/25/september-25/
cccii https://www.ngv.vic.gov.au/wp-content/uploads/2010/03/rb_flashback.pdf p. 5
ccciii ibid
ccciv ibid
cccv https://www.photo-web.com.au/GroupM/about/00.html_op.cit
cccvi Bill Pownall letter to author, op. cit
cccvii ibid
cccviii Photovision 61 catalogue, International Competition in Creative Photography, Melbourne, 9-26 May 1961, Museum of Modern Art Australia
cccix ibid
cccx *Out-of-Focus*, The Age, 8 May 1961, p. 2
cccxi ibid
cccxii ibid
cccxiii Angove's typewritten CV circa 1979
cccxiv Bill Angove – Photographer, Allanah McDonald, Australarts, London, 1966, p 32
cccxv Angove's handwritten notes, op. cit.
cccxvi Bill Pownall letter to author 4 March 2022
cccxvii https://passengers.history.sa.gov.au/node/936688
cccxviii Handwritten notes, op.cit
cccxix ibid
cccxx Mayflower Studio photo library house journal No. 1, circa 1962-63
cccxxi ibid
cccxxii ibid
cccxxiii ibid
cccxxiv ibid
cccxxv Handwritten notes, op. cit.
cccxxvi ibid
cccxxvii ibid
cccxxviii ibid
cccxxix CV, circa 1979, op. cit.
cccxxx Creating the Mood – with Colour, Photography magazine, by EWS, Undated circa 1965
cccxxxi ibid

cccxxxii ibid
cccxxxiii *Advice from a Professional*, by Frank P Evans, Sunday Times, Perth, 23 January 1972.
cccxxxiv Terry Butcher interview op cit
cccxxxv https://spacestor.com/insights/industry-trends/mid-century-modernism-a-design-movement-that-lives-on/
cccxxxvi Living the 1960s, Noeline Brown, NLA Publishing, Canberra, 2017, p. 27
cccxxxvii Cited in Australian Art and Artists in London 1950-1965, by Simon Pierse, Ashgate Publishing, Abingdon, UK, 2012.
cccxxxviii ibid
cccxxxix ibid
cccxl The Australians who set 60s Britain swinging, Vanessa Thorpe, The Guardian, 1 June 2014
cccxli The Boyds, Brenda Niall, MUP, Melbourne, 2002, p. 331
cccxlii Can You Tell What It Is Yet? Op. cit. p. 138
cccxliii Bill Pownall letter to author, op. cit
cccxliv ibid
cccxlv Creative Photography – Aesthetic Trends 1839-1960, Helmut Gernsheim, Dover (Revised), 1991
cccxlvi https://www.timeout.com/london/restaurants/kalamaras-greek-taverna
cccxlvii Stelios Platonos, Restaurateur at Kalamara, Obituary, Drew Smith, the Independent, Thursday 18 May 2006
cccxlviii Interview with Ernie and Pat Laidlaw by author, 18 November 2021, at South Perth
cccxlix He Brought Theatre to Everything He Did – Dibbs Mather 1932-2010, by Milton Cockburn, Sydney Morning Herald, 11 September 2010
cccl Editorial, Australarts, first issue, Mornington Ave Mansions, London, 1966, p. 1
cccli ibid
ccclii ibid
cccliii ibid, p. 32
cccliv Greeting card signed by Jeanne Johnson-Flint, from Paris address, undated, in possession of author
ccclv Handwritten notes, op.cit.
ccclvi Letter from Jeanne Johnson-Flint, Warwickshire, undated, in possession of author
ccclvii ibid
ccclviii https://www.facebook.com/GracewellHealthcare/posts/graceweil-of-basingstoke-formerly-pemberley-house-held-a-special-photography-exh/1241433995890894/
ccclix https://www.dumbofeather.com/conversations/ken-done-australian-icon/
ccclx Interview with author by phone 15 July 2021
ccclxi ibid
ccclxii ibid
ccclxiii Handwritten notes (undated)
ccclxiv ibid
ccclxv *Sex book model is a nice person* Charlie Anderson, Daily News, Perth, 14 January 1971, p. 18
ccclxvi Pix magazine, Date?
ccclxvii From the Other Side of the Lense, Practical Photography, London, February 1970.
ccclxviii Dare to be Different, Popular Photography, London, 1966, pp 100-102.
ccclxix ibid
ccclxx *Advice from a Professional*, op cit.
ccclxxi *I'm Really a Frustrated Painter,* op. cit.
ccclxxii ibid
ccclxxiii *What's in a Picture,* Barry Baker, Sunday Independent, 5 September 1976, p. 57
ccclxxiv ibid
ccclxxv *I'm Really a Frustrated Painter,* op. cit

ccclxxvi ibid
ccclxxvii Typed CV, circa 1979
ccclxxviii *Behind the Footlights' Glare – With a Camera* by Ray Ellinson, undated typed manuscript.
ccclxxix ibid
ccclxxx https://www.unfinishedhistories.com/history/companies/inter-action
ccclxxxi ibid
ccclxxxii Program for Lunch Hour Theatre Club production entitled *The Nudist Campers Grow and Grow*, Queensway, London, 15-27 July, year unknown.
ccclxxxiii ibid
ccclxxxiv *Behind the Footlights,* op. cit.
ccclxxxv Handwritten notes, op. cit.
ccclxxxvi Email to author, 12 January 2022
ccclxxxvii Another set of handwritten notes appearing as a draft CV or job application circa 1976.
ccclxxxviii Catalogue and Price List, Group Color, Photographic Art, typescript, undated.
ccclxxxix ibid
cccxc ibid
cccxci ibid
cccxcii ibid
cccxciii Typed CV, op. cit
cccxciv Typescript of application for lectureship, undated.
cccxcv Handwritten notes, circa 1976
cccxcvi ibid
cccxcvii https://www.parkwestgallery.com/what-is-a-serigraph-serigraphy/
cccxcviii ibid
cccxcix Handwritten notes, 1976, op cit
cd ibid
cdi https://www.arts.ac.uk/colleges/london-college-of-communication/stories/london-school-of-printing-alumni-celebrate-over-6-decades-of-friendship
cdii https://en.wikipedia.org/wiki/Sam_Haskins
cdiii https://en.wikipedia.org/wiki/Margaret_Harker
cdiv Never Too Old, by Barry Baker, Sunday Independent, 19 December 1976, p 43
cdv Handwritten notes, op cit
cdvi Notebook from Angove's 1976-77 UK visit
cdvii ibid
cdviii https://www.moma.org/artists/740
cdix https://en.wikipedia.org/wiki/Ian_Berry_(photojournalist)
cdx Angove notebook from 1976-77 UK trip
cdxi http://ceylon-ananda.com/felicitation-of-ron-lewcock-and-senaka-bandaranaike-with-guest-speaker-mira-nair/
cdxii https://www.maryevans.com/weekly/barnabys/barnabys.php
cdxiii https://www.theguardian.com/environment/2010/jun/30/john-gooders-obituary-ornithologist
cdxiv https://archival.sl.nsw.gov.au/Details/archive/110095663
cdxv https://www.siad.org/about
cdxvi Letter from A K Russell, WAIT Department of Art and Design, Bentley, 11 July 1977, in possession of author.
cdxvii ibid
cdxviii Edward Edkins interview with author, Fremantle, 13 August 2020
cdxix ibid

cdxx Magazine advertisement for Hobbycard, undated.
cdxxi https://www.dreskesomoff.com.au/profile
cdxxii Cheryl Rixon interview with author, 24 January 2022.
cdxxiii ibid
cdxxiv Jennifer Tyrie interview with author, 15 September 2020.
cdxxv ibid
cdxxvi https://aso.gov.au/titles/documentaries/wreck-batavia/clip1/
cdxxvii https://www.sbs.com.au/guide/article/2018/08/09/batavia-shipwreck-craziest-australian-horror-story-youve-never-heard
cdxxviii ibid
cdxxix *Horror Ship Lives Again,* Australasian Post, undated.
cdxxx https://en.wikipedia.org/wiki/WAY_79
cdxxxi https://api.research-repository.uwa.edu.au/ws/portalfiles/portal/37823583/THESIS_DOCTOR_OF_PHILOSOPHY_BROWN_Maria_Encarnacion_2018.pdf
cdxxxii ibid
cdxxxiii Three-page typed manuscript entitled 'Please Return to BA' undated and of unidentified authorship, possibly 1974
cdxxxiv Butcher notes to Peter Bolt, op. cit.
cdxxxv *Clean Straw for Nothing* by George Johnston, A&R Classics, Sydney, 1969, p. 7
cdxxxvi https://www.goodreads.com/book/show/1775284.Clean_Straw_for_Nothing
cdxxxvii ibid
cdxxxviii George Johnston – A Biography, Garry Kinnane, Nelson, Melbourne, 1986, p 294
cdxxxix ibid
cdxl ibid
cdxli Beverley Angove email to author, 5 February 2021
cdxlii Email correspondence to author from Peter Bolt, 8 March 2022
cdxliii ibid
cdxliv Cherie Scott phone interview with author, date not recorded
cdxlv Beverley Angove email, op.cit.
cdxlvi ibid
cdxlvii ibid
cdxlviii Email from Peter Bolt, op cit
cdxlix Beverley Angove email, op cit
cdl Darkroom Disease, Safetyline Journal, May 1992
cdli Fixing the Images, Sunday Independent, Perth, 22 October 1972, p. 5
cdlii Bill Angove: Photographer, Albany Advertiser, 26 February, 1980
cdliii A Sad Loss to Us, Living Today, February 1980
cdliv ibid
cdlv Interview with author, 13 August 2020 at Fremantle
cdlvi ibid
cdlvii Stephen Smith interview with author, 21 September 2020, at Bayswater, WA
cdlviii ibid
cdlix Death notice, *The West Australian*
cdlx ibid
cdlxi Richard and Lyn Woldendorp's email with author, 2 October 2020.

www.ingramcontent.com/pod-product-compliance
Lightning Source LLC
Chambersburg PA
CBHW041219240426
43661CB00012B/1090